REFERENCE SERIES

Air Force Combat Medals, Streamers, and Campaigns

A. Timothy Warnock
United States Air Force Historical Research Center

OFFICE OF AIR FORCE HISTORY
UNITED STATES AIR FORCE
WASHINGTON, D.C., 1990

Library of Congress Cataloging-in-Publication Data

Warnock, A. Timothy.
  Air Force combat medals, streamers, and campaigns /
A. Timothy Warnock
    339 p. cm.—(Reference series)
    Includes bibliographical references and index.
    ISBN 0–912799–66–8
    1. United States. Air Force—Medals, badges, decorations, etc.
2. United States. Air Force—History. I. United States. Air Force.
Office of Air Force History. II. Title. III. Series: Reference series
(United States. Air Force. Office of Air Force History)
UG977.W37   1990
358.4'11342'0973—dc20   90–14246
                                                             CIP

For sale by the Superintendent of Documents, U.S. Government Printing Office,
Washington, D.C. 20402

Foreword

This book is the most recent of a number of reference works prepared by the United States Air Force Historical Research Center for the use of the Air Force and the general public. They present fundamental data about such diverse subjects as Air Force organizations, specific aircraft, unit lineage and honors, and air bases. Their purpose is to provide reference data for those who will write more extensive narrative accounts of Air Force activities and operations, and for members of the service who have need for reference information on the Air Force and its activities in the past. This particular volume covers the 7 medals and streamers earned in combat by Air Force members and units in military campaigns from the beginning of military air power up to the present day.

The United States Air Force has participated in 7 theaters of war and 78 different designated campaigns since the service's origin as a part of the U.S. Army Signal Corps in 1907. In narrative, photographs, and maps, A. Timothy Warnock describes for the first time in 1 volume the combat medals, streamers, and campaigns of the Air Force in every theater. Staff officers, personnel specialists, historians, and other scholars researching the participation of military members and Air Force units can through the use of Dr. Warnock's excellent research obtain an authoritative account of Air Force combat operations organized by theater and campaign.

RICHARD H. KOHN
Chief, Office of Air Force History

Preface

In combat operations military personnel earned combat service medals and ribbons, and units of the United States Air Force (USAF) and its predecessor organizations* earned battle streamers. In this book the service medal, suspension ribbon, ribbon bar, and streamer for each of 7 theaters of war appear in color. Color plates show the obverse (front) side of the medal on the left and the reverse (back) side on the right. The narrative describes these devices, the requirements for their award, and the 78 designated campaigns in which recipients of these awards participated. Seventy-nine maps accompany the descriptions and campaign summaries. The maps generally conform in format and content to those appearing in War Department General Order No. 24, March 4, 1947, which defined the geographic parameters and periods of World War II campaigns. The campaign narratives are general and selective rather than comprehensive, with each summary highlighting aerial combat. Place names are identified and spelled as they appeared in common usage at the time of the campaigns. The pertinent orders and regulations that provided the authority for the award of medals and streamers to servicemen and their organizations are listed in the "Note on Sources."

The author is indebted to numerous individuals and organizations for their encouragement and help. Lt. Col. John F. H. Schenk, USAFR, while assigned as an Individual Mobilization Augmentee at the USAF Historical Research Center (USAFHRC), formulated the basic concept for this book and initiated research on Mexican Service and World War I. He laid the foundation on which I built. Another reservist at the Center, Col. Michael W. LeMorte, USAFR (Retired), began research on World War II Service and prepared initial drafts for some of the campaign summaries.

I am indebted to several agencies and individuals for the loan of medals and streamers. The U.S. Marine Corps Museums Branch Activities, Quantico, Virginia, and Mr. H. C. Brown, Officer-in-Charge, loaned the

---

*They are the Aeronautical Division, U.S. Army Signal Corps, August 1907 to July 1914; Aviation Section, U.S. Army Signal Corps, July 1914 to May 1918; U.S. Army Air Service, May 1918 to July 1926; U.S. Army Air Corps, July 1926 to June 1941; and the U.S. Army Air Forces, June 1941 to September 1947.

Korean and Vietnam Service Streamers. MSgt. Nicholas Halbeisen, Air Weather Service, furnished the Mexican Service Medal and the World War I Victory Medal. The USAF Museum provided the Mexican Service Streamer, and Service Streamers for World War I; American Theater, World War II Service; Asiatic–Pacific Theater, World War II Service; and European–African–Middle Eastern Theater, World War II Service. The Awards Division, Air Force Manpower and Personnel Center (now, Military Personnel Center) provided the American Campaign Medal, Asiatic–Pacific Campaign Medal, European–African–Middle Eastern Campaign Medal, Korean Service Medal, and Vietnam Service Medal. Maj. Lester A. Sliter, USAFHRC, loaned the Armed Forces Expeditionary Medal. Special thanks are owed TSgt. Rodney C. Fine at Air Force Military Personnel Center for documentation on the Vietnam campaigns, to the staffs of the Pentagon Library and the U.S. Army Center of Military History for copies of orders, circulars, and regulations, and to the Air University Library staff for research assistance.

Others read the manuscript and offered suggestions and corrections that enhanced its historical accuracy. Dr. Maurer Maurer, former Senior Historian at USAFHRC, reviewed the World War I section. Dr. Stanley L. Falk, former Chief Historian, Office of Air Force History, read the American and Asiatic–Pacific Theaters, and Dr. Martin Blumenson, formerly with the U.S. Army Center of Military History, examined the European–African–Middle Eastern Theater material, to cover World War II. Former USAFHRC Senior Historian Dr. Robert F. Futrell read the Korean Service portion. Maj. Earl H. Tilford, Jr., USAF, of the Air University Center for Aerospace Doctrine, Research, and Education, and Dr. John Schlight, Chief of the Southeast Asia Branch, U.S. Army Center of Military History, lent their expertise to the Vietnam Service section.

Still others I wish to thank include Mr. Robert S. Ryan and Mr. Herbert Huie who rendered the maps for the theaters and campaigns. At the USAF Historical Research Center, I am indebted to the late Mr. Charles A. Ravenstein, Deputy Chief of the Research Division, for his help with unit honors; Mr. Lloyd H. Cornett, Jr., former Director, USAFHRC, for his encouragement and unstinting support; and Mr. R. Cargill Hall, Chief, Research Division, who guided production of this work, counseled on details, and edited the numerous drafts. Mrs. Jacqueline B. Blamires and Mrs. Mary J. Moore, Editorial Assistants, deserve special words of appreciation for their typing and editorial efforts that converted the rough draft manuscript into a finished product. Finally, thanks are due to Mr. Herman S. Wolk and Dr. Alfred Beck, Office of Air Force History, for shepherding the manuscript through editorial reviews and to Ms. Anne E. Johnson for designing the volume and overseeing its publication. Ms. Nuala Barry of the Army Institute of Heraldry lent the medals and ribbons, and the Defense Personnel Support Center supplied the streamers for the studio photography by Mr. Cecil Webb of Air Force Graphics. Under the guidance of Chief of Air Force Graphics, Mr. Robert Bell, and Mrs. Susan J. Linders, illustrators Mrs. Kathy Jones and Mrs. Tracy A. Miller prepared the text and artwork for the printer. The drawings at the end of each major section and the book cover and jacket are the work of Mr. Stephen C. Gonyea. Any errors of omission or commission that may remain are my own.

A. TIMOTHY WARNOCK
USAF Historical Research Center

United States Air Force Historical Advisory Committee

(As of July 2, 1990)

John H. Morrow, Jr., *Chairman*
University of Georgia

Charles G. Boyd
Lieutenant General, USAF
Commander, Air University

Duane H. Cassidy
General, USAF, Retired

Merritt Roe Smith
The Massachusetts Institute
  of Technology

Dominick Graham
University of New
  Brunswick, Canada

Ira D. Gruber
Rice University

Charles R. Hamm
Lieutenant General, USAF
Superintendent, USAF Academy

Ann C. Petersen
The General Counsel, USF

Marc Trachtenberg
University of Pennsylvania

Gerhard L. Weinberg
The University of North
  Carolina at Chapel Hill

Frank E. Vandiver
Texas A&M University

The Author

A. TIMOTHY WARNOCK is a historian in the Research Division, United States Air Force Historical Research Center, Maxwell AFB, Alabama, a position he has held since October 1980. He holds a B.S. in education (1964); an M.S. in education (1967); and a Ph.D. in political science (1972) from the University of Georgia, Athens, Georgia. Prior to joining the Air Force History Program, Dr. Warnock served as Assistant Professor, Georgia Southern College, Statesboro, Georgia; Education Specialist, Air War College, Maxwell AFB, Alabama; and Adjunct Professor in Auburn University's Maxwell Graduate Program, Maxwell AFB, Alabama. He also served as Research Professor of American Politics, 1972–1978, at the Air War College, Air University. While at the Air War College, Dr. Warnock edited several textbooks anthologies, including *National Security Policy in an Open Society*, December 1978; *Army General Purpose Forces*, May 1979; *National Purpose and Values*, June 1979; *Third World Issues*, June 1979; *Strategic Appraisal of Africa*, December 1979; *The President and Congress in National Security Affairs*, February 1980; and *The International System*, June 1980.

Contents

Photographs

Air Force Combat Medals, Streamers, and Campaigns

Introduction

Decorating individuals who participated in battle is a time-honored custom. The Greeks and Romans, for example, crowned their victorious commanders with laurel wreaths, symbols which appear on many modern military decorations. The present-day system of awarding medals may be traced to the 16th century when England struck 3 separate medals to commemorate the victory in 1588 over the Spanish Armada. By the end of the 17th century, some European countries awarded medals to military members, usually high-ranking officers, who participated in a battle or campaign. By the end of the 19th century, the award of military decorations and service medals to military organizations and their members was a well-established practice in Europe.

Beginning with the Revolutionary War, the United States of America also has a long history of military awards. The Continental Congress awarded the first medal to Gen. George Washington, commemorating the withdrawal of the British from Boston in 1776. This decoration and other gold medals that Congress conferred on commanders during the war were not intended for wear, but were presented in display boxes. Congress also conferred 3 identical medals, designed for wear, on the privates involved in intercepting the British spy who implicated Benedict Arnold as a traitor. On August 7, 1782, George Washington established a decoration recognizing the meritorious actions of individual soldiers: the Badge of Military Merit. The War Department revived this decoration on Washington's 200th birthday, February 22, 1932. Redesignated the Purple Heart, it is awarded to personnel injured or wounded in combat.

These early examples of American military honors recognized individual acts of exceptional bravery, outstanding achievement, or meritorious service. This country's highest military decoration is the Medal of Honor, established by Congress for Navy and Army personnel in 1861 and 1862, respectively. Today, there are separate Medals of Honor for the Army, Navy, and Air Force.

INTRODUCTION

Distinct from valor awards for individual bravery are service
awards, given to recognize honorable military service during wars,
national emergencies, or significant military operations.* In
American practice, these service awards appeared in the 20th
century. On June 3, 1898, Congress created an award for all
officers and men who participated in the single naval engagement
in Manila Bay on May 1, 1898. Three years later Congress authorized a U.S. Naval Campaign Medal for engagements in the West
Indies in 1898. In 1905 Congress authorized campaign medals for
other military operations. Over the next 2 years, the War Department established service medals for the Civil War, the Indian
Wars, the Spanish American War, the Philippine Insurrection, and
the Boxer Rebellion, retroactively recognizing individual and unit
accomplishments in those conflicts or expeditions.

The 7 service awards appearing in these pages are presented as
combat medals to individuals and as battle streamers to units. The
medals recognize honorable, active military service during wars in
which the U.S. Air Force and its predecessor organizations participated. Each medal is a bronze disk 1 and 1/2 inches in diameter.
The embossed medals depict the nature of the war and the regions
of the world where the campaigns took place. The combat service
medal hangs from a suspension ribbon that portrays in vertical
stripes the colors of the United States, its allies, or the enemy
states. An honoree also received a *ribbon bar*, that is, a service
ribbon, to wear in place of the medal on informal occasions. The
ribbon bar is a metallic strip 1 and 3/8th inches long and 3/8ths of
an inch wide, covered with a ribbon of the same vertical design
and color as the suspension ribbon.

Distinctive metal devices, consisting of clasps, stars, and arrowheads, are often worn on the suspension ribbons. The World War I
Victory Medal may have any of 19 campaign clasps, which are
small, rectangular plates bearing a campaign name, attached to the
campaign ribbon. For later wars, a service star worn on the suspension ribbon or ribbon bar may be bronze, which represents 1

---

*In addition to decorations and service awards, individuals may receive medals or ribbons for unit awards,
such as the Presidential Unit Citation, and for special achievement, such as the Good Conduct Medal.

campaign, or silver, which represents service in 5 campaigns. The arrowhead, a bronze replica of an Indian arrowhead, appears on the suspension ribbon or ribbon bar and identifies participation in an amphibious or aerial assault landing. To qualify for an arrowhead, an Air Force recipient must have made a combat glider landing or parachute jump as a member of an organized force carrying out an assigned tactical mission to seize a beachhead or an airhead. An individual received an arrowhead for each assault credit earned, but may wear only 1 on the ribbon. On appropriate occasions, honorees may wear miniature devices in place of the regular-sized awards. A miniature medal is 1/2 the size of the regular medal, and the miniature ribbon bar is 11/16ths by 3/8ths inches. There are also service stars and arrowheads scaled to fit these smaller versions of the awards. For color illustrations of these devices, see Appendix 2, page 310.

Battle streamers awarded to Air Force units are equivalent to the combat service medals for individuals. The concept originated in antiquity when organizations carried various emblems and banners into combat to provide a rallying point around which subsidiary units were ordered. Shortly after World War I the U.S. Army became the first American military organization to adopt battle streamers, awarding them to units that directly supported or engaged in combat. An Army or an Air Force unit received 1 type of battle streamer, known as a *service streamer*, for noncombatant service in each theater of war; it qualified by having been based in or having traveled through that theater. A unit earned a *campaign streamer* if it was stationed within a designated campaign zone or engaged in combat. Since a campaign streamer is a service streamer with the name and dates of the campaign embroidered on it, any unit that earned a campaign credit did not receive an additional, unembroidered service streamer. The colors and design of the service and campaign streamers are identical to the corresponding service ribbon. These battle streamers are 4 inches wide, either 3 or 4 feet long, and swallow-tailed.

Military units participating in aerial or amphibious assault landings during World War II and the Korean conflict, like the individual service member, earned an arrowhead for each assault credit. Units could earn assault credits in 1 or more campaigns. For amphibious credit the presence of the unit on the designated beach was sufficient, but for aerial assault credit the unit had to land by parachute or glider in or near the airhead. Units responsible for dropping paratroopers or cargo and for towing gliders did not receive the arrowhead. The arrowhead device appears before the campaign name on the campaign streamer and only 1 arrowhead is embroidered on the streamer, regardless of the number of assault credits a unit might have earned in a given campaign.

Since 1908, when the U.S. Army first purchased a Wright aircraft, airmen and aviation units have participated in 7 theaters of war and 78 campaigns for which combat medals, ribbons, and streamers have been awarded. The 1st Aero Squadron of the Aviation Section, U.S. Army Signal Corps, was the first American unit to gain combat aviation experience, serving in the Mexican Expedition Campaign, March 14, 1916–February 7, 1917. The U.S. Army Air Service in World War I participated in 6 defensive sectors and 8 campaigns on the Western Front in Europe. Units of the U.S. Army Air Forces earned campaign credits during World War II in 3 different theaters: The American Theater (1 campaign), the Asiatic–Pacific Theater (23 campaigns), and the European–African–Middle Eastern Theater (18 campaigns). Air Force units participated in 10 campaigns in Korean Service and 17 campaigns in Vietnam Service.

In this volume, the narrative of each designated campaign covers combat activities in a specific location at a particular time. The names and dates of campaigns prior to Vietnam Service generally were identical for all the U.S. Armed Forces, although 9 campaigns in World War II were air campaigns with dates that differed somewhat from the ground campaigns with the same designations. In Southeast Asia during the 1960s and 1970s, however, the United States Air Force could not always identify significant events in the air war with the campaigns of the Army or Navy. Consequently, the Joint Chiefs of Staff allowed each service to designate its own campaigns, and the Air Force established campaigns for Vietnam Service that differed in name and date from those of the other services. Designated campaigns established combat credit for the individual and his unit. Campaign narratives in this book feature air power in combat operations. Important non-combat air operations occurring outside the campaign zones are not treated here. The reader must look elsewhere for descriptions of the extensive ferrying of aircraft from the United States to overseas theaters, the routine aerial transport of personnel and supplies, the vital work of air depots and repair facilities, and the vast efforts devoted to training personnel in aerial combat and support assignments.

From time to time, Air Force personnel also put their lives at risk in limited military operations around the world. These operations, such as the rescue of American citizens from Grenada in October and November 1983, or the air strikes against Libya in April 1986, are recognized through award of the Armed Forces Expeditionary Medal to participating military members. This combat service award is described in Appendix 1 because a person receiving it for service in Vietnam between July 1, 1958, and July 3, 1965, may exchange it for the Vietnam Service Medal.

For today's Air Force, the heritage of the service medal begins with the participation of aerial elements in the expedition against Mexican bandits in 1916. As the Aviation Section of the U.S. Army Signal Corps, the Air Force earned campaign credit in Mexican Service.

Mexican Service

1916-1917

Mexican Service Medal

A flowering yucca plant embossed over mountains appears on the obverse side of the Mexican Service Medal. Around the rim at the top in a semicircle are the words MEXICAN SERVICE, and around the bottom rim are the dates 1911–1917. The medal's reverse side depicts in the center an American eagle with wings spread. The eagle is perched on a cannon which rests on a cluster of crossed flags, rifles, and weapons of previous conflicts. Immediately beneath this cluster, embossed horizontally, are the words FOR SERVICE. Above the eagle, around the rim at the top, are the words UNITED STATES ARMY, and around the bottom rim in a semicircle appear 13 stars. The Mexican Service Medal is worn with a suspension ribbon, although a ribbon bar may be worn in place of the service medal. The suspension ribbon and ribbon bar are yellow, with vertical green stripes on each edge and a blue band in the center.

War Department General Order No. 155, December 12, 1917, established the Mexican Service Medal. The U.S. awarded the medal and ribbon for service in 2 military expeditions and 7 engagements in Mexico between April 12, 1911, and February 7, 1917. American airmen, as members of the Aviation Section of the U.S. Army Signal Corps, served only in the Mexican Expedition Campaign; consequently, Mexican service for which an airman received the Mexican Service Medal and Ribbon embraced the period between March 14, 1916, and February 7, 1917.

Mexican Service Streamer

The Mexican Service Streamer awarded to military units is identical to the ribbon in design and color. The 1st Aero Squadron, the sole U.S. Army aviation unit to earn Mexican service credit, qualified for the Mexican Expedition Campaign Streamer, which has embroidered on it MEXICO 1916–1917.

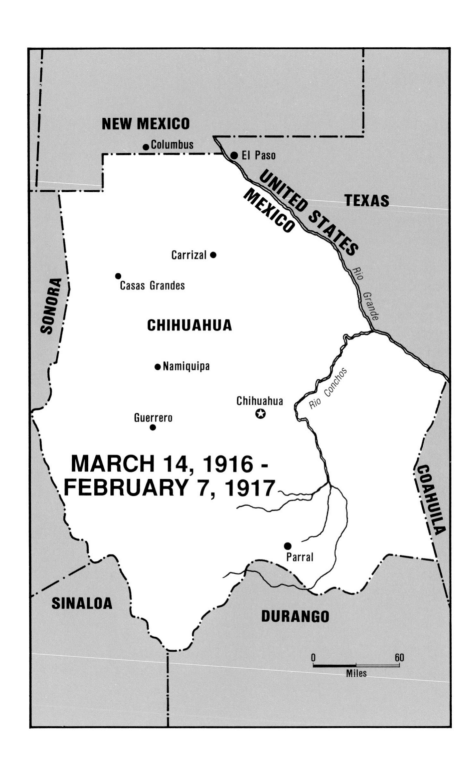

NEW MEXICO

● Columbus

● El Paso

UNITED STATES

MEXICO

TEXAS

SONORA

Carrizal ●

● Casas Grandes

CHIHUAHUA

Rio Grande

● Namiquipa

Chihuahua
☆

Rio Conchos

Guerrero
●

MARCH 14, 1916 -
FEBRUARY 7, 1917

COAHUILA

● Parral

SINALOA

DURANGO

0   60
Miles

10

Mexican Expedition Campaign:
March 14, 1916–February 7, 1917

On March 9, 1916, irregular forces of Francisco (Pancho) Villa from the Mexican state of Chihuahua raided the small town of Columbus, New Mexico, a few miles north of the U.S. border. The next day the 1st Aero Squadron, stationed 120 miles to the east at El Paso, Texas, received orders to join the Mexican Expedition being formed at Columbus by Brig. Gen. John J. Pershing. Arriving at Columbus on March 15, the squadron, under the command of Capt. Benjamin D. Foulois, made its first reconnaissance flight over Mexican territory the following day.

On March 20 the 1st Aero Squadron moved its base to Casas Grandes, Mexico, nearly 200 miles south of Columbus and about 240 miles southwest of El Paso. General Pershing, Commander of the Mexican Expedition, established his headquarters at the nearby Mormon colony of Colonia Dublan. From Casas Grandes the squadron attempted to support U.S. Armed Forces with reconnaissance and liaison missions, but its underpowered aircraft, 7 JN–2s, could not climb over the rugged Sierra Madre Mountains to reach the cavalry columns moving rapidly to the south. The squadron moved several times before arriving on April 17 at Namiquipa, Mexico, 320 miles south of Columbus and only 160 miles northwest of the city of Chihuahua.

From Namiquipa the 1st Aero Squadron flew messages received by telegraph from Pershing's headquarters to the far-ranging elements of the 7th, 10th, 11th, and 13th Cavalry Regiments. The cavalry continued to pursue Villa's forces as far as Parral, Mexico, 300 miles south of the city of Chihuahua and over 600 miles south of El Paso, Texas. But by April 20, three days after arriving in Namiquipa, the 1st Aero Squadron had crashed all but 2 of its aircraft* and returned to Columbus to await replacements. A few new Curtiss R–2s arrived before June 1, but the squadron found them underpowered and unsuited to Mexican field service. During the remainder of the Mexican Expedition the 1st Aero Squadron flew only a few more operational missions.

From the beginning, the Government of Mexico had protested the American incursion into its territory, and on June 21, 1916, Mexico's

---

*The pilots survived the crashes with various injuries.

Armed Forces attacked a detachment of U.S. cavalry at Carrizal, Mexico, 160 miles east of General Pershing's headquarters at Colonia Dublan, just outside of Casas Grandes. The diplomatic protests and military confrontation caused the U.S. to suspend operations further inside Mexico. In September 1916 General Pershing concentrated his troops at Colonia Dublan, where they remained for the next 5 months until withdrawn on February 5, 1917.

The Mexican Expedition Campaign tested the Aviation Section of the Army Signal Corps and found its aircraft far less capable and reliable than desired. But in spite of these problems, the 1st Aero Squadron did make some significant achievements. For the first time in U.S. military aviation history, photographic equipment was used for mosaic mapping. The squadron also demonstrated the importance of aircraft for reconnaissance work in a mobile operation and provided vital, albeit limited, message service for the expeditionary force. The combat support experience would soon prove beneficial: 1 year after withdrawing from Mexico, the 1st Aero Squadron and other Army aviation units would leave for France and the battlefields of World War I.

World War I Service

1917-1918

World War I Victory Medal

A winged figure of the lady Victory, holding sword and shield, graces the obverse side of the World War I Victory Medal. On the reverse side around the top rim is the inscription THE GREAT WAR FOR CIVILIZATION. Around the bottom rim are 6 stars and in the center a fasces embossed over the U.S. Coat of Arms. On either side are listed the allied and associated nations* that took part in the war against the Central Powers: FRANCE, ITALY, SERBIA, JAPAN, MONTENEGRO, RUSSIA, and GREECE are embossed on the left, and GREAT BRITAIN, BELGIUM, BRAZIL, POR-TUGAL, RUMANIA, and CHINA on the right. The medal is worn with a suspension ribbon, although a ribbon bar may be worn instead. The suspension ribbon and ribbon bar feature opposed vertical rainbows, which are from each edge violet, dark blue, light blue, green, and yellow, with a red band in the center.

War Department General Order No. 48, April 9, 1919, established the World War I Victory Medal. An individual received the decoration if he served honorably in the U.S. Army Air Service between April 6, 1917, the date of the American declaration of war against Germany, and November 11, 1918, the armistice date. Anyone serving in combat was also entitled to 1 or more rectangular bronze battle clasps, each embossed with the name of a separate campaign or defensive sector. Noncombatant service entitled a person to a service clasp embossed with the name of the allied state—England, Italy, or France—in which he served. Clasps are attached to the suspension ribbon above the medal. For each battle clasp an individual earned, he also received a Bronze Service Star to wear on his ribbon bar. The service clasp had no corresponding star because it was not a combat decoration.

World War I Service Streamer

The World War I Service Streamer, a unit award analogous to the Victory Medal, is identical to the ribbon in design and color. An Army Air Service unit based in France, England, or Italy at any time between April 6, 1917, and November 11, 1918, received a service streamer. A unit participating in a military campaign earned a campaign streamer instead of a service streamer, and a unit serving in France behind the lines in a defensive sector received a streamer embroidered with the sector's name.

---

*Associated countries declared war on one or more of the Central Powers but never formed an alliance with other Allied Nations.

Defensive Sectors of World War I

The War Department designated defensive sectors in the theater to award credit for combat in areas outside the designated campaigns. Units received embroidered streamers and individuals received battle clasps naming the defensive sectors. Air Service units earned credit for World War I participation in 6 defensive sectors named after 18th century French Provinces: Alsace, Champagne, Flanders, Ile-de-France, Lorraine, and Picardy.

Air Service units in varying numbers served within each of these defensive sectors. Only 1 unit, the 4th Balloon Company, earned credit for service in the Alsace Defensive Sector. The 12th Aero Squadron, however, moved frequently, earning combat credit in the Ile-de-France, Champagne, and Lorraine Defensive Sectors. Only a few units, including the 148th Aero Squadron, served in the Picardy Defensive Sector. Most Air Service units, among them the illustrious 1st Aero Squadron, 94th Aero Squadron, and 103d Aero Squadron, earned combat credit in the Lorraine Defensive Sector.

The 103d Aero Squadron (Pursuit) was the first to represent the Air Service in Europe; its pilots were drawn from the Lafayette Escadrille, a group of American volunteers who joined the French Air Service in 1916. On February 19, 1918, the 103d's ground crew arrived at La Noblette, a village in the Champagne Defensive Sector, just northeast of Chalons-sur-Marne, a small city 95 miles east of Paris. That same day American pilots of the Lafayette Escadrille, already in La Noblette, joined the Air Service and the 103d Aero Squadron. Pilots of the 103d subsequently achieved the Air Service's first 6 aerial victories. Although the squadron remained under control of the French, the Air Service reassigned several of its pilots to other American units to provide experienced leadership in preparation for combat. Attached to the Groupe de Combat 15, the 103d flew pursuit patrols in support of French combat operations, earning combat service credit in the Flanders and Lorraine Defensive Sectors, until it was placed under the 3d Pursuit Group in July 1918.

Meantime, on March 15, 1918, the Air Service began operations in the Champagne Defensive Sector south of St. Mihiel in a relatively quiet part of the Western Front. The 95th Aero Squadron (Pursuit) flew reconnaissance missions in unarmed Nieuports from Villeneuve-les-Vertus, a short distance from Chalons-sur-Marne. Within 3 weeks, on April 4, the 1st Aero Squadron (Observation) arrived in the sector at

Ourches, 12 miles southwest of Toul and about 25 miles southwest of Nancy. The 1st came directly from Columbus, New Mexico, where it had been based since its withdrawal from Mexico more than a year earlier. The squadron thus rejoined its former commander, Brig. Gen. Benjamin D. Foulois, who on November 27, 1917, had become Chief, Air Service, American Expeditionary Forces. On April 11, 1918, the 1st Aero Squadron (Observation) began reconnaissance flights over the front lines near Toul. A few days earlier, on April 7, the 94th Aero Squadron (Pursuit) arrived at Gengault airdrome, 2 miles northeast of Toul and 12 miles west of Nancy in the Lorraine sector. A week later, on April 14, 2 pilots of the 94th shot down a pair of enemy aircraft over the Gengault airdrome, beginning a string of aerial victories that would make the "Hat-in-the-Ring" squadron famous. The 94th earned credit for service in both the Champagne and Lorraine Defensive Sectors. As the month drew to a close, the Air Service established the 1st Corps Observation Group at Ourches airdrome, 12 miles southwest of Toul. The arrival of other new squadrons in April also contributed to the build-up of American aerial forces in the theater. Most of these units earned credit for participation in 1 or more named campaigns in World War I.

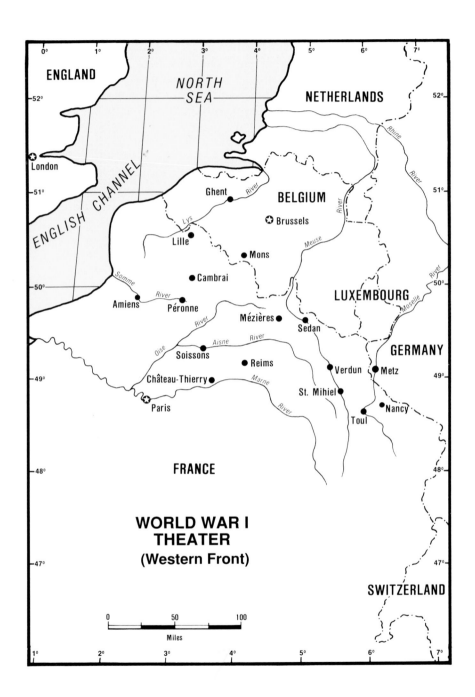

ENGLAND

NORTH
SEA

NETHERLANDS

London

ENGLISH CHANNEL

Ghent

BELGIUM

Brussels

Lille

Mons

Cambrai

LUXEMBOURG

Amiens

Péronne

Mézières

Sedan

GERMANY

Soissons

Reims

Verdun

Metz

Château-Thierry

St. Mihiel

Paris

Toul

Nancy

FRANCE

**WORLD WAR I
THEATER**
(Western Front)

0   50   100
Miles

SWITZERLAND

20

World War I Campaigns
March 21–November 11, 1918

Designated Campaigns of World War I

The War Department designated 13 campaigns in World War I;
however, U.S. Army Air Service units qualified for campaign streamers in only 8 of them, all on the Western Front, between March 21 and
November 11, 1918. No Air Service units participated in the
Cambrai, Aisne, Montdidier-Noyon, Ypres-Lys, and Vittorio-Veneto
Campaigns, although some American pilots and observers attached to
other Allied air services flew combat missions in these campaigns and
earned the appropriate battle clasps. In essence, Western Europe
comprised the World War I theater of operations for U.S. Army Air
Service units.

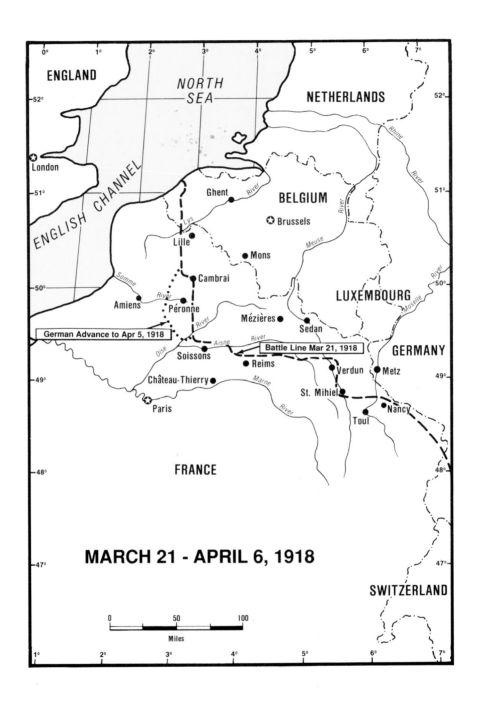

ENGLAND

NORTH SEA

NETHERLANDS

London

ENGLISH CHANNEL

Ghent

BELGIUM

Brussels

Lille

Mons

Cambrai

Amiens

Péronne

Mézières

Sedan

LUXEMBOURG

Soissons

Reims

German Advance to Apr 5, 1918

Battle Line Mar 21, 1918

GERMANY

Château-Thierry

Verdun

Metz

St. Mihiel

Nancy

Paris

Toul

FRANCE

MARCH 21 - APRIL 6, 1918

SWITZERLAND

0   50   100

Miles

Somme Defensive:
March 21–April 6, 1918

On March 21, 1918, the Germans, following the plan of Gen. Erich F. Ludendorff, launched an attack against the right flank of the British sector, in the vicinity of Péronne, France, on the Somme River, 100 miles north of Paris. General Ludendorff intended to split the British forces from the French troops to the south. Three German armies, the Seventeenth, the Second, and the Eighteenth, attacked on a 60-mile front, driving toward the southwest. The British Third Army held the German Seventeenth and Second Armies to only small gains along the northern portion of the front. Farther south, the German Eighteenth had greater success against the British Fifth Army. By March 22 the Germans had broken through the British lines and advanced rapidly 30 miles to the southwest toward Amiens. The drive exposed the flank of the British Third Army, forcing its withdrawal as well.

The Commander of the British Expeditionary Force, Field Marshal Sir Douglas Haig, threw service troops into the line as reserves and called for French reinforcements. Some French units arrived piecemeal and short of artillery and ammunition because the French commander, Marshal Henri Philippe Pétain, concentrated instead on organizing the French Third and Sixth Armies along a new east to west defensive line located 15 to 20 miles south of the Somme River. Marshal Pétain was concerned about protecting Paris, which German long-range artillery shelled from a distance of 65 miles. Upset with the lack of support from the French, Field Marshal Haig insisted on the appointment of a Supreme Allied Commander. On April 3 the Allies named French Marshal Ferdinand Foch to this post. Meanwhile, on March 27, the German Eighteenth Army captured the town of Montdidier, 60 miles north of Paris, thus creating a small gap between British and French forces. But the Allies quickly closed it, denying the enemy an opportunity to destroy the divided British and French Armies and achieve a strategic victory before the Americans arrived in Europe in full force.

Four units of the Air Service, American Expeditionary Forces (AEF), entered combat during the Somme Defensive: the 22d Aero Squadron of the 2d Pursuit Group, the 28th Aero Squadron of the 3d Pursuit Group, and the 17th and 148th Aero Squadrons of the 4th Pursuit Group. These units had arrived in France in early March before the Somme Defensive and were assigned to various British squadrons for training. None of the American squadrons possessed aircraft, and apparently, the 17th and 148th arrived without pilots. During the Somme Defensive several pilots of the 22d squadron flew with the British on observation and photographic missions, and pilots of the 28th served as aircrew members on day bombing and photographic missions. By April 6, 1918, a stout British defense had stopped the German advance about 15 miles east of Amiens.

Lys:
April 9–27, 1918

On April 9, 1918, almost immediately after their advance was halted near Amiens, the Germans began a new offensive along the Lys River north of the city. General Ludendorff still hoped to destroy the British forces in France and sought to cut off the English Channel ports of Dunkirk and Calais. The German Sixth Army scattered the Portuguese 2d Division in an attack along the southern bank of the Lys River and advanced some 3 to 5 miles westward until checked by elements of the British First and Second Armies. The next day, the German Fourth Army advanced along the northern bank of the Lys where the British Second Army had been weakened by the withdrawal of reserves to the south the day before.

As the Germans penetrated the front, Field Marshal Sir Douglas Haig, the British commander, requested immediate reinforcements from the Supreme Allied Commander. Facing other commitments, Marshal Foch sent less than half the needed support, but the British effort on April 12–17 succeeded in stopping the enemy after an advance of 10 miles. The German Fourth Army gained a few hundred yards more in a surprise attack on the 25th, but to no avail. Once again, although suffering heavy casualties, enemy troops failed to breach Allied defenses.

The only American Air Service unit that participated in the Lys Campaign, the 28th Aero Squadron, was divided and assigned to the British. On April 9 the headquarters and Flights A and B were attached to the Royal Flying Corps's 20th Squadron, equipped with Bristol fighters, and stationed near Troissereux. Flight C was moved to Boisdinghem on the 12th to join the 206th Squadron, Royal Flying Corps, and fly de Havilland daytime bombers. Also on April 12 the rest of the 28th Aero Squadron relocated to Alquines and was attached to the British 98th Squadron, equipped with the same day bomber. Pilots and observers of the 28th flew with the British on day bombing and reconnaissance missions behind German lines until the end of the Lys Campaign.

American ground forces to the southeast, near St. Mihiel in Lorraine, came under fire for the first time during the Lys Campaign on April 20, when the Germans launched an abortive attack on the positions of the U.S. Army 26th Division. At this time, British and French leaders tried to persuade Gen. John J. Pershing, Commander of American

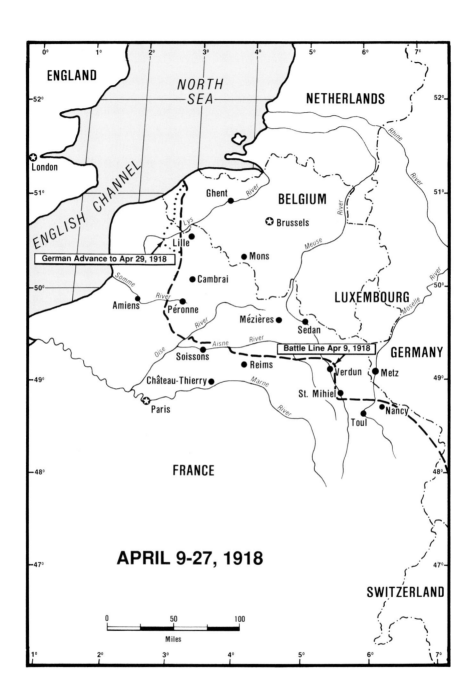

ENGLAND

NORTH SEA

NETHERLANDS

London

ENGLISH CHANNEL

Ghent

BELGIUM

Brussels

Lille

German Advance to Apr 29, 1918

Mons

Cambrai

LUXEMBOURG

Amiens

Péronne

Mézières

Sedan

GERMANY

Soissons

Reims

Battle Line Apr 9, 1918

Verdun

Metz

Château-Thierry

St. Mihiel

Nancy

Paris

Toul

FRANCE

APRIL 9-27, 1918

SWITZERLAND

0   50   100

Miles

Expeditionary Forces, to commit American troops along the front where needed as reserves. This scheme would place small groups of American servicemen under the direct control of numerous French and British commanders. General Pershing steadfastly refused, although he remained willing to commit entire U.S. divisions for service under Allied Command. The Allies ultimately agreed that the AEF would remain intact under Pershing's command and fight as an independent force. General Pershing, having secured Allied agreement in principle to the separate American force, later relented and some smaller units did operate at times under British and French control. One month after the end of the Lys Campaign, on May 29, 1918, Brig. Gen. (later, Maj. Gen.) Mason M. Patrick succeeded General Foulois as the Chief of Air Service, AEF.

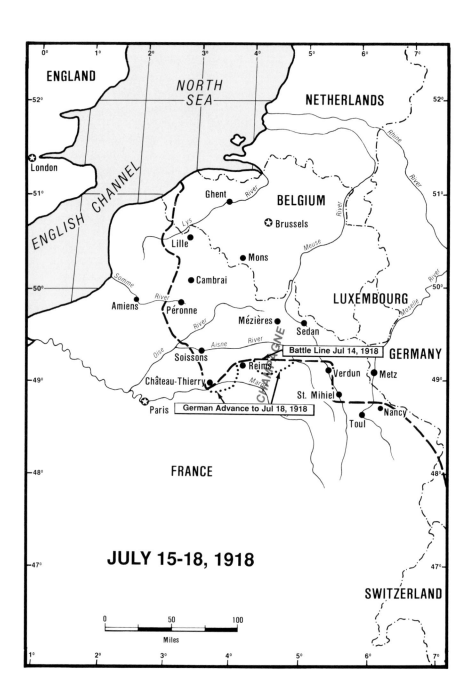

ENGLAND

NORTH
SEA

NETHERLANDS

London

ENGLISH CHANNEL

Ghent

River

BELGIUM

Rhine

River

Brussels

Lys

Lille

Mons

Meuse

River

Cambrai

LUXEMBOURG

River

Somme

Amiens

River

Péronne

Moselle

Mézières

Soissons

Oise

Aisne

River

Sedan

CHAMPAGNE

Battle Line Jul 14, 1918

GERMANY

Château-Thierry

Reims

Marne

Verdun

Metz

St. Mihiel

Paris

German Advance to Jul 18, 1918

Nancy

Toul

FRANCE

JULY 15-18, 1918

SWITZERLAND

0   50   100

Miles

Champagne–Marne:
July 15–18, 1918

At the end of June 1918 two American air units, the 1st Pursuit Group and the I Corps Observation Group, having gained combat experience in the Toul area, moved west to airdromes near Château-Thierry, a town which the Germans had captured a few weeks earlier.* These units formed the nucleus of the First Air Service Brigade, a temporary organization under the command of Col. William (Billy) Mitchell. During the first 2 weeks of July the 1st Pursuit Group, flying older Nieuports against a larger and more experienced enemy air force, lost 8 pilots, half captured when forced down behind German lines and half killed in action. Among the latter was the son of former President Theodore Roosevelt, Quentin, whom a German pilot shot down on July 14. Despite these losses, the group scored 9 aerial victories.

The Germans attempted to break Allied defenses on the Western Front in a 2-pronged attack on July 15. The Allies had pinpointed the time of the attack within 24 hours and determined the general location, assisted in part by the 1st Corps Observation Group, which conducted visual and photographic reconnaissance that contributed to Allied intelligence. Early on the morning of the 15th Colonel Mitchell flew a reconnaissance mission to locate the enemy bridgehead over the Marne River. After informing Allied Headquarters, he dispatched pursuit aircraft to strafe enemy troops crossing the Marne on pontoon bridges. Attacking between Soissons, on the Aisne River, and Reims, 40 miles to the east on the Vesle River, the German Seventh Army pushed south across the Marne River between Château-Thierry, about 55 miles northeast of Paris, and Epernay, 25 miles east of Château-Thierry. The Germans drove 2 Italian divisions from their positions southwest of Reims before the U.S. 3d Division, aided by the French, stopped the German advance.

In the second prong of the attack, the German First Army made practically no gains east of Reims, where the French Fourth Army,

---

*Between April 17 and July 15, 1918, the Germans launched 2 other ground offensives, designated the Aisne and the Montdidier-Noyon Campaigns (War Department General Order No. 48, April 9, 1919). Enemy troops seized a salient between Soissons, Château-Thierry, and Reims. During this time Air Service units and pilots flew combat missions elsewhere along the Western Front and especially near Toul, but no Air Service unit qualified for campaign credit in the Aisne Campaign, May 27–June 5, 1918, or the Montdidier-Noyon Campaign, June 9–13, 1918.

reinforced with British units, had prepared a strong defense in expectation of the battle. The Allies also had ample warning of this attack, provided for the most part through aerial photography by the Air Service 1st Corps Observation Group. The 1st Pursuit Group aggressively strafed German ground forces, escorted observation and bombardment aircraft, and flew air defense patrols over the battle area. The American pilots also adopted new tactics. Instead of relying on the large, closely massed formations favored by the British and French or on the small independent formations of 3 to 5 aircraft employed around Toul, the 1st Pursuit Group began to fly in formations of 12 to 15 aircraft organized in mutually supporting flights of 4 or 5, with 1 flight usually remaining high as cover. During the 3-day battle, the group destroyed 8 enemy aircraft, and the Germans killed 2 American pilots and captured another.

On July 18 the German High Command, directing exhausted and ill-equipped troops and facing well-prepared Allied defenses and the threat of an Allied counter offensive between the Aisne and Marne River, terminated the Champagne-Marne offensive. Aerial reconnaissance and air defense performed by the 1st Pursuit Group and other elements of the First Air Service Brigade had helped the Allies successfully defend Reims.

Aisne–Marne:
July 18–August 6, 1918

On July 18, 1918, in a unified operation under the Supreme Allied Commander, Marshal Ferdinand Foch, the Allies (France, Great Britain, Italy, and the United States) counterattacked in the region between the Aisne and Marne Rivers. Striking along a front that extended from Soissons in the northwest to Château-Thierry in the south, and to Reims in the northeast, the Allies succeeded in rolling back the German forces. Eight American divisions participated in the offensive. The U.S. 1st and 2d Divisions spearheaded the main attack by the French Tenth Army just south of Soissons. The French also employed 350 tanks in support of the initial assault. Caught by surprise, the enemy suffered heavy casualties, and many demoralized troops surrendered. However, German leaders quickly began an orderly withdrawal. The first ground given up was the Marne River beachhead on July 19, only a few days after its capture. Enemy ground forces covered their retreat to a line along the Aisne and Vesle Rivers with machine gun and artillery rear guards, while the German Air Force supported the withdrawal with reconnaissance, strafing, and air defense flights.

Allied air forces, including components of the American Air Service, countered the German presence in the air and supported the Allied summer offensive. In fact, in spite of inclement weather early in the morning of July 18, an American pilot and his observer flew over the lines without fighter escort to confirm what the Allied leaders suspected, that the enemy troops were retreating on all fronts. For the next 3 weeks the I Corps Observation Group located and identified the shifting front lines and helped direct artillery fire on enemy batteries. Often the observation pilots had to fly at low altitudes where their aircraft were especially vulnerable to ground fire. The group lost 10 pilots and observers to ground fire and enemy pursuit attacks, but managed to shoot down 2 enemy aircraft. Meanwhile, the 1st Pursuit Group was busy escorting photographic reconnaissance planes, performing low-level strafing, and conducting offensive patrols to establish air superiority over local areas of operation. The 1st Pursuit Group destroyed 16 enemy aircraft during the campaign, but lost 15 pilots killed or captured.

July 6—a few days before the Aisne-Marne Campaign began—marked the first time Air Service balloonists operated in combat. In all, 3 balloon companies participated in the campaign, losing 8 balloons to

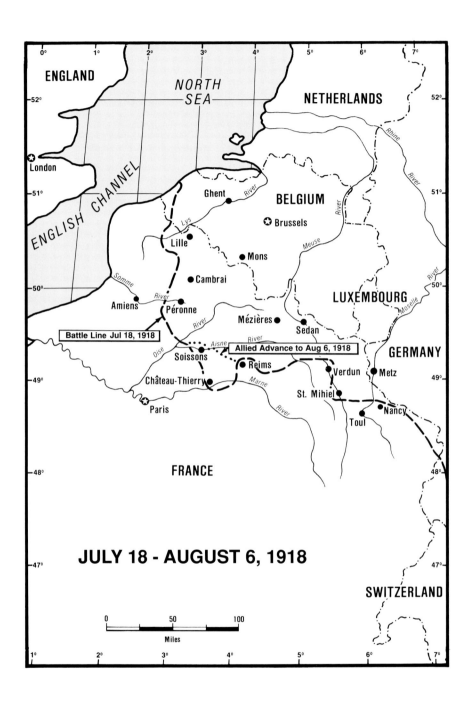

ENGLAND

NORTH
SEA

NETHERLANDS

London

ENGLISH CHANNEL

Ghent

BELGIUM

Brussels

Lys

Lille

Mons

Meuse River

Cambrai

LUXEMBOURG

Somme

River

Amiens

Péronne

Mézières

Sedan

Moselle River

GERMANY

River

Battle Line Jul 18, 1918

Oise

Aisne

River

Allied Advance to Aug 6, 1918

Soissons

Reims

Verdun

Metz

Château-Thierry

Marne

St. Mihiel

Paris

River

Nancy

Toul

FRANCE

JULY 18 - AUGUST 6, 1918

0   50   100

Miles

SWITZERLAND

enemy aircraft and 1 to artillery fire, while providing valuable artillery spotting service.

By August 6 the German forces had retreated 20 miles and established defensive lines along the Vesle River, a tributary of the Aisne flowing between Reims and Soissons. The Aisne-Marne Campaign eliminated any threat to Paris and dashed German hopes for a decisive victory. American air units—the 1st Pursuit Group, the I Corps Observation Group, and the 3 balloon companies—provided a nucleus of veteran forces for the continuing expansion of American Air Service activities in Europe.

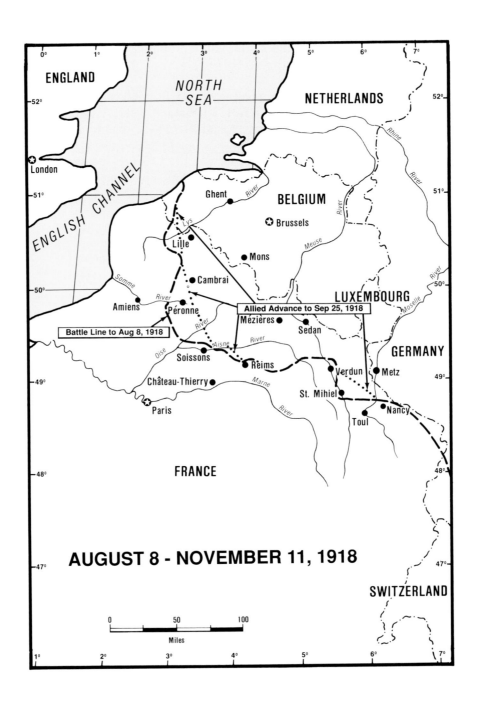

ENGLAND

NORTH
SEA

NETHERLANDS

London

ENGLISH CHANNEL

Ghent

BELGIUM

Brussels

Rhine River

Lille

Mons

Meuse River

LUXEMBOURG

Cambrai

Somme River

Amiens

Péronne

Allied Advance to Sep 25, 1918

Mézières

Sedan

Moselle River

GERMANY

Battle Line to Aug 8, 1918

Oise River

Soissons

Aisne River

Reims

Verdun

Metz

Château-Thierry

Marne

St. Mihiel

Nancy

Paris

River

Toul

FRANCE

AUGUST 8 - NOVEMBER 11, 1918

SWITZERLAND

0   50   100

Miles

Somme Offensive:
August 8–November 11, 1918

The Allies surprised the Germans on August 8, 1918, with a general offensive along the front of the Amiens Salient between the Oise and Somme Rivers in northeastern France. Field Marshal Sir Douglas Haig, the Allied commander for this operation, directed the British Fourth Army and the French First Army against the German Eighteenth and Second Armies. Canadian and Australian/New Zealand corps spearheaded the offensive along the north and south banks of the Somme River, attacking behind tanks and, to achieve surprise, without the preliminary artillery barrage. To the south, the French advanced after a 45-minute artillery bombardment along the Oise River. The French Third Army joined the battle on August 10, forcing the Germans to give up Montdidier, a town that they had captured less than 5 months previously. Then on the 21st the British Third Army added its efforts along a 15-mile front south of Arras, located 45 miles north of Montdidier and slightly more than 100 miles north of Paris, and succeeded in driving the Germans as much as 6 miles eastward.

The Allies used airplanes and tanks to help reduce strongpoints that the infantry could not breach alone and steadily and methodically pushed the German forces eastward. By September 2, under constant Allied pressure, the enemy had withdrawn to a defensive position that ran between Reims in the south and the town of Cambrai in the north, on the Schelde River. German forces held Cambrai so tenaciously that the Allies failed to capture it until late October.

On August 8, the first day of the Somme Offensive, foggy weather grounded the air forces early in the morning, but by the end of the day Allied aircraft were engaging the enemy in the air and supporting the advance on the ground. Two American units under British control, the 17th Aero Squadron (Pursuit) and the 148th Aero Squadron (Pursuit), participated in this campaign from airdromes near Amiens, a town on the Somme River. The 17th and 148th flew offensive patrols against German aircraft and performed low-level bombing, strafing, and reconnaissance missions. On August 11–12, in the first American aerial bombardment mission, Air Service units successfully struck railroad yards a few miles behind the enemy front.

The Somme Offensive merged in September with the Allied assaults undertaken all along the Western Front. These actions continued to force the Germans to retreat until the armistice on November 11, 1918. American participation in the Somme Campaign and the Oise-Aisne Campaign that followed was limited to some extent because the U.S. commander, Gen. John J. Pershing, was organizing the American Expeditionary Forces for the St. Mihiel offensive.

Oisne–Aisne:
August 18–November 11, 1918

On August 18, 1918, the Allies broadened the offensive against the Amiens Salient, attacking along its southern edge in a 30-mile stretch between the Oise and Aisne Rivers. Three days later the French took the village of Lassigny, 25 miles northwest of Soissons. The American Expeditionary Forces contributed only 3 infantry divisions, the 28th, 32d, and 77th, to this effort. Meantime, to the north in Flanders, the U.S. II Corps aided the British in reducing the Lys Salient. By September 4 the Germans had established their defenses along the Hindenburg Line, a position they had occupied before their spring offensives. The German leadership, by now convinced that the war had to be ended, considered how this might be accomplished without giving up all the conquered territory. In September the Oise-Aisne Campaign, like the Somme Offensive, merged in a general Allied assault.

The American Air Service limited its support of this campaign to 1 balloon company, 1 observation squadron, and 3 pursuit squadrons. The 4th Balloon Company and the 27th Aero Squadron provided observation and reconnaissance support for the French ground forces. During the first few weeks of the campaign, the 94th and 95th Aero Squadrons (Pursuit) flew close air support missions and offensive aerial patrols until the units were relocated near Toul on September 1–2 in preparation for the St. Mihiel Campaign. The 88th Aero Squadron (Pursuit) remained behind, flying missions mostly along the Vesle River between Soissons, 60 miles northeast of Paris, and Reims, 35 miles farther east. On September 2 the 88th lost an aircraft with its pilot and observer, but destroyed an enemy plane. With the American squadron aiding newly arrived French pursuit units, the Allies soon gained air superiority in the area. Finally, on September 11, the 88th moved to a base 10 miles southwest of Verdun and about 145 miles east of Paris. Here, the squadron joined other Air Service units preparing for the planned offensive against the St. Mihiel Salient.

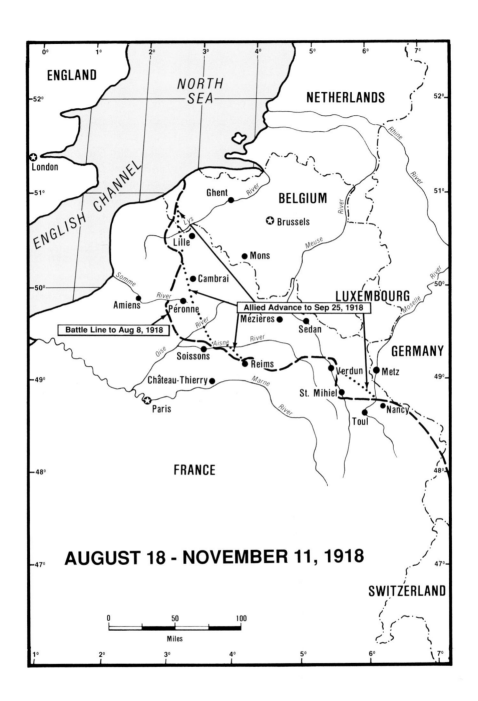

ENGLAND

NORTH SEA

NETHERLANDS

London

ENGLISH CHANNEL

Ghent

Rhine River

BELGIUM

Brussels

Lys

Lille

Mons

Meuse River

Cambrai

LUXEMBOURG

Somme River

Amiens

Péronne

Allied Advance to Sep 25, 1918

Mézières

Sedan

Moselle River

GERMANY

Battle Line to Aug 8, 1918

Oise River

Aisne River

Soissons

Reims

Verdun

Metz

Château-Thierry

Marne River

St. Mihiel

Nancy

Paris

Toul

FRANCE

AUGUST 18 - NOVEMBER 11, 1918

SWITZERLAND

0   50   100
Miles

38

St. Mihiel:
September 12–16, 1918

The roots of the St. Mihiel Campaign dated back to July 24, 1918, when Allied leaders authorized the formation of a separate American Army under the command of Gen. John J. Pershing, who also led the American Expeditionary Forces in Europe. General Pershing assumed command of the First U.S. Army on August 11 and began to plan for the reduction of the St. Mihiel Salient, located between the Moselle and the Meuse Rivers in eastern France. At the apex of the salient was the village of St. Mihiel on the Meuse River. German forces had already begun to withdraw, and from September 12 to 16 the First U.S. Army, with the help of a French colonial corps, overtook the enemy positions and stabilized a new line along a 35-mile front from Pont-à-Mousson on the Moselle River northeast to the village of Fresnes, about 25 miles north of St. Mihiel.

The First Army Air Service, consisting of American, British, and French units under the command of Col. William (Billy) Mitchell, supported the ground forces with more than 1,500 aircraft of all types. During the first 2 days of the campaign, poor weather kept most of the aircraft on the ground, although some observation and aerial patrol missions were flown. Once the weather cleared on September 14, the pursuit squadrons quickly established air superiority over the salient. Observation and pursuit squadrons suffered relatively few losses, but the outcome was quite different for bombardment aircraft, particularly for the Air Service's newly organized and outfitted 1st Day Bombardment Group.

On September 10 the 1st Day Bombardment Group, based at Amanty, 15 miles to the southwest of Toul, received DH–4 single-engine bomber aircraft built in the United States and equipped with the Liberty engine. The DH–4, with a top speed of 124 miles per hour, was virtually the only aircraft of American manufacture to see combat during World War I. On the 12th, after only minimal training, the group sent 15 bombers on 3 separate missions, but lost 8 to enemy fire, with poor bombing results. Two days later flying weather improved, and the group again attempted bombing missions, only to suffer more losses. In the 4-day campaign, a single bombardment squadron, the 96th, lost 16 pilots and observers and 14 aircraft—a loss rate greater than any other Air Service squadron during the war. The debut of the American-built bomber proved a disappointment because of inadequate defensive weapons, slow speed, and mechanical prob-

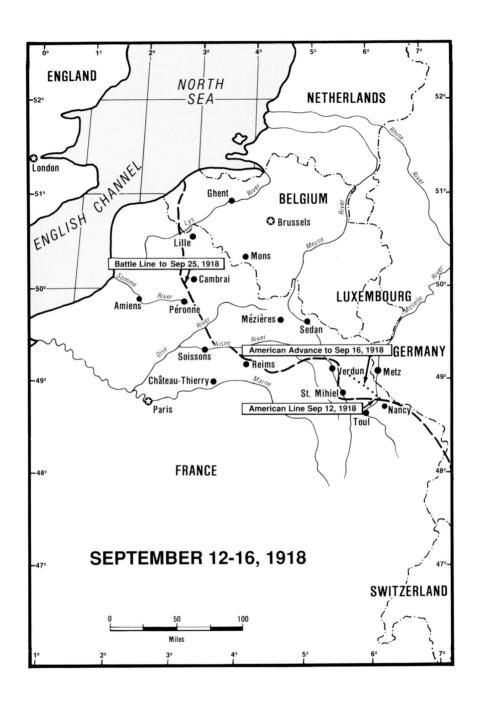

ENGLAND

NORTH SEA

NETHERLANDS

London

ENGLISH CHANNEL

Ghent

BELGIUM

Lys River

Brussels

Rhine River

Lille

Mons

Meuse River

Battle Line to Sep 25, 1918

Cambrai

LUXEMBOURG

Somme River

Amiens

Péronne

Mézières

Sedan

Moselle River

River

Oise

Aisne

River

Soissons

Reims

American Advance to Sep 16, 1918

GERMANY

Verdun

Metz

Château-Thierry

Marne

St. Mihiel

American Line Sep 12, 1918

Nancy

Paris

Toul

FRANCE

SEPTEMBER 12-16, 1918

SWITZERLAND

0   50   100

Miles

40

lems. Limited aircrew training and the use of small formations also contributed to high losses from aggressive German pursuit aircraft.

The First Army Air Service units nonetheless achieved some notable milestones in support of the ground offensive; they flew 3,300 missions within 4 days, destroying 12 enemy balloons, shooting down 60 enemy aircraft, and dropping 75 tons of bombs. Overall, the Allied air forces' contribution to the campaign operation was substantial. U.S. forces, both ground and air, achieved their objectives in the St. Mihiel Campaign and eliminated a potential threat to American forces during the last major Allied offensive of the war.

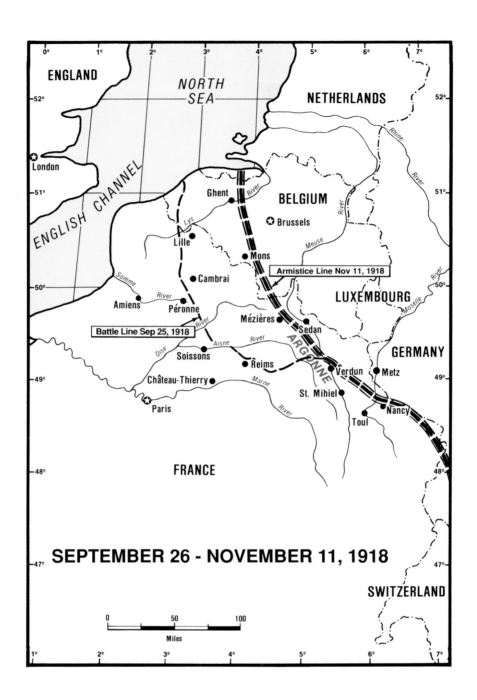

ENGLAND

NORTH
SEA

NETHERLANDS

London

ENGLISH CHANNEL

Ghent

Rhine
River

BELGIUM

Brussels

River

Lys

Lille

Mons

Armistice Line Nov 11, 1918

Meuse
River

Cambrai

LUXEMBOURG

Somme

River

Amiens

Péronne

Mézières

River

Sedan

Moselle
River

Battle Line Sep 25, 1918

ARGONNE

Oise

Aisne

River

GERMANY

Soissons

Reims

Verdun

Metz

Château-Thierry

Marne

St. Mihiel

Paris

River

Nancy

Toul

FRANCE

SEPTEMBER 26 - NOVEMBER 11, 1918

SWITZERLAND

0   50   100

Miles

Meuse–Argonne:
September 26–November 11, 1918[*]

On September 26, 1918, the Allies launched a general offensive all along the Western Front. General Pershing's U.S. First Army attacked on a 24-mile sector from the eastern banks of the Meuse River just north of Verdun to the Aisne River on the western edge of the Argonne Forest. The American objective was the railroad between Metz, on the Moselle River 178 miles northeast of Paris, and Mézières, about 90 miles northwest of Metz on the Meuse River. In October French forces joined U.S. troops to widen the front on the east, and by November 11 the combined armies had forced a German retreat from Lille to Ghent in the north and from Reims to Verdun in the south. By the time of the Meuse-Argonne Campaign, the Air Service had sufficient battle experience to revise its tactics and exploit its air superiority. Between September 26 and October 1, American pursuit airplanes claimed 100 German airplanes and 21 balloons shot down. The day before the campaign began, on September 25, Capt. Edward V. (Eddie) Rickenbacker assumed command of the 94th Aero Squadron (Pursuit). By the end of the war he had become the leading American ace, and his "Hat-in-the-Ring" squadron had scored more aerial victories than any other Air Service squadron.

American observation squadrons worked effectively with infantry and artillery forces, although the wooded, rugged terrain in the U.S. First Army sector made identification of friendly troops especially difficult. Inclement weather during much of the campaign increased the problem. But because the Air Service pursuit squadrons maintained air superiority over the front lines, most losses of observation aircraft resulted from ground fire.

Air Service bombardment groups that flew missions into enemy territory to bomb communications centers, railroads, troop concentrations, and other battlefield interdiction targets again suffered much heavier losses than did either pursuit or observation squadrons. The DH–4 continued to experience mechanical trouble. Bombardment

---

[*]The Vittorio-Veneto Campaign (October 24–November 4, 1918) in northern Italy was the only U.S. World War I campaign outside France. Although no Air Service unit participated in this campaign, 80 American pilots served with the Italians between June 20 and November 4, 1918. These Air Service pilots flew a total of 65 missions, bombing airfields, munition dumps, bridges, railroads, and troop concentrations. Among them was Maj. Fiorello H. La Guardia, then a New York Congressman and later to become mayor of New York City.

squadrons flying the French Breguet suffered fewer losses than those equipped with the American-made aircraft.

On November 6, as part of the Allied offensive, U.S. Armed Forces under General Pershing cut the Metz-Mézières railroad that anchored the enemy defensive line near Sedan, on the Meuse River a few miles southeast of Mézières, thus helping precipitate the final collapse of the German and Austrian forces. As early as October 6, German leaders had requested an armistice, but the U.S. (and the Allies) would not negotiate with the existing government. A revolt in the first week in November overthrew the German monarchy, and on November 9 a newly formed Socialist government proclaimed a republic. Within 2 days, at 5:00 a.m. on November 11, the German and Allied leaders signed an armistice that took effect at 11:00 a.m. the same day, thereby ending the hostilities of World War I.

From April to November 1918 the Air Service, American Expedition-ary Forces, had expanded from a single observation squadron assigned on the front to 45 assigned squadrons of all types, with 767 pilots, 481 observers, and 23 aerial gunners and equipped with 740 airplanes. Many other squadrons and personnel were in training or engaged in support functions in the rear areas. American air units flew 35,000 combat hours, took 18,000 photographs, and bombed 150 targets with 137.5 tons of bombs. In April 1918 no balloon companies existed in France, but by Armistice Day there were 35 companies, of which 23 served on the front. The balloons made 1,642 ascensions and flew a total of 3,111 hours. In the official aerial victory credits, U.S. aircraft accounted for 624 enemy airplanes and 60 balloons; American losses to German aerial action amounted to 289 airplanes and 35 balloons. Although constituting only 10 percent of the Allied Air Forces on Armistice Day, the Air Service, American Expeditionary Forces, provided the extra air power needed to assure Allied air superiority over the Western Front in the final campaigns.

The U.S. had relied on its Allies for most of the warplanes it used during World War I, while the fledgling Air Service concentrated on observation and pursuit functions, with bombardment operations playing only a secondary role. But in the 2 short decades of peace that followed, American aeronautical technology advanced dramati-cally. U.S. Army airmen, meantime, developed doctrines of air power which would be tested in World War II.

World War II Service

1941-1946

The Theaters

Unlike previous and subsequent wars in which U.S. participation was confined to a single continent, region, or country, World War II embraced practically the entire globe. Allied efforts to defeat the Axis powers in World War II involved the marshaling of manpower, the production of war materiel, and the deployment of forces on a scale never achieved before or since. On November 6, 1942, President Franklin D. Roosevelt issued Executive Order No. 9265 which established 3 combat service medals, 1 for each of 3 designated theaters around the world. The American Theater included all of North and South America (except Greenland and Alaska) and surrounding waters. The European–African–Middle Eastern (EAME) Theater embraced Europe, Africa, the Middle East, and Greenland, as well as the eastern Atlantic and western Indian Ocean. The largest of the 3 by far, however, was the Asiatic–Pacific (AP) Theater, which included Asia, Australia, Alaska, the Pacific Islands, most of the Pacific Ocean, and the eastern half of the Indian Ocean. Of these 3 theaters, the American Theater saw the least amount of combat—most of it confined to coastal waters, the Gulf of Mexico, and the Caribbean Sea.

World War II Service

American Theater

1941-1946

American Campaign Medal

The American Campaign Medal depicts on the lower half of the obverse side a sinking submarine. In the center background is a navy cruiser underway, with a B–24 aircraft flying overhead. In a semi-circle around the rim at the top are the words AMERICAN CAM-PAIGN. The reverse side of the medal is identical to the Asiatic–Pacific and European–African–Middle Eastern Campaign Medals. All 3 have in profile facing to the viewer's left a bald eagle perched on a rock. In the upper right quadrant above the eagle's back are embossed horizontally the words UNITED STATES OF AMERICA; in the lower left quadrant below the eagle's breast are the dates 1941–1945. The medal is worn with a suspension ribbon, although a ribbon bar may be worn in its place. The suspension ribbon and ribbon bar are bright azure with the colors of the United States—blue, white, and red—running in a vertical stripe down the center. A white and a black stripe, representing the colors of Germany, appear vertically near each edge, with the colors of Japan, a red and a white stripe, next to and inside the German colors.

Executive Order No. 9265, November 6, 1942, established the American Campaign Medal. A member of the U.S. Armed Forces earned the decoration if between December 7, 1941, and March 2, 1946, he or she engaged in combat within the American Theater, served for at least 1 year within the Continental U.S., was on permanent assignment in any other part of the American Theater, served on temporary duty for 30 consecutive or 60 nonconsecutive days in the theater but outside the U.S., or had a permanent assignment in an aircrew making frequent flights within the theater. Anyone who served with a unit awarded battle credit for the Antisubmarine Campaign, American Theater, also received a Bronze Service Star.

American Theater Streamers

The American Theater Service Streamer, a unit award analogous to the medal for the individual, is identical to the ribbon in design and color. A unit received this service streamer if it was based in the Continental U.S. for at least 1 year or in any other part of the theater at any time between December 7, 1941, and March 2, 1946. A unit in transit outside the U.S. through the American Theater also qualified. Units participating in the Antisubmarine Campaign, American Theater, earned that campaign streamer instead of the service streamer.

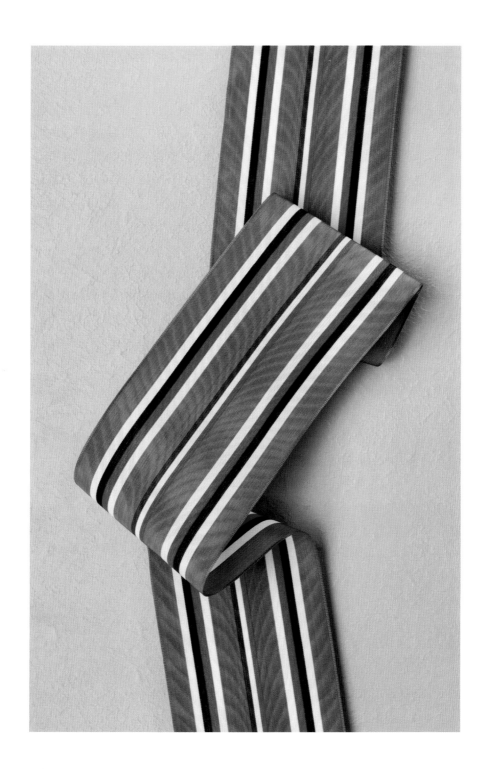

ARCTIC

OCEAN

GREENLAND

ALASKA

CANADA

EUROPEAN-
AFRICAN-
MIDDLE
EASTERN
THEATER

UNITED STATES

EUROPE

ATLANTIC

OCEAN

PACIFIC

OCEAN

AFRICA

SOUTH AMERICA

AMERICAN
THEATER

ASIATIC-
PACIFIC
THEATER

52

Designated Campaign
of the American Theater

The only combat operations within the American Theater involved antisubmarine warfare; thus the only campaign credit a unit or an individual could earn was the Antisubmarine Campaign, American Theater. A unit that conducted antisubmarine operations in the American Theater and in any one of the other World War II theaters qualified for the Antisubmarine Campaign Streamer in each theater. Individuals serving with a unit in more than 1 theater also earned the medal and ribbon for each theater along with a Bronze Service Star for each campaign. For example, the 4th Antisubmarine Squadron earned the Antisubmarine Campaign Streamer, American Theater, and the Antisubmarine Campaign Streamer, European–African–Middle Eastern Theater. A member of the squadron in both theaters received the American Campaign Medal and Ribbon, with a Bronze Star signifying the Antisubmarine Campaign, American Theater, and the EAME Campaign Medal and Ribbon with another Bronze Service Star signifying the Antisubmarine Campaign, EAME Theater. The entire American Theater constituted the combat zone for Antisubmarine Campaign credit, and the campaign dates extended from December 7, 1941, when Japan attacked Pearl Harbor, to September 2, 1945, when Japan formally surrendered.

Antisubmarine Campaign, American Theater: December 7, 1941–September 2, 1945[*]

Immediately following the attack on Pearl Harbor, the War Department assigned responsibility for aerial antisubmarine warfare to the United States Army Air Forces (AAF). The U.S. Navy, because it lacked the aircraft necessary for these missions, could not at that time undertake long-range aerial antisubmarine patrols. AAF units in the American Theater were therefore pressed into service to fly extensive patrols over U.S. coastal waters on the east and west coasts, and in the Caribbean Sea, the Gulf of Mexico, the Atlantic Ocean off Newfoundland, and the eastern and western approaches to the Panama Canal.

On the west coast, the Second and Fourth Air Forces began patrols on December 8, 1941, primarily with medium bombers, up to 200 miles offshore. The following January a reorganization left the entire burden of antisubmarine operations to the Fourth Air Force, which continued to patrol the west coast until late 1943. Japanese submarines could not operate effectively at such great distances from their Western Pacific bases, although some did occasionally shell West Coast installations, including a refinery near Santa Barbara, California, in February 1942. Throughout the war, AAF aircraft did not sink a single Japanese submarine near the U.S. west coast.

The AAF concentrated its efforts on antisubmarine patrols off the east coast of the United States, where the threat was very serious indeed. The I Bomber Command began flying missions on December 8, 1941, and for the next few months attempted as best it could to counter the German U–boat threat to Allied shipping in the Western Atlantic. During this period, before the employment of microwave radar capable of locating surfaced vessels at night, few AAF aircraft successfully attacked German submarines. But constant aerial patrols forced the submarines to submerge frequently and to stay down for long intervals, thereby hampering U–boat interception of Allied vessels.

By March 1942 antisubmarine aircraft began to interfere significantly with German submarine attacks against Allied shipping along the Atlantic coast. So the enemy shifted the focus of U–boat attacks to the Gulf of Mexico and the Caribbean Sea, and in May the Allies lost more vessels

---

[*]See Theater Map

there than in the western reaches of the Atlantic Ocean. On May 26, to counter this increasing threat, I Bomber Command created the Gulf Task Force, operating initially from Charleston, South Carolina, and later from Miami, Florida. Sightings of and attacks against submarines increased steadily from April through June, and this ultimately encouraged the enemy to shift to areas not effectively covered by air patrols. By October Germany redeployed its submarines to the North Atlantic convoy area and the approaches to Northwest Africa, in an effort to counter the Allied invasion in Morocco and Algeria. During November enemy submarines destroyed more Allied and neutral shipping than in any month since June.

At this critical time, on October 15, 1942, the Army Air Forces Antisubmarine Command (AAFAC), newly activated and placed under the operational control of the U.S. Navy, assumed the organization and functions of I Bomber Command. On November 20 the AAFAC organized the squadrons it had inherited from I Bomber Command into 2 wings: the 25th Antisubmarine Wing, headquartered in New York and responsible for patrols in the Eastern Atlantic; and the 26th Antisubmarine Wing, with headquarters in Miami and in charge of activities in the Gulf of Mexico. The next month the command also began operating a few B–24 Liberators equipped with advanced microwave radar capable of detecting surfaced submarines at night, and in 1943 these aircraft became the primary antisubmarine patrol airplanes.

German U–boats continued to interdict Allied and neutral shipping in the North Atlantic throughout the winter of 1942 and the first half of 1943. In April 1943 the AAF sent additional B–24s to AAFAC in Newfoundland to reinforce the effort in the North Atlantic. Early that month a detachment of the 25th Antisubmarine Wing, consisting of 3 squadrons, arrived at St. Johns, Newfoundland. Although the Germans increased their attacks in March and April, the Newfoundland-based squadrons inflicted sufficiently heavy losses to prompt the enemy to begin withdrawing its submarines from the Northwest Atlantic in May. No longer needed in Newfoundland, the 3 AAF squadrons moved to England in May. Other AAFAC squadrons continued flying patrols over the Western Atlantic, the Gulf of Mexico, and the Caribbean Sea long after the enemy had withdrawn most of its submarines from these areas.

On August 31, 1943, with the submarine threat markedly reduced, the AAF inactivated the AAFAC, and the U.S. Navy, using B–24s and other aircraft inherited from the command, assumed complete responsibility for antisubmarine operations in the American Theater, as well as in the European–African–Middle Eastern and Asiatic–Pacific Theaters.

World War II Service

Asiatic Pacific Theater

1941-1946

Asiatic–Pacific Campaign Medal

An amphibious landing in the tropics is shown on the obverse side of the AP Campaign Medal. In the center foreground are 2 helmeted soldiers holding rifles; behind them appears a leafed palm tree embossed over a landing craft with disembarking troops. In the background on the horizon are a battleship, an aircraft carrier, and a submarine, with 2 aircraft flying above the carrier. The words ASIATIC–PACIFIC CAMPAIGN are embossed in a semicircle around the top rim. The reverse side, identical to the American and EAME Campaign Medals, depicts a bald eagle in profile facing the viewer's left and perched on a rock. In the upper right quadrant, embossed horizontally above the eagle's back, are the words UNITED STATES OF AMERICA, and in the lower left quadrant below the eagle's breast are the dates 1941–1945. The medal is worn with a suspension ribbon, although a ribbon bar may be worn instead. The suspension ribbon and ribbon bar are yellow with 3 vertical stripes, blue, white, and red—the colors of the U.S.—in the center. Three more vertical stripes, white, red, and white—representing the colors of Japan—appear near each edge.

Executive Order No. 9265, November 6, 1942, established the Asiatic–Pacific Campaign Medal. A member of the U.S. Armed Forces earned this decoration if he or she participated in combat, had a permanent assignment, or served on temporary duty at least 30 consecutive or 60 nonconsecutive days within the theater. The individual received a Bronze Service Star for each campaign in which he or she participated or a Silver Service Star in place of 5 Bronze Stars. The stars are worn on the suspension ribbon or the ribbon bar. Participants in airborne or amphibious assault landings are entitled to wear an arrowhead on the suspension ribbon or the ribbon bar; a recipient may wear only 1 arrowhead regardless of the number of assault credits earned.

Asiatic–Pacific Theater Streamers

The AP Theater Service Streamer is identical to the ribbon in design and color. A unit received this service streamer if it was based in the theater at any time between December 7, 1941, and March 2, 1946, or if it traveled through the theater for at least 30 days. A campaign streamer has the name and dates of the campaign embroidered on it. A unit received a campaign streamer instead of the service streamer if it served within or flew combat missions into the combat zone during a designated campaign. Units participating in amphibious or airborne assault landings received a campaign streamer with an embroidered arrowhead preceding the name and dates.

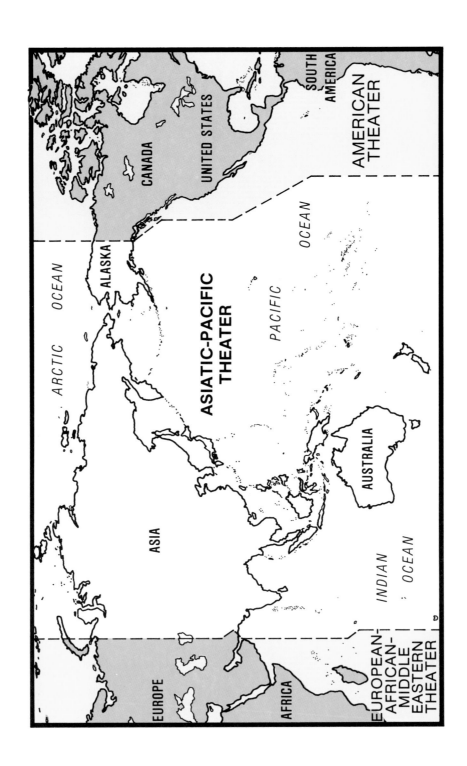

Asiatic–Pacific Theater Campaigns
December 7, 1941–September 2, 1945

Designated Campaigns of the Asiatic–Pacific Theater

The War Department designated 21 campaigns for the Asiatic–Pacific Theater. Each campaign had a designated combat zone and specific dates for campaign credits; campaign dates extended from December 7, 1941, the date of the Japanese attack on Pearl Harbor, through September 2, 1945, when Japan formally surrendered. For service within the theater during the 6 months after Japan surrendered, units and individuals could earn no campaign credits but received the Asiatic–Pacific Theater Service Streamer or the Asiatic–Pacific Campaign Medal and Ribbon. The first campaign summarized in this theater is the Central Pacific.

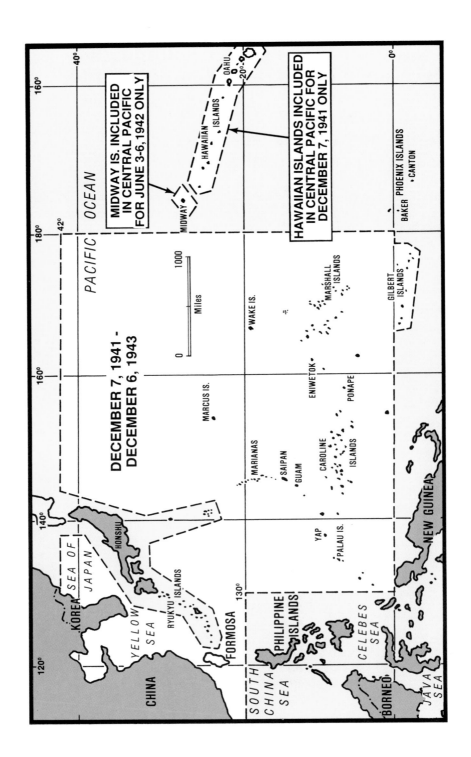

62

Central Pacific:
December 7, 1941–December 6, 1943

For the United States, World War II began on December 7, 1941, when Japanese forces attacked Pearl Harbor in the Territory of Hawaii. Besides successfully striking U.S. Navy ships and installations at Pearl Harbor on Oahu Island, the Japanese bombed and strafed AAF installations at Hickam Field on the south side of Pearl Harbor, Wheeler Field, 12 miles to the northwest of Hickam Field, and Bellows Field, about 7 miles northeast of Hickam on Mokapu Point. Only the small airfield at Haleiwa, on the north coast of Oahu Island and about 17 miles northwest of Hickam Field, escaped attack. Six pilots of the 47th Pursuit Squadron based at Haleiwa Field effectively engaged enemy aircraft during the battle. But the Hawaiian Air Force was caught completely by surprise, and the Japanese delivered a devastating blow at a cost of about 50 aircraft, many of them lost in accidents on the return, crash-landing on aircraft carriers in rough seas.

The Japanese attack destroyed 64 of the 231 aircraft assigned to the Hawaiian Air Force, damaged 88, and left only 79 in flyable condition. Over 200 AAF personnel were killed or missing after the attack. AAF installations at Hickam Field suffered especially severe damage.

Continuing the offensive in the Pacific, on December 10, 1941, Japan captured Guam and 2 weeks later overwhelmed the American defenders on Wake Island. During the first few months of 1942, while Japan pursued offensives in the East Indies and Indochina, the U.S. mobilized its forces and the Navy harassed enemy bases in the Central Pacific. In late May Japanese military leaders prepared to draw out the U.S. Navy with a surprise attack on Midway Island, 1,200 miles northwest of Oahu Island, but American armed forces, having broken an important Japanese code, this time expected the attack.

The Hawaiian Air Force, redesignated the Seventh Air Force in February 1942, participated in the Battle of Midway with a special task force of B–17s and B–26s. Twelve B–17s were flown to Midway Island on May 30–31, 1942, where they joined U.S. Marine aircraft in long-range reconnaissance to locate the Japanese fleet. On June 3 nine B–17s at high altitude bombed a fleet of enemy transports about

570 miles west of Midway, but to no effect.* American naval aircraft located the Japanese carrier task force the next day. Even as the enemy carrier aircraft bombed Midway, AAF B–17s and B–26s based there joined U.S. Navy carrier aircraft to attack the Japanese fleet. The enemy task force lost all 4 of its aircraft carriers to U.S. Navy attacks, and on June 6 the remainder of the fleet, stripped of air cover, turned back to Japan. The Seventh Air Force Commander, Maj. Gen. Clarence L. Tinker, exploited the Japanese defeat with an attack by B–17s on June 7 against Wake Island, but Tinker and his aircraft were lost. His successor, Maj. Gen. Willis H. Hale, commanded the Seventh until April 1944.

The Battle of Midway proved a decisive victory for the United States, but another 18 months would elapse before American forces could mount a serious offensive in the Central Pacific. Meanwhile, the Americans began to reconnoiter the first target planned for this offensive: the Gilbert Islands, located almost 2,400 miles southwest of Pearl Harbor. Seventh Air Force bombers flew a few reconnaissance and bombing missions against Wake Island and the Gilbert Islands between June 1942 and November 1943. In preparation for the offensive, the 11th and 30th Bombardment Groups moved in November 1943 from Hawaii to airfields in the Ellice Islands, only 550 to 850 miles southeast of Tarawa and Makin Islands, the Japanese strongholds in the Gilberts. From the 13th through the 17th of the month, the 2 groups bombed both Tarawa and Makin in preparation for assault landings on November 20. The U.S. Army 27th Infantry Division easily captured Makin, but the 2d Marine Division suffered heavy casualties before overwhelming Japanese troops on Tarawa on November 24. At the close of the Central Pacific Campaign on December 6, 1943, the United States was at last in a position to attack Japanese positions in the Western Pacific.

---

*The 1921 Army Air Service demonstration attacks on tethered German warships off the Virginia Capes had been successful, but the AAF leaders found bombing ships underway at sea from high altitude much more difficult. The most effective aerial bombing of naval ships on the high seas in World War II would be done by dive bombers and medium bombers operating at low altitude, not by heavy bombers at high altitude.

Philippine Islands:
December 7, 1941–May 10, 1942

On December 8, 1941, just a few hours after Japanese naval aircraft attacked Pearl Harbor, enemy pilots bombed and strafed U.S. installations in the Philippine Islands. The Japanese air forces directed their heaviest blow against Clark Field, a large air base about 55 miles northwest of the capital, Manila, which is on the west coast of Luzon, the northernmost and largest of the Philippine Islands. Only a few P–40s and P–35s managed to take off from Clark Field to engage the Japanese aircraft in combat. The first bombs destroyed Clark's communication center, and AAF controllers could not contact fighters patrolling other sections of Luzon. The enemy also successfully bombed Iba Field up the coast, about 70 miles northwest of Clark Field, again with little opposition from American fighter aircraft. Antiaircraft defenses proved ineffective against the Japanese bombers and fighters, which severely damaged both Clark and Iba Fields. Early the next morning enemy forces bombed Nichols Field, just south of Manila, and again inflicted heavy damage while suffering few losses.

The V Bomber Command had gathered most of the B–17s in the Philippines at Clark Field to prepare for a mission against Formosa, but authorities at Clark failed to receive warning of the enemy air attack that came shortly after noon on December 8. Of the 17 or 18 B–17s on the ground, all were destroyed. Two B–17 squadrons, totaling 16 aircraft, that the Commander of the Far East Air Force (FEAF), Maj. Gen. Lewis H. Brereton, had sent 3 days earlier to Del Monte airfield on Mindanao Island, survived the Japanese attack, as did a B–17 on a long-range reconnaissance mission. During the 2-day siege of the Philippines, 55 of the 105 P–40s as well as 25 to 30 other aircraft were lost to enemy bombers; no more than 15 P–35s remained operational. Eighty men were killed and about 150 wounded.

On the night of December 9–10, AAF pilots flying reconnaissance missions sighted an enemy convoy north of Luzon. General Brereton had moved the B–17s from Mindanao to Luzon on the 9th, enabling the FEAF to mount attacks as Japanese forces landed the next day in northern Luzon. This did little more than harass the enemy troops at a cost of several more B–17s, P–35s, and P–40s. Unable to obtain reinforcements or supplies, American air and ground forces in the Philippines fought a delaying action. In the days that followed, AAF pursuit aircraft achieved few aerial victories while suffering continu-

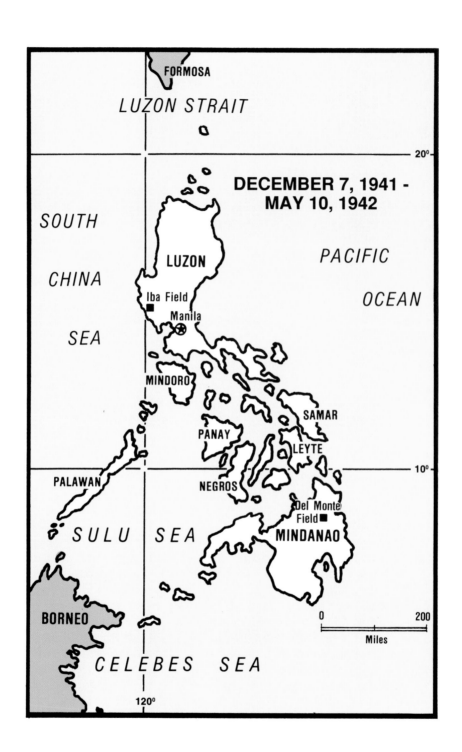

FORMOSA

LUZON STRAIT

**DECEMBER 7, 1941 -
MAY 10, 1942**

20°

SOUTH

CHINA

SEA

PACIFIC

OCEAN

LUZON

Iba Field ■

Manila ⊗

MINDORO

SAMAR

PANAY

LEYTE

10°

PALAWAN

NEGROS

S U L U   S E A

Del Monte
Field ■

MINDANAO

0   200

BORNEO

Miles

C E L E B E S   S E A

120°

ous attrition. On the 11th FEAF moved its remaining B–17s from Luzon to Del Monte Field on Mindanao Island, 600 miles south of Clark Field. The B–17s flew reconnaissance missions for several days, but as Japanese troops advanced southward on Luzon between December 16 and 18, the AAF evacuated its few remaining bombers to Australia. But U.S. aerial operations resumed the next week. From December 22 to 24, 19th Bombardment Group B–17s, stationed at Darwin, Australia, attacked enemy shipping and harbor facilities in the Philippines, having staged through Del Monte Field for refueling and rearming.

AAF personnel that remained in the Philippine Islands fought as infantry, integrated with Army ground troops. By January 1, 1942, Gen. Douglas MacArthur, U.S. Army Commander, withdrew his American and Filipino troops on Luzon to the Bataan Peninsula on the west side of Manila Bay, while U.S. and Filipino forces continued fighting the Japanese on Mindanao Island. The American forces on the Bataan Peninsula stymied the enemy until forced to surrender on April 9. Meanwhile, on March 11, General MacArthur, under orders of President Franklin D. Roosevelt, departed Corregidor by Navy patrol boat and boarded a B–17 at Del Monte Field for the flight to Australia. A remnant that retreated to Corregidor, the small island fortress at the entrance of Manila Bay, continued to resist. Japanese troops established a toe hold on Corregidor on May 5–6, and the decimated U.S. forces surrendered. Shortly afterward, American troops remaining elsewhere also surrendered; Japan had secured the Philippines.

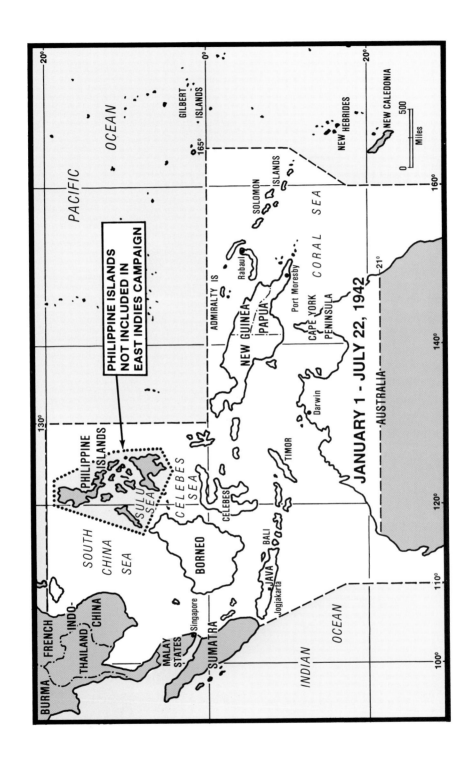

PHILIPPINE ISLANDS
NOT INCLUDED IN
EAST INDIES CAMPAIGN

JANUARY 1 - JULY 22, 1942

East Indies:
January 1–July 22, 1942

While still engaged in the conquest of the Philippines, the Japanese occupied Malaya and attacked The Netherlands East Indies. The Allies, i.e., the United States, Great Britain, Australia, and The Netherlands, decided to defend the East Indies from Java. As early as January 1942 the AAF began to send pursuit aircraft originally intended for the Philippine Islands to Java and ferried B–17s to the East Indies via the South Atlantic, North Africa, the Middle East, and India. The trickle of replacement aircraft, however, just made up for Allied combat losses.

Rapid enemy advances, unpredictable tropical weather, and long distances combined with shortages of aircraft, spare parts, gasoline, personnel, and supplies to hamper severely air operations from Java. The AAF units on the island, nominally under the control of Far East Air Force,* operated nearly independently because of the 1,300-mile distance between FEAF headquarters at Darwin, Australia, and the airfields on Java. Bomber targets in the Philippines were 1,500 miles away, and the B–17s stationed on Java had to refuel at bases on the Celebes and Borneo, about 750 miles closer to the targets. During January 1942 the heavy bombers also undertook long-range bombing missions against targets on the Malay Peninsula. Unfortunately, the Allied defenders on Java possessed only a few pursuit airplanes and a limited number of antiaircraft guns, so on February 3 a Japanese air attack force easily inflicted heavy damage and escaped with minor losses. The AAF belatedly rushed available P–40 aircraft from Australia to Java, and by February 16 an entire air defense squadron was operational.

Meantime, Japan rapidly consolidated its positions in the Southwest Pacific. On January 23 Japanese forces captured Rabaul, situated on the northern tip of New Britain Island, the largest of the Bismarck Archipelago and about 830 miles northeast of Cape York, Australia. The enemy invaded Sumatra on February 14 and captured Singapore the next day. On the 18th the Japanese landed on Bali, just east of Java, choking the Allied ferrying route from Australia and preventing further transport by air of pursuit aircraft to Java. Ten days later, the

---

*FEAF was redesignated Fifth Air Force on Feb. 5, 1942.

enemy landed on the island's northern coast. Long-range Allied aircraft had already begun to evacuate Jogjakarta Air Base, near Java's southern coast, on February 25, and within 2 weeks, on March 9, The Netherlands East Indies surrendered to Japan.

Allied military operations in the Southwest Pacific remained minimal during March and April 1942, while the United States and Australia consolidated and strengthened their forces. Then on May 7 and 8 an American naval task force in the Coral Sea southeast of New Guinea achieved an important strategic victory by turning back a Japanese armada headed for Port Moresby, the Allies' toehold on Papua's southeast coast, 350 miles northeast of Australia's Cape York Penin-sula. In this engagement, known as the Battle of the Coral Sea, Fifth Air Force units assisted the Navy with long-range reconnaissance missions.

The thwarting of the assault did not deter Japanese military action against the last Allied outpost in Papua. From May through July Port Moresby came under frequent enemy air attack. The Americans and Australians, defending the base with obsolete P–39s and P–400s,* suffered heavy losses. Other elements of the Fifth Air Force, flying from Australian bases and staging through Port Moresby, sent a few aircraft at a time to bomb Rabaul on New Britain Island, already a major Japanese naval and air base from which the enemy supported its operations, including air raids, in New Guinea. As circumstances permitted, the AAF also bombed other Japanese installations in New Guinea. Japanese military leaders meantime prepared for another assault on Port Moresby.

---

*An export version of the P–39.

Papua:
July 23, 1942–January 23, 1943

In July 1942 Japan occupied Buna and Gona on the northern coast of New Guinea, only 100 miles northeast of Port Moresby. The only opposition came from Australian and AAF fighters and bombers, which flew from Port Moresby to bomb and strafe Japanese forces as they moved ashore. The enemy quickly built an airstrip at Buna and from there continued the raids on Allied facilities at Port Moresby. From Gona, Japanese troops pushed inland to seize the key pass over the Owen Stanley Mountains on August 12. Later in the month the Japanese advanced within 30 miles of Port Moresby before stiff Allied defenses, supported by tactical air forces, stopped them. Australia's 7th and the U.S. Army's 32d Infantry Divisions began to force the Japanese back over the mountains in mid-September. Allied air transports brought in the first elements of the 32d Infantry Division on September 15 to augment the exhausted Australian troops that faced the enemy near Port Moresby. The Fifth Air Force, under its new Commander, Maj. Gen. George C. Kenney, since September 3, established air superiority over Papua. It provided close air support and ferried supplies and reinforcements to the Allied troops fighting in the jungles of the Owen Stanley Mountains.

In the weeks that followed, resupply of the front-line ground forces occurred most frequently by airdrop. Pilots flew at 400 to 500 feet and dropped the supplies free-fall in bundles. As the Allied troops advanced, they constructed small airstrips close to the front so that troop carrier units could fly in reinforcements and supplies and fly out the wounded. Between November 13, 1942, and January 23, 1943, Allied air units dropped or landed over 2,000 tons of rations and supplies for the Allied troops advancing against Buna.

The AAF also conducted an interdiction effort during October and November 1942; B–17s from Australia and Port Moresby frequently flew bombing missions against Japanese facilities, targeting especially the primary naval installation at Rabaul on New Britain. By November 3 the Fifth Air Force had moved several fighter squadrons and a heavy bombardment squadron to Milne Bay, at the southeastern extremity of Papua, New Guinea, more than 200 miles east of Port Moresby. Other fighter units and several medium bombardment squadrons moved from Australia to Port Moresby. In November–December Fifth Air Force medium and heavy bombers bombed and strafed Japanese vessels attempting to reinforce Buna, discouraging

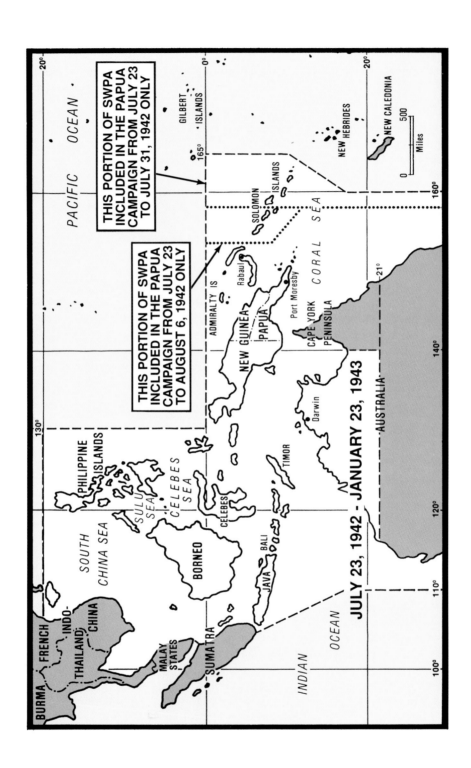

THIS PORTION OF SWPA INCLUDED IN THE PAPUA CAMPAIGN FROM JULY 23 TO JULY 31, 1942 ONLY

THIS PORTION OF SWPA INCLUDED IN THE PAPUA CAMPAIGN FROM JULY 23 TO AUGUST 6, 1942 ONLY

JULY 23, 1942 - JANUARY 23, 1943

the resupply efforts. Having crossed the Owen Stanley Mountains, the Australians successfully stormed Gona on December 9; a few weeks later, on January 23, 1943, the Japanese evacuated their positions near Buna.

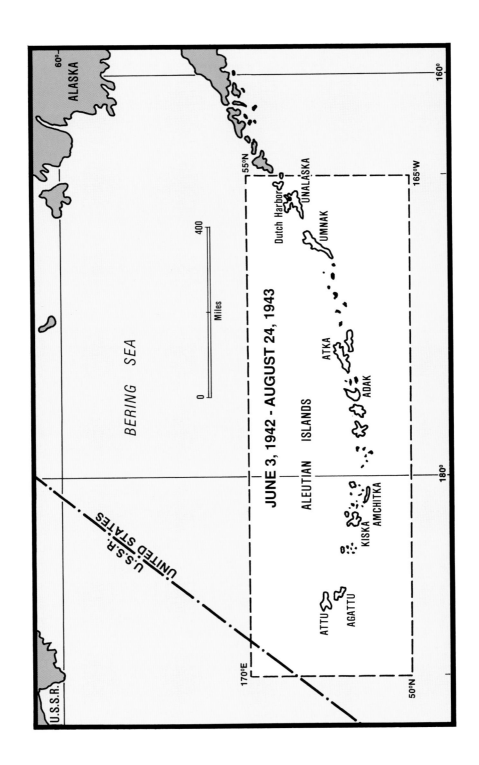

JUNE 3, 1942 - AUGUST 24, 1943

ALEUTIAN ISLANDS

ALASKA

BERING SEA

U.S.S.R.

U.S.S.R.
UNITED STATES

ATTU
AGATTU

KISKA
AMCHITKA

ADAK

ATKA

UMNAK
UNALASKA
Dutch Harbor

Miles
0   400

60°
55°N
50°N

160°
165°W
180°
170°E

74

Aleutian Islands:
June 3, 1942–August 24, 1943

Coinciding with the Battle of Midway in the Central Pacific between June 3 and 7, 1942, a Japanese task force attacked Dutch Harbor, a U.S. Navy installation on Unalaska Island, almost 800 miles southwest of Elmendorf Field, which was the headquarters of the Eleventh Air Force, commanded by Col. Lionel H. Dunlap. The AAF's westernmost base, a newly constructed airfield, was located on Umnak Island, 70 miles from Dutch Harbor. On June 3, P–40 pilots from Umnak shot down the first Japanese aircraft (a scout seaplane) to be destroyed in aerial combat in the Aleutian Islands. The next day, while the enemy attacked Dutch Harbor, P–40 pilots shot down 4 more Japanese aircraft but lost 2 of their own. That same day the AAF attempted several attacks on the Japanese carrier force, but the ships escaped damage. Breaking off the attack on Dutch Harbor after 2 days, the Japanese on June 6 landed on Kiska, 700 miles to the west of Dutch Harbor. A day later another force took Attu, the westernmost of the Aleutian Islands, 900 miles from Dutch Harbor.

Both Japanese and American forces in the Aleutians were small, and inclement weather severely hampered combat flying. The entire Eleventh Air Force in June 1942 consisted of 1 heavy and 2 medium bombardment squadrons, 3 fighter squadrons, and 1 transport squadron. B–17s and B–24s flying from Umnak bombed enemy ships and installations whenever weather permitted. But bomb loads were reduced to make room for additional fuel tanks needed for the 1,200-mile round trip between Umnak and Kiska, and so the heavy bombers inflicted little damage. To overcome the extreme range, on August 30 the U.S. landed a force on Adak Island, 340 miles closer to the Japanese-occupied Aleutians. Flying from a new airfield on Adak and escorted by fighters, Eleventh Air Force B–24s attacked harbor installations at Kiska on September 14. Subsequent bombing raids were somewhat more successful from Adak, but bad weather and distance continued to hamper efforts to interdict Japanese forces in the Aleutians. On January 12, 1943, U.S. Army forces landed on Amchitka Island, 200 miles west of Adak and only 80 miles from Kiska, and by February 16 Amchitka's newly constructed airstrip was ready for fighter aircraft. From this base, the Eleventh Air Force, commanded since March 8 by Maj. Gen. William O. Butler, achieved air supremacy over Attu and Kiska. On March 26 the U.S. Navy turned back a Japanese naval task force attempting to resupply Japanese troops.

For the next 6 weeks, in preparation for an assault landing at Attu, the Eleventh Air Force flew numerous missions against enemy facilities both at Attu and Kiska, with generally good results. P–40s and P–38s flying from Amchitka proved effective as fighter-bombers, and reconnaissance missions provided a good estimate of the number of Japanese troops on Attu. By this time the Eleventh Air Force had destroyed most of the enemy aircraft stationed in the Aleutians, and AAF aerial losses were attributed to poor weather and flak. On May 11 the Army's 7th Infantry Division landed on Attu. Eleventh Air Force provided air cover for the landings and, on the few days when weather permitted pilots to find their targets, provided close air support for the advancing troops. On May 29 the Japanese commander ordered a last-ditch attack that ended with the 7th Infantry Division in command of Attu.

Flying from Adak, Attu, and Shemya (an Aleutian Island 35 miles east of Attu), the Eleventh, sometimes joined by naval aircraft, bombed the remaining Japanese facilities at Kiska through June, July, and August. A joint force of U.S. Army and Canadian troops landed on Kiska on August 15, only to discover that Japan, under cover of cloud and fog, had already evacuated its garrison on July 29 and slipped past the U.S. Navy blockade to return to the Kuriles. After August 24, 1943, the Eleventh Air Force would use its bases in the Aleutian Islands to mount aerial raids on Japanese positions in the Kurile Islands, 1,200 to 1,500 miles southwest of Attu.

Guadalcanal:
August 7, 1942–February 21, 1943

One year before the U.S. 7th Infantry Division landed on vacated Kiska Island in the Aleutians, on August 7, 1942, the 1st Marine Division landed on the South Pacific island of Guadalcanal, one of the Solomon Islands located 850 miles east of Port Moresby, Papua, New Guinea. B–17s of the 11th Bombardment Group flying from Espiritu Santo, the largest of the New Hebrides Islands, 600 miles southeast of Guadalcanal, provided reconnaissance for the assault landing. Advancing in the face of slight resistance, the Marines soon captured the half-completed Japanese air base on Guadalcanal, which was promptly named Henderson Field.

Recognizing that American control of Henderson Field ultimately meant control of the air, Japanese troops launched vigorous ground attacks to retake the air base, while enemy aircraft bombed it repeatedly. On August 9, U.S. naval forces withdrew. A few days later, B–17s from Espiritu Santo flew covering missions for naval transports returning with supplies for the battling Marines. Despite persistent bombing, Navy Seabee engineers completed Henderson Field, and on August 20 the Marines landed several fighter aircraft. Two days later the 67th Fighter Squadron flew in 5 P–400s.* The P–400 pilots provided close air support for the ground troops and dive-bombed enemy sea-going vessels, but most of the air support, including high-altitude interception of Japanese bombers, fell to the more versatile Marine fighter aircraft.

Intense fighting continued on Guadalcanal throughout the year, and on the night of October 13–14, enemy warships bombarded Henderson Field so effectively that it was temporarily knocked out of operation. AAF C–47 transports bringing in supplies used a dirt strip nearby, while the few remaining AAF and Marine fighters attacked Japanese reinforcements landing on Guadalcanal, with only limited success. From October 23 to 25 the enemy army fought hard to break the Marine perimeter at Henderson, suffered heavy losses, and again withdrew. The P–400 pilots provided particularly effective close air support during this battle. U.S. naval air and sea forces then combined with AAF reinforcements from Espiritu Santo Island to destroy

---

*Export version of the P–39 Airacobra.

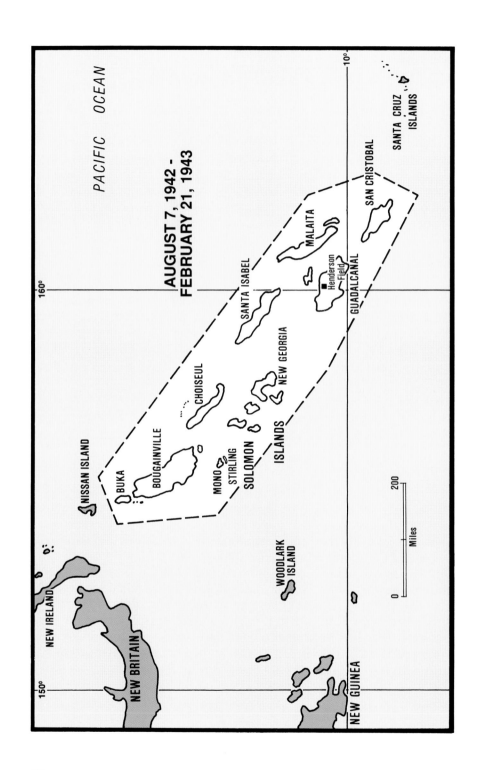

PACIFIC OCEAN

AUGUST 7, 1942 -
FEBRUARY 21, 1943

10°

SANTA CRUZ
ISLANDS

160°

MALAITA

SANTA ISABEL

SAN CRISTOBAL

Henderson
Field

GUADALCANAL

NISSAN ISLAND

CHOISEUL

NEW GEORGIA

BUKA

BOUGAINVILLE

MONO

STIRLING

SOLOMON   ISLANDS

150°

NEW IRELAND

NEW BRITAIN

WOODLARK
ISLAND

0   200

Miles

NEW GUINEA

78

newly arrived Japanese transports and their escorts, thus denying replacements for the enemy troops lost in the fighting. As the U.S. Marines widened the perimeter about Henderson Field during November 1942, engineers once again repaired the runway. In November and December, the 11th and 5th Bombardment Groups, flying north from Espiritu Santo Island on heavy bombardment and long-range reconnaissance missions, began to stage* through Henderson Field. This coincided with the arrival of the U.S. Army American Division and the 25th Infantry Division to relieve the weary Marines and strengthen American positions.

As demands on the AAF increased throughout the Pacific, the U.S. Army activated the Thirteenth Air Force on January 13, 1943, and a week later moved its headquarters from New Caledonia to Espiritu Santo in order to provide administrative and operational control over air force units in the South Pacific. The Thirteenth's first Commander was Maj. Gen. Nathan F. Twining. One month before, on December 17, 1942, the U.S. Army XIV Corps had launched a series of offensives on Guadalcanal that eventually forced the Japanese secretly to remove their remaining troops from the island. The enemy completed the evacuation during the night of February 7, 1943, leaving the United States victorious in its first major amphibious operation of the war. During the last offensive, P–39s of the 347th Fighter Group from Henderson Field provided close air support for Army troops. Engineers, meantime, improved Henderson Field, by mid-January permitting B–17s to fly bombardment missions from Guadalcanal against Japanese shipping at Bougainville, a large island 400 miles to the northwest.

---

*"To stage" means to refuel and rearm aircraft.

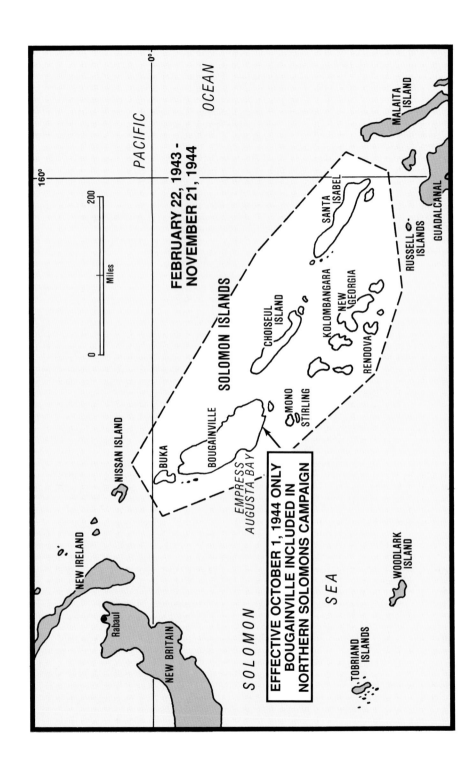

PACIFIC OCEAN

0°

160°

200

0

Miles

FEBRUARY 22, 1943 -
NOVEMBER 21, 1944

SOLOMON ISLANDS

MALAITA ISLAND

SANTA ISABEL

RUSSELL ISLANDS

GUADALCANAL

CHOISEUL ISLAND

KOLOMBANGARA

NEW GEORGIA

RENDOVA

NISSAN ISLAND

BUKA

BOUGAINVILLE

MONO
STIRLING

EMPRESS AUGUSTA BAY

EFFECTIVE OCTOBER 1, 1944 ONLY
BOUGAINVILLE INCLUDED IN
NORTHERN SOLOMONS CAMPAIGN

NEW IRELAND

Rabaul

NEW BRITAIN

SOLOMON SEA

WOODLARK ISLAND

TOBRIAND ISLANDS

Northern Solomons:
February 22, 1943–November 21, 1944

Beginning in October 1942, the AAF and naval aviation units bombed Japanese positions in the northern Solomons. Then on February 21, 1943, U.S. forces landed on Banika, one of the Russell Islands 65 miles north of Guadalcanal. These islands provided bases for Navy and AAF operations against Rabaul on New Britain. For the next few months, Thirteenth Air Force bombers pounded enemy installations in the Solomons, particularly Munda Air Base on New Georgia Island, about halfway between Guadalcanal and Bougainville. In April Japanese air forces attacked American installations in the southern Solomons, but to little effect. Thirteenth Air Force and U.S. Navy fighter pilots successfully intercepted them, destroying 59 aircraft in aerial combat while losing only 13 American fighters. Meantime, on April 18, the AAF dealt the Japanese a severe blow. P–38 pilots of the 12th, 68th, and 339th Fighter Squadrons from Henderson Field on Guadalcanal intercepted and shot down the aircraft carrying Admiral Isoroku Yamamoto, Commander in Chief, Combined Fleet of the Navy of Japan, en route from Rabaul, New Britain Island, to visit installations on Bougainville Island. Japan had lost one of its most important military leaders.

In June 1943 Japanese air forces again attacked U.S. installations on Guadalcanal, but suffered disproportionate losses in combat. All the while, U.S. Army, Navy, and Marine aircraft bombed and strafed enemy positions throughout the Solomons in preparation for the assault on New Georgia Island. On June 30 American forces captured Rendova Island, located just southwest of New Georgia. AAF pilots who provided cover for the Rendova landing forces destroyed 24 Japanese aircraft.

Beginning on July 2 the U.S. Army's 25th, 37th, and 43d Infantry Divisions, reinforced by Marine battalions, assaulted New Georgia Island. The Thirteenth Air Force, now commanded by Brig. Gen. Ray L. Owens, provided air cover and close air support for the ground forces and flew long-range reconnaissance and bombardment missions over the Solomons. While C–47 pilots dropped provisions to U.S. troops mired in swamps on New Georgia, B–25s flying at low altitude proved especially adept at blasting enemy shipping out of the water. In spite of strong enemy resistance, on August 5 U.S. ground troops captured Munda Air Base, one of the enemy's principal military installations in the Solomons. Japanese ships and barges slipped in during the night of August 25 to withdraw remaining troops from New Georgia.

During the battle for New Georgia, the Thirteenth Air Force bombed the enemy airfield on Kolombangara Island, just to the northwest of New Georgia, so extensively that Japanese aircraft could not use it to threaten American air superiority. U.S. forces subsequently by-passed Kolombangara and prepared to assault Bougainville Island, the last enemy stronghold in the Solomons. Japanese forces possessed 2 airfields on the northern end of Bougainville, 2 on the southern end, an airfield and seaplane base on the east coast, and another airfield on Buka Island, just north of Bougainville.

Throughout September and October the Thirteenth Air Force, flying from Munda and other recently captured sites in the Solomons, bombed and strafed these Japanese installations incessantly in an effort to suppress enemy air power over Bougainville Island. On October 27 the New Zealand Armed Forces, under the cover of AAF P–38s, captured the Treasury Islands, Mono and Stirling, 80 miles southwest of Empress Augustus Bay on the west coast of Bougainville. A few days later, on November 1, the U.S. 3rd Marine Division landed at Empress Augustus Bay with little opposition.

For the next 2 months, the AAF attacked Japanese shipping near Bougainville and enemy air bases on the island, flew close air support missions for ground troops, and intercepted enemy aircraft. By mid-December the U.S. could claim air superiority, and by the end of the year American troops had isolated the remaining Japanese garrisons on Bougainville. Army engineers quickly constructed 3 airfields in the Empress Augusta Bay area.   From these fields AAF long-range bombers raided Rabaul, on New Britain Island, 200 miles northwest of Bougainville. Maj. Gen. Hubert R. Harmon commanded the Thirteenth Air Force from January 7, 1944, until succeeded by Maj. Gen. St. Clair Streett on June 15. U.S. forces secured a large area around Empress Augusta Bay, Bougainville, by January 1944, and although Japanese troops remaining in the Solomon Islands continued scattered and sometimes ferocious resistance until November 1944, these rear-guard actions would have little effect on the outcome of the war.

Bismarck Archipelago:
December 15, 1943–November 27, 1944

After the Japanese defeat in the Solomons, the Allies, particularly the United States, New Zealand, and Australia, prepared to isolate and destroy enemy forces and facilities at Rabaul on New Britain and Kavieng on New Ireland in the Bismarck Archipelago north of New Guinea. The Fifth Air Force, operating from Port Moresby and other New Guinea bases, began frequent bombing of Rabaul in September 1943. Three months later, on December 15, the Fifth Air Force began close air support of the U.S. Army's 1st Cavalry Division, which landed at Arawe, New Britain, 280 miles northeast of Port Moresby. Fifth Air Force fighters over Arawe also inflicted heavy losses on Japanese aircraft sent to attack the Allied beachhead.

Following the Arawe landing, the Fifth Air Force heavily bombed Japanese facilities at Cape Gloucester on the western tip of New Britain, reducing enemy opposition to the landing there of the U.S. 1st Marine Division on December 26. During the operation, an enemy air force sank an American destroyer and damaged several other ships, but at a cost of 48 aircraft downed by U.S. Navy and Fifth Air Force fighters and antiaircraft fire. In all, between December 15 and 31 Japan lost an estimated 163 aircraft over Arawe and Cape Gloucester. Following a heavy bombardment by B–24s on December 29, 1943, U.S. Marines the next day overran the Japanese airfield at Cape Gloucester. As the new year began, American engineers rebuilt the airfield, and on February 13, 1944, a Fifth Air Force fighter squadron moved from New Guinea to Cape Gloucester, New Britain Island.

With the Fifth Air Force engaged on the western end of New Britain, the Thirteenth Air Force, operating from new bases on Bougainville, began bombing the key Japanese military installations at Rabaul on the northeastern end of the island. On December 19, 1943, Thirteenth Air Force B–24s made their first raid on Rabaul, relying on Navy and Marine fighters for escort. Enemy fighter and antiaircraft defenses were at first strong enough to down U.S. aircraft on practically every mission. The Thirteenth continued the raids, however, and under the pressure of constant aerial attacks through January and February 1944, Japanese air power at Rabaul, without adequate reinforcements, steadily deteriorated. On February 19 the South Pacific Command announced a victory in the air battle at Rabaul, although the Allies continued strikes against the installations there for several more weeks.

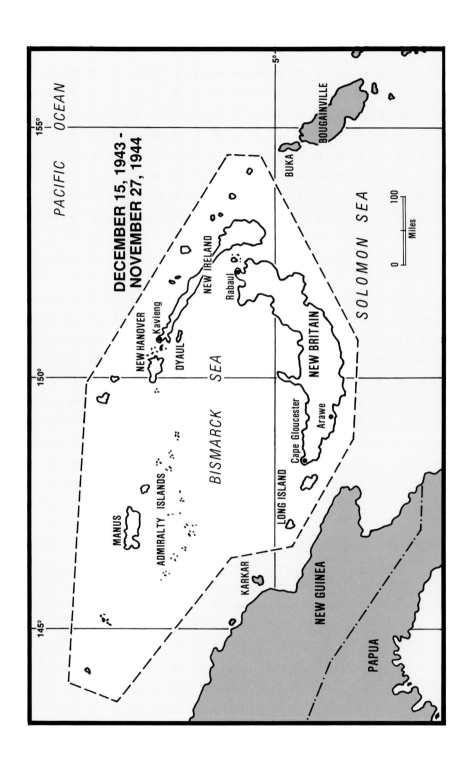

DECEMBER 15, 1943 -
NOVEMBER 27, 1944

PACIFIC
OCEAN

155°

5°

BOUGAINVILLE

BUKA

NEW IRELAND

SOLOMON SEA

100

Miles

0

Kavieng

NEW HANOVER

Rabaul

DYAUL

NEW BRITAIN

150°

BISMARCK SEA

Cape Gloucester

Arawe

MANUS

ADMIRALTY ISLANDS

LONG ISLAND

145°

KARKAR

NEW GUINEA

PAPUA

84

Late in February the Fifth Air Force, operating from bases on the northern coast of New Guinea, attacked Japanese airfields at Kavieng, New Ireland, 150 miles northwest of Rabaul. By the end of the month, Kavieng had been reduced to rubble. AAF pilots also found good hunting in the Bismarck Sea, damaging or sinking a number of enemy ships engaged in evacuating personnel from Rabaul and Kavieng.

Early in 1944 the Fifth Air Force also began to fly reconnaissance and bombing missions over the Admiralty Islands on the northern edge of the Bismarck Sea. The primary targets were Momote airfield on Los Negros Island, 220 miles northwest of Cape Gloucester, and Lorengau airdrome, on nearby Manus Island, less than 5 miles west of Momote. After aerial reconnaissance showed little evidence of strong Japanese defenses in the Admiralty Islands, the U.S. 1st Cavalry Division landed on Los Negros on February 29 and captured Momote airfield. When enemy opposition on the ground proved greater than expected, the Fifth Air Force provided an extra measure of close air support, and B–17s dropped supplies to the Army troops. By March 8 Japanese resistance had virtually ended, and the next day a Royal Australian Air Force (RAAF) squadron of P–40s arrived at Momote. Having secured Los Negros, the Allies prepared to attack Manus Island. The Fifth Air Force bombarded the town of Lorengau and a nearby airdrome before the Allied landing on March 15, and on D–Day AAF aircraft joined the RAAF P–40s to provide air cover and close air support. Three months later, on May 18, the Allies officially closed the Admiralties operation, which completed the isolation of Rabaul, Kavieng, and other enemy positions in the Bismarck Archipelago. Fighting in the area nevertheless continued sporadically until November 1944.

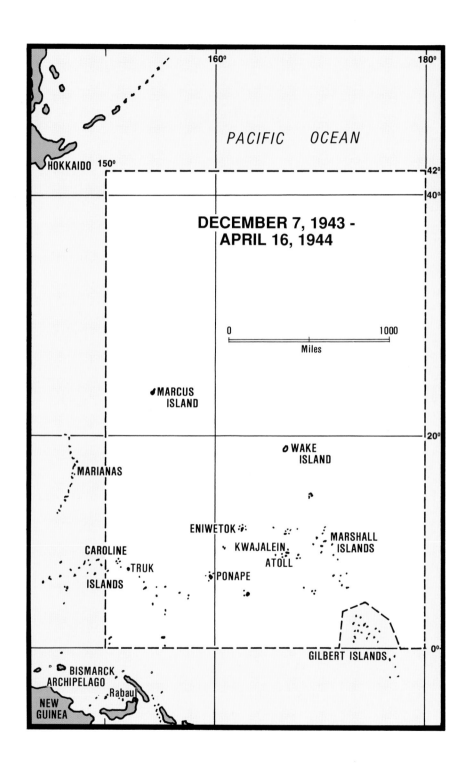

PACIFIC OCEAN

HOKKAIDO

DECEMBER 7, 1943 - APRIL 16, 1944

0   1000
Miles

MARCUS ISLAND

WAKE ISLAND

MARIANAS

ENIWETOK

KWAJALEIN ATOLL

MARSHALL ISLANDS

CAROLINE ISLANDS

TRUK

PONAPE

GILBERT ISLANDS

BISMARCK ARCHIPELAGO

Rabaul

NEW GUINEA

Eastern Mandates: December 7, 1943–April 16, 1944

While the Fifth and Thirteenth Air Forces were helping reduce Rabaul and other Japanese strongholds in the Bismarck Archipelago, the Seventh Air Force participated in the drive across the Pacific Ocean. In the Marshall Islands, which cover a 400,000-square-mile area about 2,100 miles southwest of Pearl Harbor, the Japanese possessed significant bases on Roi, Kwajalein, Jaluit, Mille, Maloelap, and Wotje Atolls. After December 7, 1943, these installations became targets of the Seventh Air Force, which flew from the recently conquered Gilbert Islands, about 600 miles south of the Marshalls. The Seventh conducted reconnaissance over the Marshall Islands, attacked Japanese shipping in the area, and repeatedly bombed the enemy's bases.

By the end of 1943 U.S. Navy carrier-based aircraft, with some help from the Seventh Air Force, could claim air superiority over the Marshall Islands, and on January 31, 1944, the Army's 7th Infantry Division assaulted Kwajalein, while the 4th Marine Division went ashore on Roi and Namur Islands, some 50 miles to the north. Applying lessons learned in the Gilbert Islands assaults, the American forces annihilated the 8,000 Japanese troops on the 3 islands within a week. U.S. casualties totaled less than 400 dead and about 1,000 wounded. B–24s of the Seventh Air Force provided support, dropping bombs from altitudes as low as 4,000 feet and strafing enemy positions. On February 14 the Seventh began to fly missions against Ponape Atoll on the western edge of the Marshalls, a 2,200-mile round trip for the B–24s stationed at Tarawa Island in the Gilberts. Within a week, between February 16 and 20, U.S. Marine and Army troops captured Eniwetok Atoll in the Marshall Islands. Relying on the Seventh Air Force and Navy fighters to suppress Japanese air power, U.S. forces by-passed the Japanese bases at Jaluit and Wotje and "island-hopped" across the Pacific.

After the capture of Eniwetok, the AAF was ready to attack Truk Atoll, site of a large Japanese air and sea base. One of the Caroline Islands, Truk is located about halfway between Rabaul on New Britain, almost 800 miles to the south, and Saipan Island in the Marianas, more than 700 miles to the northwest. On February 16–17 an American naval carrier force attacked the enemy's installations at Truk, inflicting severe damage before withdrawing virtually unscathed. The next month Seventh Air Force moved its 2 B–24 groups from the Gilbert Islands to Kwajalein Atoll in the Marshalls. The

Seventh made its first heavy bombing attack on Truk Atoll on March 14–15; two weeks later, on the 29th, the Thirteenth Air Force, flying from the Solomon Islands, also made its initial bombing raid on the island. For the next 6 months AAF heavy bombers raided Truk and other enemy bases in the Carolines almost daily, helping to destroy Japan's air and sea power in the area and allowing U.S. ground forces to by-pass Truk and invade the Mariana Islands in the Western Pacific Basin.

Western Pacific:
April 17, 1944–September 2, 1945

With the Thirteenth Air Force continuing the raids against Truk, the Seventh Air Force, now commanded by Maj. Gen. Robert W. Douglass, Jr., turned to the Marianas, attacking Saipan Island on April 18, 1944. The Seventh was responsible for bombardment of Saipan prior to the American invasion; the unit also alternated with the Thirteenth in bombing installations on Truk until June 19, 1944, when the Seventh assumed sole responsibility for the raids. The Thirteenth Air Force, under the command of Maj. Gen. St. Clair Streett, then concentrated on the near-daily bombing of Japanese bases on Woleai Atoll, 850 miles west of Truk, and Yap Island, almost 1,000 miles northwest of the Admiralties.

On June 15, 1944, the 2d and 4th Marine Divisions assaulted Saipan, the first American objective in the Marianas. Japan dispatched a carrier task force from the Philippines to counter the invasion, and, on June 19, less than 200 miles southwest of Saipan, Japanese naval aviators attacked the U.S. Navy's Fifth Fleet, which guarded the approaches to the island. This engagement became known as the Battle of the Philippine Sea. Possessing more training and experience than their Japanese counterparts, American naval pilots shot most of the enemy out of the sky. Japan lost more than 300 aircraft in what would be called "The Great Marianas Turkey Shoot." American losses totaled 30 aircraft. Also on June 19 U.S. submarines sank 2 Japanese aircraft carriers. The next day the American naval force pursued the retreating Japanese, sinking another carrier, shooting down more than 150 aircraft, and all but ending the Japanese naval threat in the Western Pacific. The American Navy lost 130 aircraft, mostly because pilots ran out of fuel and had to ditch at sea.

On June 22 a squadron of AAF P–47s catapulted from 2 Navy aircraft carriers and landed at Saipan's Isley Field. These Seventh Air Force fighters, soon reinforced, helped provide air cover and close air support for the ground troops battling the Japanese on the island. Organized enemy resistance on Saipan ended on July 9, and the P–47s turned to bombing and strafing nearby Tinian Island. U.S. naval aviators attacked Japanese positions on Guam, 250 miles south of Saipan, in preparation for its recapture; on July 21 U.S. forces landed on Guam and by August 10 had defeated the Japanese defenders. Meantime, on July 24 the 4th Marine Division landed on Tinian. Seventh Air Force P–47s marked the beach for the assault troops and

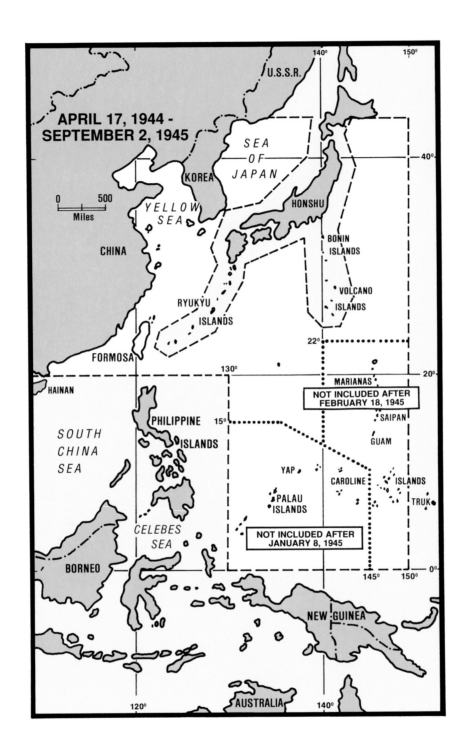

APRIL 17, 1944 -
SEPTEMBER 2, 1945

U.S.S.R.

SEA
OF
JAPAN

KOREA

HONSHU

YELLOW
SEA

BONIN
ISLANDS

CHINA

VOLCANO
ISLANDS

RYUKYU

ISLANDS

FORMOSA

MARIANAS

HAINAN

NOT INCLUDED AFTER
FEBRUARY 18, 1945

PHILIPPINE

SAIPAN

SOUTH
CHINA
SEA

ISLANDS

GUAM

YAP

CAROLINE

ISLANDS

PALAU
ISLANDS

TRUK

CELEBES
SEA

NOT INCLUDED AFTER
JANUARY 8, 1945

BORNEO

NEW GUINEA

AUSTRALIA

0   500
Miles

140°   150°
40°
130°   20°
22°
15°

120°   140°
145°   150°
0°

bombed and strafed enemy positions. In providing close air support on Tinian, the P–47 pilots used new ordnance, a napalm "fire bomb" of jellied gasoline, to good effect. By August 1 U.S. Marines had defeated the Japanese on Tinian. The remaining Mariana Islands, lacking enemy installations of consequence, presented no difficulty to the Americans. Saipan and Tinian, only 1,200 miles from Tokyo, now provided the United States with crucial bases for a strategic air offensive against the Japanese home islands.

With the Marianas secure, the XIII Bomber Command began strikes against the Palau Islands, 800 miles southwest of the Marianas, in preparation for Allied landings at Angaur Island, southernmost of the Palaus, and at Peleliu Island, a few miles north of Angaur. The bombardment missions destroyed many Japanese installations on the Palau Islands, and on September 15 the U.S. 1st Marine Division landed on Peleliu. Two days later the U.S. 81st Infantry Division easily overwhelmed the Japanese on Angaur, but the Marines battled tenacious Japanese defenders for almost a month before capturing Peleliu. Army engineers immediately began to rebuild the air bases on these islands. In late October 1944 the Seventh Air Force dispatched the first squadron of a heavy bombardment group to Angaur in preparation for attacks against Japanese positions in the Philippines.

At the beginning of 1945, the island of Formosa near mainland China remained perhaps the most heavily fortified of Japanese positions outside Japan. In 1943 Fourteenth Air Force had bombed targets there, and in the fall of 1944 B–29s flew from forward bases in China to bomb the island's military installations. Later, in January 1945, Fifth Air Force bombers and fighters, operating from Clark Field in the Philippine Islands, began a 6-month air campaign against enemy airfields, railways, fuel dumps, harbor facilities, shipping, and industrial targets. The Fifth Air Force dominated Formosan air space by April 1945, although the enemy concealed sufficient aircraft on the island to launch numerous suicide air attacks against the U.S. Navy during assault landings that month on Okinawa.

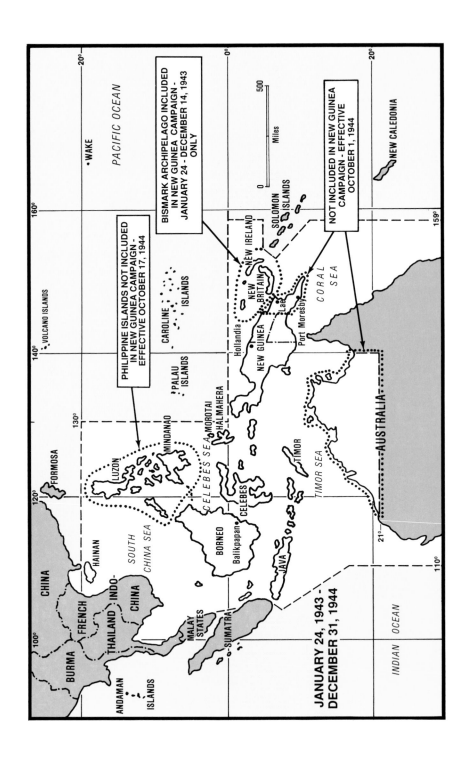

BISMARK ARCHIPELAGO INCLUDED IN NEW GUINEA CAMPAIGN - JANUARY 24 - DECEMBER 14, 1943 ONLY

PHILIPPINE ISLANDS NOT INCLUDED IN NEW GUINEA CAMPAIGN - EFFECTIVE OCTOBER 17, 1944

NOT INCLUDED IN NEW GUINEA CAMPAIGN - EFFECTIVE OCTOBER 1, 1944

JANUARY 24, 1943 - DECEMBER 31, 1944

92

New Guinea:
January 24, 1943–December 31, 1944

The Japanese, after losing Buna and Gona on the northern coast of New Guinea in January 1943, retreated to Lae, 175 miles north of Port Moresby. Meanwhile, the Fifth Air Force engaged Japanese air forces over New Guinea in a battle for air superiority. On February 6, for example, AAF pilots attacked separate enemy formations and shot down 29 aircraft without losing a single fighter.

One month later, between March 2 and 4, 1943, tipped off by signal intelligence, Fifth Air Force medium and heavy bombers in the Bismarck Sea intercepted a Japanese troop convoy steaming from Rabaul on the northeastern tip of New Britain Island, to Lae, almost 400 miles to the southwest. Encouraged by the Fifth Air Force Commander, Lt. Gen. George C. Kenney, B–25 pilots had developed a skip-bombing technique, in which bombs were ricocheted off the water. Using this tactic, U.S. and Australian aircraft destroyed all the troop transports and several of the escorts. In this crushing defeat for the Japanese, Allied fighters destroyed some 50 Japanese aircraft flying air cover for the convoy, while losing only 5 aircraft.

Early in 1943 the Fifth moved its aircraft to airfields at Port Moresby and Milne Bay. Good fighter cover and a radar early warning system protected these bases successfully from enemy air attacks. In March and April the AAF built a major air base at Dobodura, halfway up the northern coast between Milne Bay and Lae. Troop carrier units poured men and supplies into Dobodura to reinforce Allied forces for the advance against Lae. From March through June 1943, Fifth Air Force fighter units escorted troop carrier aircraft and intercepted Japanese bomber formations. The twin-engined P–38s, recently arrived in the Southwest Pacific, proved especially effective in aerial combat. Also during the spring, Fifth Air Force medium and heavy bombers attacked enemy positions along the northern coast of New Guinea.

Allied forces advanced from Buna westward toward Lae from July through September 1943. Fifth Air Force fighters provided aerial cover against Japanese air attack, while troop carriers dropped supplies to the advancing troops and bombers attacked airfields at Wewak, 300 miles west of Lae.   On September 4 Australian forces landed south of Lae, and the next day air transports dropped paratroopers at Nadzab, just north of the island. These forces took Lae on September 16.

The next objective was Finschhafen, on the tip of the Huon Peninsula, about 70 miles east of Lae. After first isolating the enemy by repeatedly attacking airfields and interceptors, the Fifth Air Force directly supported the ground troops during the assault. The decimated Japanese air forces gave little opposition. On October 2 the Allies captured Finschhafen and immediately repaired the airfields for local air support and long-range reconnaissance and bombardment operations.

Allied forces continued the westward advance in New Guinea, capturing some enemy strongholds and by-passing others, notably Wewak. During March 1944 the Fifth Air Force destroyed enemy installations at Wewak, then turned to the bombardment of Hollandia, a major objective 220 miles northwest of Wewak. On April 22 Allied forces landed on the beaches east and west of the island. Another assault force captured Aitape, 123 miles southeast of Hollandia, and within 2 days the Fifth Air Force was using the airstrip at Aitape to support the Hollandia operations. After 5 days of fighting, Allied troops captured Hollandia on April 27, 1944.

The Allies on May 17–19 attacked the Japanese base at Wakde, about 100 miles northwest of Hollandia. Then, on the 27th, they assaulted Biak Island, close to 160 miles northwest of Wakde. The V and XIII Bomber Commands extensively bombed enemy positions before the assaults, and Fifth Air Force provided close air support and dropped supplies to the troops on Biak. Engineers had an airstrip operational at Wakde by May 21 and another on Biak by June 17, only 2 days after Lt. Gen. Ennis C. Whitehead succeeded General Kenney as Fifth Air Force Commander.* The Allies quelled the strongest Japanese resistance on Biak by July 22 and mopped up isolated pockets by August 20. Having destroyed Japan's bases in New Guinea, on September 15 Allied troops landed on Morotai Island, about 300 miles northwest of New Guinea and within 400 miles of Mindanao, southernmost of the Philippines. During the rest of 1944, in preparation for the invasion of the Philippines, Allied air forces frequently struck the oil center at Balikpapan, Borneo, as well as other military targets in Borneo, Celebes, and the Philippines.

---

*General Kenney assumed command of the Far East Air Forces, established on July 31, 1944, and activated on August 3 to direct the Fifth and Thirteenth Air Forces and Royal Australian Air Force and Dutch units based at Darwin. (Not to be confused with Far East Air Force at Clark Field in 1941.)

Leyte:
October 17, 1944–July 1, 1945

On October 17, 1944, the United States began the invasion of the Philippine Islands. By-passing Mindanao, the southernmost and second largest of the islands, elements of the U.S. Army 6th Ranger Infantry Battalion landed on Suluan and Dinagat Islands and the next day on Homonhon Island. These islands, just north of Mindanao, guarded the entrances to Leyte Gulf, and their capture cleared the way for the assault on Leyte Island. On the 20th, after U.S. naval mine-sweepers had cleared the channels to the gulf, the Army X and XXIV Corps landed unopposed near Dulag, halfway up Leyte's east coast, while the 21st Infantry Regiment landed unopposed on the southern tip of the island. Two days later Gen. Douglas MacArthur came ashore, fulfilling his promise to return to the Philippines, made more than 2 years before. Navy aircraft provided all of the aerial support for these operations because pursuit elements of the Fifth and Thirteenth Air Forces on Morotai Island, 600 miles southeast of Leyte, were too far removed to engage the Japanese effectively.

During the Battle of Leyte Gulf, between October 23 and 26, the U.S. Navy's Third and Seventh Fleets in 4 separate actions destroyed most of the Japanese fleet in the Philippines. Admiral William F. Halsey commanded the Third Fleet, and Admiral Thomas C. Kinkaid led the Seventh Fleet. For the first time, Japanese air attacks on U.S. naval forces included "kamikaze" suicide aircraft.

Meantime, from October 22 to 24, headquarters and ground echelon personnel of Fifth Air Force units moved ashore at Tacloban to aid engineers in readying an airstrip for AAF aircraft. During the next 2 days, enemy aircraft conducted several destructive raids on U.S. positions. Thirty-four P–38s landed at the Tacloban airstrip on the 27th, becoming the first AAF airplanes stationed in the Philippine Islands since 1942. By the end of the day, P–38 pilots had shot down 4 Japanese aircraft over Tacloban. Despite a vigorous fighter defense, for the next 2 weeks enemy aircraft continued to bomb and strafe the airfield regularly and effectively. As of mid-November the air raids were less frequent, but Japanese aircraft harassed Allied forces periodically until the beginning of 1945.

While Fifth Air Force fighters struggled to protect the airstrip at Tacloban and U.S. forces elsewhere on Leyte Island, AAF bombers attacked Japanese installations throughout the central and southern

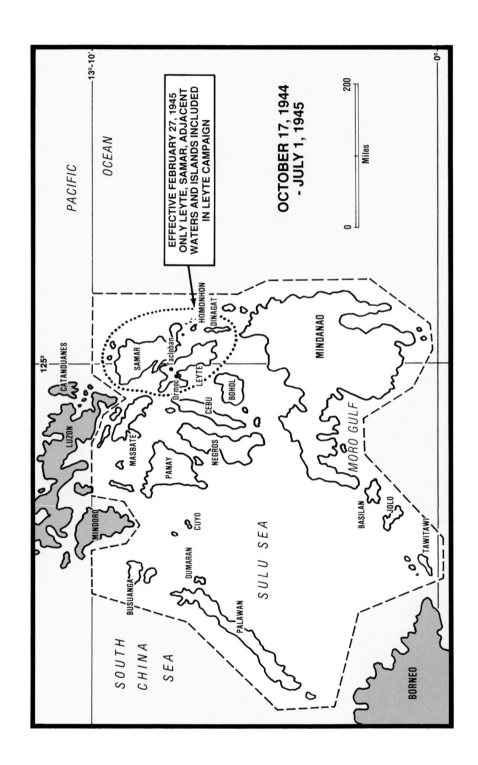

PACIFIC

OCEAN

SOUTH
CHINA
SEA

EFFECTIVE FEBRUARY 27, 1945
ONLY LEYTE, SAMAR, ADJACENT
WATERS AND ISLANDS INCLUDED
IN LEYTE CAMPAIGN

OCTOBER 17, 1944
- JULY 1, 1945

200

0   Miles

13°-10'

125°

CATANDUANES

LUZON

MINDORO

MASBATE

PANAY

CUYO

DUMARAN

BUSUANGA

PALAWAN

SULU SEA

NEGROS

CEBU

SAMAR

Tacloban

LEYTE

Ormoc

BOHOL

HOMONHON

DINAGAT

MINDANAO

MORO GULF

BASILAN

JOLO

TAWITAWI

BORNEO

0°

Philippines. Both V and XIII Bomber Commands, flying from Morotai Island, dropped tons of bombs almost daily on enemy air and harbor installations on the islands of Mindanao, Negros, Cebu, Palawan, Panay, and Masbate. On these raids American bombers also destroyed numerous Japanese aircraft, mostly on the ground. As a result, during the first 2 weeks of November 1944, Japanese air power in the southern Philippines was destroyed. AAF bombers also joined naval aircraft in seeking out and attacking Japanese transports attempting to land reinforcements and supplies on Leyte.

On December 7, 1944, the Army's 77th Infantry Division made another landing on Leyte, at Ormoc, on the west coast 32 miles southwest of Tacloban. AAF fighters from Tacloban covered the landing and shot down an estimated 53 enemy aircraft, while Japanese suicide attacks resulted in the loss of 3 U.S. naval vessels. On this third anniversary of the attack on Pearl Harbor, AAF and Marine aircraft also destroyed virtually all of the cargo vessels of a Japanese convoy landing troops at San Isidro Bay, 35 miles north of Ormoc. Most of the troops got ashore, but without their equipment. In these 2 actions on the 7th the United States lost only 4 aircraft. By December 26 U.S. military leaders were confident of the reconquest of Leyte Island, although the Japanese continued to offer sporadic resistance until May 1945.

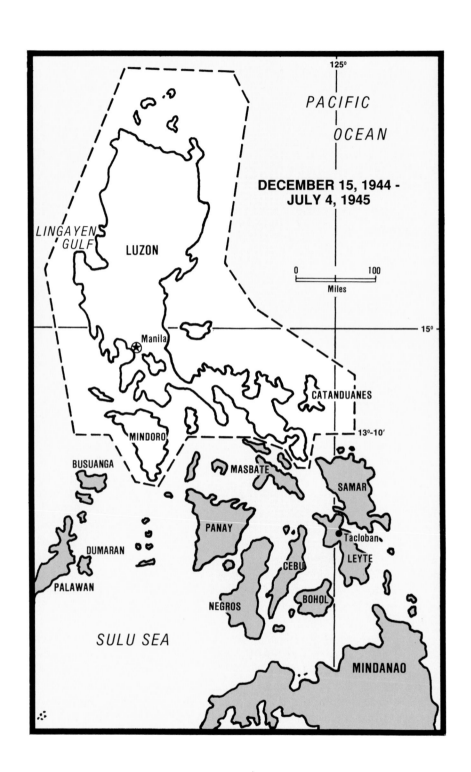

PACIFIC

OCEAN

**DECEMBER 15, 1944 -
JULY 4, 1945**

LINGAYEN
GULF

LUZON

0   100
Miles

15°

Manila

CATANDUANES

MINDORO

13°-10'

BUSUANGA

MASBATE

SAMAR

PANAY

Tacloban

DUMARAN

CEBU

LEYTE

PALAWAN

BOHOL

NEGROS

SULU SEA

MINDANAO

Luzon:
December 15, 1944–July 4, 1945

While the battle for Leyte Island ran its course, on December 15, 1944, U.S. Army forces landed on the southern tip of Mindoro Island, 280 miles northwest of Tacloban and less than 200 miles south of Manila, capital of the Philippines. Japanese pilots again resorted to suicide attacks and sank 2 U.S. ships in the assault force in spite of a vigorous air defense from AAF, Navy, and Marine fighters. Opposition from Japanese ground troops was minimal, however, and within 5 days British and American engineers completed a temporary runway called Hill Field. Operating from this airfield, on December 26 AAF pilots attacked a small Japanese naval force sent to bombard the beachhead on Mindoro. The AAF lost 3 B–25s, 7 P–38s, 10 P–47s, and 6 P–40s to enemy fire and crashes because of low fuel, night flying, and poor weather. But American installations and forces on the beachhead suffered little damage, and the enemy fleet turned away.

Aerial attacks against U.S. shipping bound for Mindoro were far more threatening than the hesitant naval attack. Between December 18, 1944, and January 7, 1945, Japanese pilots regularly attacked American convoys, and, using suicide tactics, sank several ships. By Christmas Fifth Air Force units on Mindoro were critically low on gasoline and munitions. To ease the fuel situation, from January 3 to 10, C–46s and C–47s flew in drums of gasoline, enabling the 310th Bombardment Wing on Mindoro to continue its attacks on enemy supply ships in the area. As early as December 22, V Bomber Command's B–24s had begun bombing Japanese installations at Clark Field on Luzon. Then V Fighter Command aircraft from Leyte attacked targets on Luzon, while other AAF units on Mindoro bombed railroads and highways in the central and southern parts of the island. Meantime, Fifth Air Force moved additional units to Mindoro so that sufficient aircraft and personnel would be available to support the planned assault on Luzon Island.

On January 2–5, 1945, the U.S. Navy's Seventh Fleet departed Leyte to sail almost 500 miles north to Lingayen Gulf, on the west coast of Luzon Island and about 120 miles northeast of Manila. As the ships approached the gulf on January 6, Japanese "kamikaze" pilots attacked the fleet savagely, temporarily threatening the amphibious landings. Navy aircraft bombed and strafed enemy airfields in northern Luzon over the next 2 days, and Fifth Air Force struck the heavily defended airdromes at Clark Field near Manila. These attacks destroyed most of the remaining enemy aircraft, and only a few suicide pilots flew against Allied forces on January 9, when the Sixth Army, commanded by Gen. Walter Krueger, made its assault on Luzon. By January 18 AAF and Navy fliers had eliminated the Japanese air forces on the island. Fifth Air Force fighters then turned to close air support of ground forces and the interdiction of roads, railways, and bridges.

On January 29 and 31, 1945, the U.S. Eighth Army, under the command of Gen. Robert L. Eichelberger, landed 2 task forces, one near Subic Bay, 35 miles north of the mouth of Manila Bay, and the other south of Manila Bay. The Army's 37th Infantry Division battled into Manila on February 4. During the rest of the month, bitter house-to-house fighting ensued, but by March 4 the U.S. troops, aided by Filipino irregulars, cleared the last of the Japanese soldiers from the city. All the while, AAF aircraft bombed and strafed Corregidor, the island fortress in Manila Bay that American troops had held so tenaciously 3 years before. Japanese forces on Corregidor now prevented American use of Manila Harbor; consequently, on February 16 amphibious forces landed on the beach and Fifth Air Force C–47s dropped over 2,000 paratroopers elsewhere on the island. By February 27th Corregidor was secured.

On Luzon, AAF tactics proved especially effective in close air support of the ground troops. Japanese forces often occupied fortified caves and bunkers, from which they could impede the American advance. The Fifth Air Force B–24s dropped 1,000- and 2,000-pound bombs on these targets and were followed by fighter-bombers with napalm. Thus U.S. soldiers were able to advance. Less than 7 months after landing on Luzon, by July 4, 1945, U.S. forces had defeated the Japanese, although some enemy forces continued to hold out until the war ended.

Southern Philippines:
February 27–July 4, 1945

In the assaults against Leyte and Luzon Islands, the United States had by-passed substantial Japanese garrisons in The Netherlands East Indies, Borneo, and the southern Philippines. The Indies and Borneo were left to the Allied forces of The Netherlands and Australia, while the U.S. concentrated on defeating the remaining enemy forces in the Philippines. As the U.S. Sixth Army and the Fifth Air Force completed the conquest of Luzon, the Eighth Army and the Thirteenth Air Force, under the command of Maj. Gen. Paul B. Wurtsmith since February 19, set about retaking the southern Philippines. On February 28 the 41st Infantry Division landed unopposed on the east coast of Palawan, westernmost of the larger islands, near Puerto Princesa, almost 400 miles southwest of Manila. Army engineers immediately began rebuilding the concrete airstrip at Puerto Princesa, but it was not ready until March 24, too late for the landing on Zamboanga Peninsula on the southwestern tip of Mindanao Island.

Eighth Army forces landed at Zamboanga on March 10, after the Fifth and Thirteenth Air Force's heavy bombers had thoroughly bombed the area. The Marines provided aerial cover for the landing itself. Encountering a determined Japanese resistance, the Eighth Army called frequently on the AAF for close air support. The Thirteenth Air Force moved fighter units to reconditioned Zamboangan airfields in April and May to provide aerial support for further landings in the southern Philippines.

In March and April American forces captured Tawitawi and Jolo Islands of the Sulu Archipelago, located in the straits between Borneo and Mindanao. At the same time, the Army's 40th Infantry Division took Panay Island, 250 miles south of Manila, and Negros Island, just south of Panay. The Army's Americal Division, which aided in the capture of Negros, also captured Cebu, just east of Negros, and landed on Bohol, between Leyte and Cebu Islands. In each instance the Japanese defenders withdrew to the island's interior, permitting U.S. forces to secure their initial objectives with little opposition. The real work for the ground forces came in clearing the interior of Japanese troops.

By mid-April 1945 the only sizable Japanese force remaining in the southern Philippine Islands was on Mindanao, concentrated around Davao Gulf. On April 2, XIII Bomber Command dispatched medium

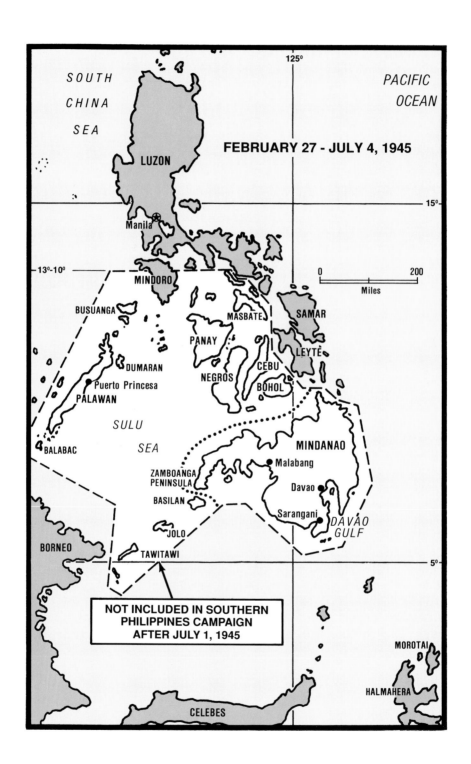

SOUTH
CHINA
SEA

PACIFIC
OCEAN

125°

FEBRUARY 27 - JULY 4, 1945

LUZON

15°

Manila

13°-10°

MINDORO

0   200
Miles

BUSUANGA

MASBATE

SAMAR

PANAY

LEYTE

DUMARAN

NEGROS

CEBU

Puerto Princesa

BOHOL

PALAWAN

SULU
SEA

MINDANAO

Malabang

BALABAC

ZAMBOANGA
PENINSULA

Davao

BASILAN

Sarangani

DAVAO
GULF

JOLO

BORNEO

TAWITAWI

5°

**NOT INCLUDED IN SOUTHERN
PHILIPPINES CAMPAIGN
AFTER JULY 1, 1945**

MOROTAI

HALMAHERA

CELEBES

and heavy bombers to hit the cities of Davao and Sarangani, 70 miles south of Davao, and other targets along the southwest coast of Mindanao. The bombers also struck Japanese positions at Malabang, 100 miles northwest of Davao, and Parang, 5 miles south of Malabang. On April 17 U.S. troops landed at Parang and Malabang and by the 26th had reached Digos, 20 miles south of Davao. When the ground forces outran their supply lines, the 403d Troop Carrier Group resupplied them in aerial drops from C–54s or landed C–47s on rough airstrips that Filipino guerrillas had carved from the jungle. Marine fighter aircraft provided most of the close air support on Mindanao, but from time to time the Army called on AAF fighters for napalm strikes on entrenched enemy positions. American troops took Davao on May 3, and Japanese forces retreated to the central mountainous region where they fought until Japan surrendered in August. On July 4, 1945, Gen. Douglas MacArthur, Commander of the Allied forces in the Philippine Islands, proclaimed the end of the Philippines campaigns.

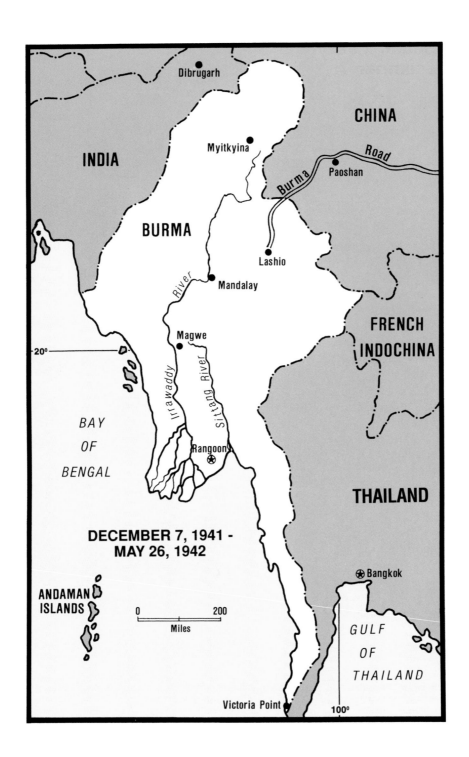

DECEMBER 7, 1941 -
MAY 26, 1942

Burma, 1942:
December 7, 1941–May 26, 1942

Japanese forces occupied Thailand on December 8, 1941, and preparations began for an invasion of Burma. On December 23 the enemy seized Victoria Point, a British air base at Burma's southernmost tip, but did not invade Burma from Thailand until a few weeks later, January 15, 1942. Japanese troops then moved rapidly against weak British defenses, crossing the Sittang River to threaten Rangoon, the capital city located on the Irrawaddy River delta in southern Burma.

Meantime, on December 23, 1941, pilots of the American Volunteer Group (AVG)* engaged Japanese bombers and fighters in the first aerial combat in Burma, inflicting heavy losses on an enemy formation that bombed Rangoon. The AVG continued the aerial defense of Rangoon until the first week in March, when it withdrew to Magwe on the Irrawaddy River, 275 miles north of Rangoon. During the rest of the Burma Campaign, the AVG frequently provided close air support for Allied ground forces and in aerial combat exacted a heavy toll of Japanese aircraft.

On March 7, 1942, Japanese troops captured Rangoon, effectively blocking further shipment to China of American Lend-Lease supplies. Five days later Generalissimo Chiang Kai-shek, head of China's government, sent his Fifth and Sixth Armies under the nominal command of his American Chief of Staff, Lt. Gen. Joseph W. Stilwell, into Burma to aid the British. Meanwhile enemy troops advanced against Mandalay, almost 200 miles north of Magwe in central Burma, and against Lashio, the southern terminus of the Burma Road over which the U.S. shipped supplies to China. The Japanese offensive forced British troops westward into India and the Chinese northeastward into China. Reinforced with veteran troops, the Japanese forces captured Lashio on April 29.

Except for the AVG, American fliers played only a minor role in the defense of Burma. On February 12, 1942, the AAF activated the

---

*The AVG, popularly known as the Flying Tigers, consisted of American pilots and mechanics recruited by Claire Chennault to fly for the Chinese Air Force. The group had the unofficial sanction of the U.S. government, and in July 1942 those among the Flying Tigers who so chose were inducted into the Army Air Forces as the 23d Pursuit Group. Most of the rest eventually joined one or another of the services.

Tenth Air Force and assigned it in the China–Burma–India Theater. Its first commander in India was Maj. Gen. Lewis H. Brereton. From March 8 through 12, the entire Tenth Air Force, consisting of only 6 heavy bombers, transported troops and supplies from India to Magwe, Burma. Gradually the AAF added aircraft, equipment, and personnel to the Tenth. During the next 2 months its pilots flew ammunition, fuel, and supplies to Allied forces and evacuated the wounded. After the fall of Mandalay on May 1, the C–47 pilots began to fly out troops whenever possible and airdropped supplies to columns of British soldiers retreating into India. General Stilwell refused to fly out; instead, he marched to India through the jungles with his staff and remnants of British units. By May 26, 1942, Japan had conquered virtually all of Burma.

India–Burma:
April 2, 1942–January 28, 1945

As of April 1942 the Japanese dominated Singapore, the Malay
Peninsula, Sumatra, Thailand, and most of Burma. The Tenth Air
Force flew its first combat mission on the second of the month, when
3 heavy bombers attacked enemy shipping near Port Blair in the
Andaman Islands, 450 miles southwest of Rangoon, Burma.

Because China could no longer receive supplies over the Burma Road,
the AAF in June 1942 began a long-range airlift from India over the
Himalaya Mountains. By then, Brig. Gen. Earl L. Naiden was the
Tenth's Commander, but he was relieved in August by Maj. Gen.
Clayton L. Bissell. American pilots assigned to the Tenth Air Force
flew the "Hump," as the air route was known throughout the war. The
Hump Route, which extended from bases in northeastern India to
Kunming, China, about 650 miles to the east, involved flying at
altitudes up to 21,000 feet over the Himalaya Mountains in fog, rain,
and strong winds. Japanese fighters often attacked the transports as
they flew over northern Burma. These difficulties were only part of
the problem of establishing the Hump Route, because in 1942 the
Tenth Air Force had few serviceable aircraft, virtually no spare parts,
and too few personnel to operate more than a shoestring transport
service. The situation improved, however, in October when more
aircraft became available and the Air Transport Command took over
the Hump flights. The airlift over the Himalayas supplied Allied
forces in China until, in January 1945, Allied forces reopened the
Burma Road.

During the last week of June 1942, the AAF sent most of the Tenth
Air Force's personnel, its bombers, and several transport aircraft to
the Middle East, leaving only a skeleton force in India.* For the rest
of the year the Tenth Air Force restricted its missions to the protection
of the Hump airlift route and the defense of British and U.S. air bases
in extreme northeast India in the State of Assam.

In November 1942, having received B–24s, the Tenth Air Force began
the long-range bombing of targets at Mandalay in central Burma,
Bangkok in Thailand, and Port Blair in the Andaman Islands. During

---

*See Egypt-Libya Campaign, p. 139

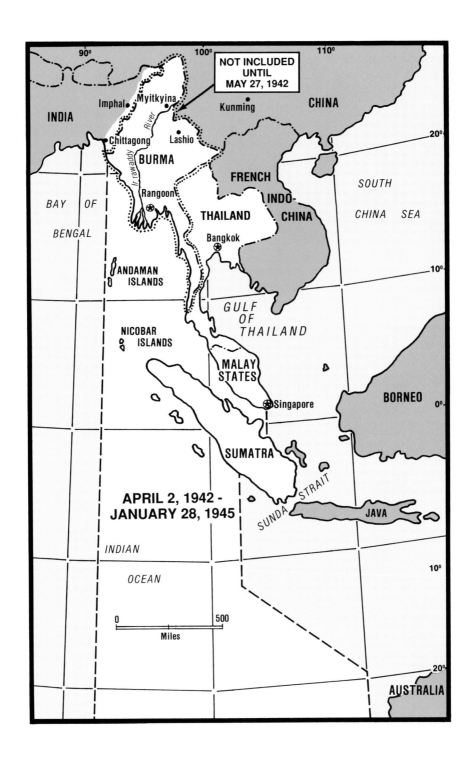

90°　　　　100°　　　　　　　　　　　　110°

NOT INCLUDED
UNTIL
MAY 27, 1942

Imphal● ●Myitkyina
INDIA　　　　　　　　　　●Kunming　　　CHINA

●Chittagong　　　●Lashio　　　　　　　　　　　20°

BURMA

FRENCH

Rangoon●　　　　　　INDO-

THAILAND　　CHINA

●Bangkok

BAY　OF

BENGAL

ANDAMAN
ISLANDS

SOUTH

CHINA　SEA

GULF
OF
THAILAND　　　　　　　　　　10°

NICOBAR
ISLANDS

MALAY
STATES

⊗Singapore　　　　　BORNEO　　0°

SUMATRA

APRIL 2, 1942 -
JANUARY 28, 1945

SUNDA STRAIT　　JAVA

INDIAN

OCEAN　　　　　　　　　　　　　　　10°

0　　　　　　500

Miles

20°

AUSTRALIA

Ir rawaddy River

108

1943 Royal Air Force (RAF) and AAF fighters supported British and Chinese ground troops in Burma, and heavy bombers struck targets in southern Burma and the Andaman Islands to hinder Japanese resupply and reinforcement of their forces in Burma. Tenth Air Force medium bombers and P–47s carrying 1,000-pound bombs continually disrupted enemy traffic between Rangoon and the battle front in northern Burma. Throughout the fall and winter of 1943–1944, the AAF and RAF cooperated in bombing raids to destroy Rangoon Harbor. Although the Allies lost aircraft on practically every mission, the enemy also suffered constant losses of aircraft in Burma. Because of this attrition and the continued build-up of the Tenth Air Force, under the command from August 1943 of Maj. Gen. Howard C. Davidson, by mid-1944 the AAF dominated the skies over Burma.

At the end of 1943 the only Allied forces that had reentered Burma were Chinese troops under the command of Lt. Gen. Joseph W. Stilwell. As the new year began, the Chinese slowly advanced southeastward from the India-Burma border toward Myitkyina on the Irrawaddy River, almost 600 miles north of Rangoon. On March 5, 1944, the British sent a special force into central Burma behind enemy lines to harass Japanese troops during the Chinese offensive. The AAF's 1st Air Commando Group airlifted the British unit and provided much of its close air support. When the British special force began operations, however, Japanese troops crossed the Chindwin River on March 6 and attacked British positions near Imphal, India, almost 50 miles west of the India-Burma border. The British repulsed the Japanese invasion on May 17, just as Chinese troops reached Myitkyina, Burma. The Japanese held Myitkyina until August 3 before withdrawing to the east bank of the Irrawaddy River. Enemy forces fought delaying actions during 1944 as they gradually withdrew into central Burma. On January 28, 1945, Chinese troops reopened the Burma road between Lashio and Kunming, once again allowing the movement of men and supplies overland between India and China. Allied successes in Burma also encouraged Generalissimo Chiang Kai-shek to keep the Chinese in the war against Japan.

The besieged British forces at Imphal, the British special force, and the Chinese troops in Burma received their supplies primarily by air transport of the Eastern Air Command, which the Allies created on December 15, 1943, to direct air power in India and Burma.

Throughout the India-Burma Campaign, air transport proved indispensable. When the Japanese cut roads or isolated Allied forces, aerial resupply often became the only way to support continued operations.

Central Burma:
January 29–July 15, 1945

By January 29, 1945, Allied forces, primarily British and Chinese troops supported in the air by the RAF and AAF, occupied most of northern Burma. The battle line ran roughly 280 miles northeast from Minbya on the Bay of Bengal to a point on the Irrawaddy River about 12 miles north of Mandalay in central Burma, then north for more than 90 miles along the Irrawaddy before turning east to Kunlong on the Salween River, 470 miles northeast of Rangoon. Eastern Air Command transports flew to bases a short distance behind this battle line, bringing reinforcements and supplies to the ground troops and returning casualties to medical facilities at Ledo, India, about 450 miles north of Mandalay, Burma. In February alone, AAF transports brought out over 3,000 casualties from Burma, in addition to those flown out by British air transports. Meantime, through late winter and early spring, the Tenth Air Force's P–47s and B–25s struck at Japanese positions and troop concentrations in close support of the advancing Allied ground forces. In February 1945 the Japanese withdrew their air forces from Burma, removing a long-standing threat to the Himalaya airlift route across northern Burma and forfeiting supremacy in the air to the Allied air forces.

The British XV Corps, during March 1945, pushed down the coast of the Bay of Bengal, while the British Fourteenth Army advanced southward on a broad front through the jungles and plains of central Burma. The Chinese worked their way from the northeast toward Mandalay. The Commander of the Fourteenth Army, Lt. Gen. Sir William J. Slim, who perceived that the Japanese intended to trap British forces as they tried to cross the Irawaddy River to take Mandalay, sent 1 of his corps south to cross in the rear of the enemy's positions. This successful tactic permitted the Allies to surround Mandalay with minimal losses. The Japanese defenders of the city, nevertheless, held Fort Dufferin against repeated assaults. Air attacks, supplemented by British artillery, finally broke the walls of the fort, and on March 21 Mandalay fell to the Allies while the remaining Japanese troops withdrew to the south and east. Advancing Allied troops still received practically all of their supplies and reinforcements by air transport from India. Military leaders, concerned that the monsoon season beginning in May would halt the tremendous aerial flow of materiel and personnel, decided in favor of an amphibious assault on Rangoon.

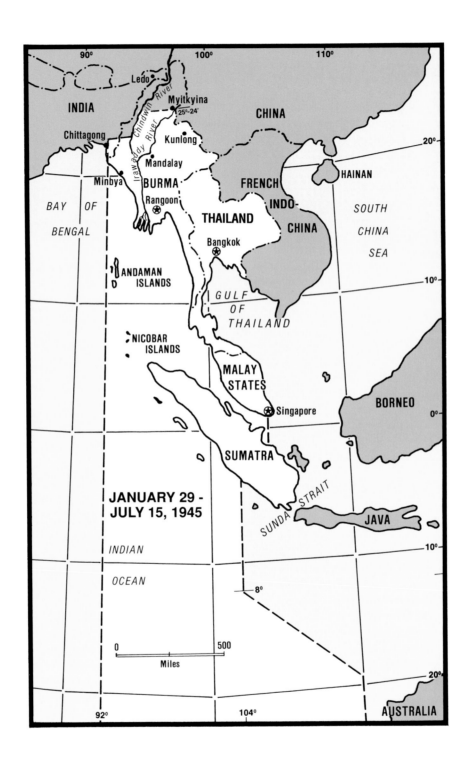

JANUARY 29 - JULY 15, 1945

112

In preparation for the assault, between April 26 and May 2, Tenth Air Force heavy bombers smashed enemy gun emplacements and troop concentrations along the banks of the Rangoon River. By May 1 Allied armies advancing overland from Mandalay reached Pegu, 40 miles northeast of Rangoon. The next day troop carriers airdropped 800 Ghurkas of the British Army at Elephant Point, 20 miles south of Rangoon, and then a British corps made an amphibious landing nearby on the banks of the Rangoon River. When Allied troops entered the city on the 3rd, they found that the Japanese had already left. The recapture of Burma was complete, although isolated groups of enemy soldiers continued fighting until July 15. Allied air superiority, effective air transport, and the interdiction of the enemy's airfields, railroads, and other means of transportation markedly contributed to success in the Central Burma Campaign.

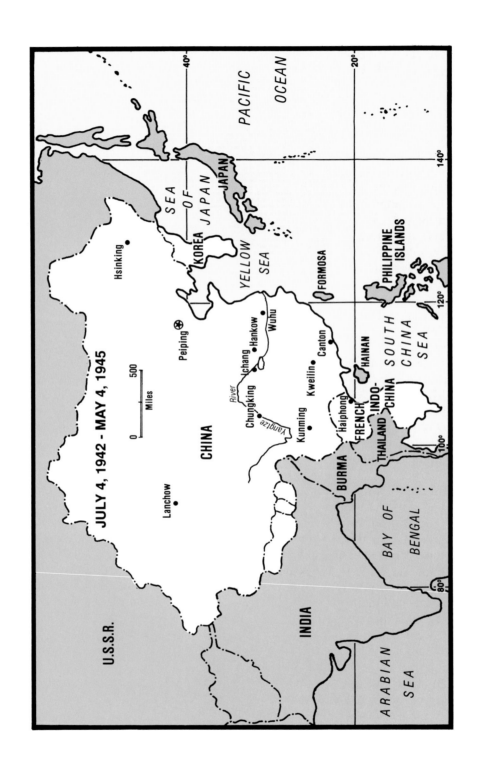

JULY 4, 1942 - MAY 4, 1945

U.S.S.R.

Hsinking

Lanchow

CHINA

Peiping

Chungking

Ichang   Hankow   Wuhu

Kunming   Kweilin   Canton

Yangtze River

Haiphong

FRENCH INDO-CHINA

BURMA

THAILAND

HAINAN

FORMOSA

KOREA   JAPAN

SEA OF JAPAN

YELLOW SEA

PACIFIC OCEAN

PHILIPPINE ISLANDS

SOUTH CHINA SEA

INDIA

BAY OF BENGAL

ARABIAN SEA

500

Miles

0

40°   20°   140°   120°   100°   80°

China Defensive:
July 4, 1942–May 4, 1945

On July 4, 1942, the China Air Task Force (CATF), a unit of the Tenth Air Force, assumed responsibility for the air defense of China, a mission previously performed by the American Volunteer Group. Several members of the AVG, including its founder, Brig. Gen. Claire L. Chennault, formed the nucleus of the CATF. General Chennault established the task force's headquarters at Kunming in southwest China. Kunming, over 1,200 miles from Peiping, was the eastern terminus of the AAF airlift of supplies from India to China. Major CATF bases located near Kunming were: Yunani, 150 miles west; Nanning, 350 miles southeast; Kweilin, 475 miles east; Hengyang, 625 miles east; Chungking, 350 miles northeast; and Chengtu, 380 miles north. From these airfields, task force aircraft attacked Japanese targets at Hankow on the Yangzte River, at Canton and Hong Kong on the coast, and at Haiphong, French Indochina—besides protecting CATF installations from enemy attack.

Between December 1942 and March 1943 the China Air Task Force curtailed its offensive operations because of a shortage of fuel. Then in March the AAF activated the Fourteenth Air Force to replace the CATF. The Fourteenth, under the command of General Chennault, slowly increased the frequency and scope of its offensive missions, and for the first time, on May 4, B–24s flew a long-range mission, bombing installations on Hainan Island, a 1,200-mile round trip from Kunming. The B–24s soon settled into a routine of flying 2 or 3 bombing missions followed by a resupply flight over the Himalayas to India to bring back fuel and bombs for the next few missions. From May to August 1943 the Japanese Air Force repeatedly attacked Fourteenth Air Force bases and while losing aircraft in these raids, exacted a toll of AAF fighters. By August 1 enemy attacks had severely depleted Fourteenth Air Force fighter aircraft. During this time, from July to December, American heavy and medium bombers concentrated their efforts on enemy shipping and harbor installations along the Chinese coast. But the Fourteenth Air Force, small in size and short of supplies, had to be content with restricted operations throughout 1943.

In the first few months of 1944, the Fourteenth Air Force had few resources with which to operate. The Japanese launched a ground offensive in southern China on May 26 seeking, among other objectives, to capture key Allied air bases. Enemy troops moved south from the Yangtze River in a 400-mile front from Ichang, 700 miles southwest of Peiping, eastward to Wuhu, 620 miles southeast of the capital city. The Fourteenth suspended most of its bombing operations and turned to close air support of Chinese forces. These missions included intercepting enemy aircraft, attacking shipping on rivers and lakes near Hankow, and striking troop columns, positions, transports, roads, and bridges. On August 8 the Japanese captured Hengyang, easternmost of the Fourteenth Air Force's bases. By mid-November the enemy had overrun 6 more of the Fourteenth's installations. But although Japanese ground forces repeatedly defeated the poorly trained and equipped Chinese troops, the Japanese Air Force failed to maintain air superiority in southwest China. Only occasionally did enemy pilots subject the Chinese troops to concentrated air attacks.

In December 1944 the AAF airlifted 2 Chinese divisions, more than 25,000 troops, from Burma to China to help blunt the Japanese advance; nevertheless, by May 1945 the enemy had seized 4 more Fourteenth Air Force bases. However, Chinese troops, now reequipped by the expanding Hump airlift* and better trained, prepared to take the offensive in their homeland.

---

*In July 1942 AAF aircraft delivered only 85 tons of supplies over the Hump from India to China. A year later, the Air Transport Command airlifted 2,916 tons per month to China. By July 1944 that figure was 18,975 tons and a year later 71,042 tons.

China Offensive:
May 5–September 2, 1945

In April 1945 the Japanese launched another offensive from Paoking, 500 miles northeast of Kunming, China. Enemy troops advanced slowly on a broad front immediately southwest of Tungting Lake, 700 miles south of Peiping. In previous battles Chinese ground forces often broke early, enabling the enemy to achieve its objectives in spite of being outnumbered. In the battle for Chihkiang, however, the Japanese force of 60,000 troops faced the Chinese Sixth Army of some 100,000 men trained and equipped under the guidance of the Commanders of the China–Burma–India Theater, Gen. Joseph W. Stilwell and his successor, Gen. Albert C. Wedemeyer. The invaders could no longer be assured of the battle's outcome.

Besides well-trained and equipped ground forces, the Japanese had to contend with a more effective Chinese Air Force. The Chinese American Composite Wing (CACW), in particular, consisted of Chinese personnel led by American commanders and was the only Chinese Air Force unit regularly engaged in combat. The P–51s of the CACW's 5th Fighter Group provided close air support for ground forces, and B–25s of the 3d and 4th Bombardment Squadrons, Medium, flew battlefield interdiction missions. The wing sent air-ground liaison teams to the battle area to direct the pilots to targets. When a Chinese commander requested air support, the air-ground team relayed the request to 5th Fighter Group headquarters, which tasked P–51s to the mission. The CACW relied heavily on napalm bombs to flush the enemy from their foxholes, but the P–51's .50-caliber machine gun proved the most important weapon in close air support.

With the support of the CACW, the Chinese Sixth Army quickly brought the Japanese offensive to a halt and on May 5, 1945, launched a strong counterattack. By the 15th the enemy retreated eastward—a turning point of the war in China. Throughout June Japanese forces rapidly abandoned hard-won positions in southwest China as Chinese troops pressed a major offensive.

In July 1945, the Tenth Air Force moved from Burma to China, joining the Fourteenth Air Force to provide air support for Chinese forces. At this time, although the Burma Highway was now in use, AAF transports continued to airlift most of the supplies to China. American aircraft met little resistance from Japanese fighters during their interdiction and close air support missions. The railway interdic-

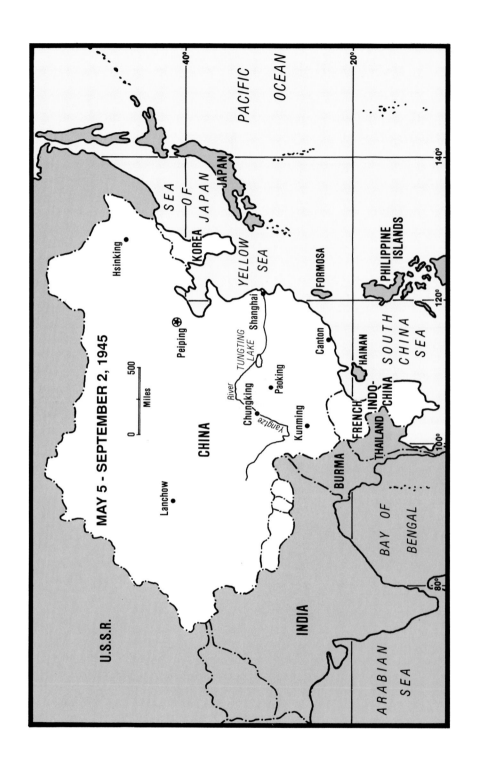

MAY 5 - SEPTEMBER 2, 1945

tion campaign proved particularly successful, forcing the Japanese to rely heavily on motor and animal transport at night. By the end of July the Japanese had withdrawn from much of central China and the Chinese coast, abandoning positions at Canton and as far north as the Yellow River. By VJ Day in August, the only sizable Japanese force remained in North China and faced invading forces of the Soviet Union in Manchuria.

The sudden collapse of Japanese forces in China was part of the general defeat of Japan. For the Allies, China remained throughout the war a peripheral theater. The AAF operated in China at the end of the longest supply line in the world, and the Fourteenth Air Force was the only AAF organization that depended almost entirely on air transport for resupply. In spite of many obstacles, including limited supplies, a small force, primitive conditions, and a mission that concentrated on supporting battered Chinese ground forces during much of the war, the Fourteenth Air Force gained and held air superiority over southern and central China during 1944 and 1945.

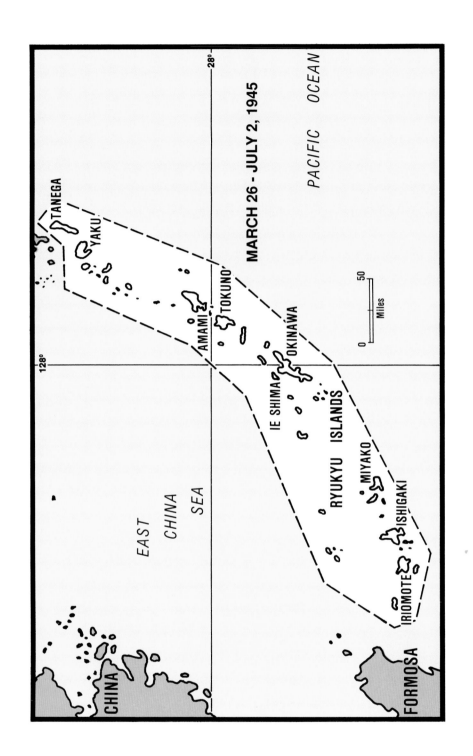

MARCH 26 - JULY 2, 1945

PACIFIC OCEAN

TANEGA

YAKU.

TOKUNO

AMAMI

OKINAWA

128°

28°

IE SHIMA

MIYAKO

RYUKYU ISLANDS

ISHIGAKI

IRIOMOTE

EAST CHINA SEA

CHINA

FORMOSA

50

0

Miles

120

Ryukyus:
March 26–July 2, 1945

By March 1945 U.S. Armed Forces had captured the Philippine Islands in the Southwest Pacific, the Marianas in the West Pacific, and Iwo Jima in the Bonins. The U.S. was now ready to move against the Ryukyu Islands, located between Formosa and the southernmost island of Japan, Kyushu. The first target among the Ryukyus was the largest island, Okinawa, located 950 miles northeast of Clark Field in the Philippines. Because the distance to Okinawa was too far from the nearest airfield for AAF fighter aircraft to operate, the U.S. Navy provided aerial cover for the fleet and close air support for the landing forces.

On March 26–27 American forces seized several small islands west of the southern tip of Okinawa. Five days later, on April 1, the U.S. Fifth Fleet, under the command of Adm. Thomas L. Sprague, landed Lt. Gen. Simon B. Buckner's Tenth Army, consisting of the Army XXIV Corps and the III Marine Amphibious Corps, at Hagushi Beach on the island's west coast.

During the weeks that followed, Japanese pilots made numerous suicide attacks on the American fleet and inflicted some of the heaviest naval losses of the war. The enemy expended its air strength in 2,000 to 3,000 suicide sorties between March 1 and mid-April. Near Iwo Jima and Okinawa, the U.S. Navy lost 36 ships sunk or scuttled, 28 so badly damaged they could not be repaired, and 42 more put out of action for more than a month. Naval fighters, busy defending ships against enemy attacks, were often unavailable for close air support of the ground forces. On April 4 the Tenth Army captured 2 Okinawan airfields, Yontan and Kadena, and within 3 days Marine and Seventh Air Force fighters could land and take off at Yontan. Thereafter, Marine and Seventh Air Force pilots assumed the close air support mission on Okinawa.

On April 16 an element of the U.S. Army 77th Infantry Division assaulted Ie Shima and in 6 days of fierce fighting secured this 11-square-mile island just off the northwest spur of Okinawa. U.S. engineers had rebuilt the all-weather strip on Ie Shima by May 12, allowing the AAF to dispatch units to fly against Okinawan targets.

Meanwhile, on Okinawa U.S. ground forces captured the northern two-thirds of the island before the end of April 1945, but a determined

Japanese defense of the southern tip virtually halted the ground advance. The enemy had constructed mutually supporting strong points, pill boxes, and elaborate caves with connecting tunnels. On June 22, 1945, after nearly 2 months of bitter fighting, U.S. Marine and Army troops captured the last organized enemy position on Okinawa. The victory in the Ryukyus was expensive to both sides. The United States suffered almost 50,000 casualties, while Japan lost over 110,000 troops. But the benefits were clear: the U.S. gained additional bases from which the Seventh Air Force could bomb the Japanese home islands.

Air Offensive, Japan: April 17, 1942–September 2, 1945

The first American bombing raid on Japan took place on April 17, 1942, when a U.S. Navy carrier, the USS *Hornet*, sailing almost 800 miles east of Japan, launched 16 B–25s. Led by Col. James H. Doolittle, the aircrews bombed Tokyo and other cities before attempting to fly across the Sea of Japan to friendly bases in China. Although all of the B–25s were lost, most of the AAF aircrews survived and eventually returned to duty. This first bombing mission, which inflicted little physical damage on the Japanese, nevertheless boosted public morale in the U.S. tremendously.

Bombing attacks were resumed more than 2 years later, on June 15, 1944, when the Twentieth Air Force, activated in April 1944 and under the direct command of AAF Commanding General H. H. Arnold in Washington, began flying B–29 missions against targets in Japan from bases in China. At the time the Chinese bases were the only ones from which the bombers could reach Japan. Because of the distance, the aircraft could carry only partial bomb loads and could hit only targets on Kyushu, the southernmost island of Japan, and the southern tip of Honshu Island, immediately to the north of Kyushu. In addition, the B–29s had to haul bombs and fuel across the Himalaya Mountains for every mission against Japan. The Twentieth Air Force flew its last mission from China on January 6, 1945, bombing the city of Omuta on the northwest coast of Kyushu Island.

Meantime, on November 24, 1944, the XXI Bomber Command of the Twentieth Air Force, led by Brig. Gen. Haywood S. Hansell, Jr., began the strategic bombing of Japan from air bases in the recently captured Mariana Islands. These B–29 raids consisted of high-altitude daylight missions, employing high explosives that had proved effective against concentrated European industrial targets. Japan's industry, however, was widely dispersed, targets were frequently obscured by cloud cover, and thus strategic bombardment produced poor results.

In early March 1945 Maj. Gen. Curtis E. LeMay, having replaced General Hansell in January, shifted to adopt low-altitude night missions, dropping incendiary instead of high-explosive bombs on cities. Aircrews stripped the B–29s of armor and guns, except for tail guns, so that at altitudes of 7,000–10,000 feet the bombers could carry almost 3 times the tonnage they carried on high-altitude missions. The XXI Bomber

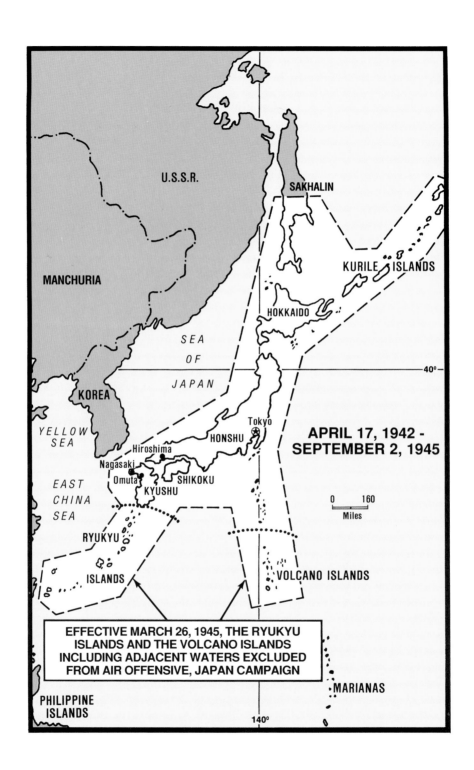

U.S.S.R.

SAKHALIN

MANCHURIA

KURILE   ISLANDS

HOKKAIDO

SEA
OF
JAPAN

40°

KOREA

YELLOW
SEA

Tokyo

HONSHU

Hiroshima

Nagasaki

Omuta

KYUSHU

SHIKOKU

APRIL 17, 1942 -
SEPTEMBER 2, 1945

EAST
CHINA
SEA

0   160

Miles

RYUKYU

ISLANDS

VOLCANO ISLANDS

EFFECTIVE MARCH 26, 1945, THE RYUKYU
ISLANDS AND THE VOLCANO ISLANDS
INCLUDING ADJACENT WATERS EXCLUDED
FROM AIR OFFENSIVE, JAPAN CAMPAIGN

MARIANAS

PHILIPPINE
ISLANDS

140°

Command flew its first low-altitude mission on March 9–10 against Tokyo. The results were devastating. About 15–16 square miles of the city burned, and over 84,000 people died in the fires. Between March and August 1945 the B–29s destroyed most of Japan's major cities in fire-bombing raids. Twentieth Air Force B–29s also sowed mines in Japanese navigable territorial waters and supported the Ryukyus Campaign, bombing airfields on Kyushu Island from which the Japanese launched "kamikaze" attacks.

The Fifth, Seventh, and Eleventh Air Forces also participated in the Air Offensive, Japan. As early as November 9, 1943, the Eleventh Air Force, flying B–24s from the Aleutian Islands, bombed targets in the Kurile Islands northeast of Hokkaido, the northernmost island of Japan. The Eleventh Air Force flew its last mission over the Kuriles on August 24, 1945. The Seventh and Fifth Air Forces, after the establishment of bases on Okinawa in April 1945, flew missions against Japanese shipping and targets on Kyushu.

On August 10, 1944, the Seventh Air Force began bombing Iwo Jima in the Volcano Islands, 850 miles south of Tokyo. Iwo Jima was well-suited for a forward air base, and on February 19, 1945, the 4th and 5th Marine Divisions, the 3rd being held in reserve until the beachhead was established, landed on the southeast coast to battle stubborn Japanese defenders. These 3 divisions made up the Fifth Amphibious Corps, commanded by Maj. Gen. Harry Schmidt. By March 16 the Marines had crushed the defenders. The next day several B–29s returning from missions over Japan made emergency landings on the island, and by the end of the war more than 2,200 B–29s had landed on Iwo Jima. On April 7 the VII Fighter Command moved to Iwo Jima to escort B–29s attacking Japan.

Throughout the summer of 1945, Japan remained under constant aerial attack, but its leaders refused to surrender. On August 6 a B–29 of the 509th Composite Group dropped an atomic bomb on Hiroshima, a city on the southern end of Honshu Island, 420 miles southwest of Tokyo. The explosion destroyed two-thirds of the city and killed almost 80,000 people. Three days later, on August 9, another B–29 dropped a second atomic bomb on Nagasaki, located on the western side of Kyushu Island, 600 miles southwest of Tokyo, with somewhat lesser but comparable destruction. The next day Japan's leaders requested a cease-fire, and on the 15th the Far East Air Forces began to transport advance occupation troops to Tokyo. The Japanese formally surrendered on September 2, 1945, thus ending World War II.

Antisubmarine, Asiatic–Pacific Theater: December 7, 1941–September 2, 1945*

Army Air Forces units and personnel received credit for the Antisubmarine Campaign, Asiatic–Pacific Theater, if they engaged in antisubmarine operations outside of specified combat zones or times established for other campaigns. The only AAF unit credited with the Antisubmarine Campaign, Asiatic–Pacific Theater, was the 333d Fighter Squadron stationed in Hawaii. It flew antisubmarine patrols outside the Central Pacific Campaign zone between September 1942 and July 1943.

*See Theater Map.

Air Combat, Asiatic–Pacific Theater: December 7, 1941–September 2, 1945*

Personnel and units that participated in combat operations within the theater that could not be credited under other campaigns, received credit for Air Combat Campaign, Asiatic–Pacific Theater. For example, in April 1944, before the beginning of the Western Pacific Campaign, Fourteenth Air Force bombers, escorted by fighter groups, attacked targets in Formosa. Later in the year, between October and December, Fifth Air Force units flew bombing and reconnaissance missions over Luzon, northernmost of the Philippine Islands, before the Luzon Campaign began. From May through July 1945, Thirteenth Air Force bombardment groups provided close air support for Australian troops in Borneo, after the New Guinea Campaign ended. Also, in July and August 1945, following the end of the Central Burma Campaign, Tenth Air Force fighter-bombers supported Allied troops in Burma with bombing and strafing missions. Other air combat operations at various times and locations likewise fell under the Air Combat Campaign, Asiatic–Pacific Theater.

For the United States, the war in the Asiatic–Pacific Theater began before and ended after the war in the European–African–Middle Eastern Theater. On the whole, in the Asiatic–Pacific Theater, the AAF played a secondary role to the U.S. Navy's air power, but was the primary air force in the EAME Theater.

---

*See Theater Map.

World War II Service

European African Middle Eastern Theater

1941-1945

EAME Campaign Medal

At the top on the obverse side are the words EUROPEAN AFRICAN MIDDLE EASTERN CAMPAIGN. In the center foreground is a landing craft filled with troops. The craft appears under the bow of a landing vessel (an LST), which has an antiaircraft gun firing from its forward deck. In the left background, another ship is barely visible beneath a plume of smoke; a fighter aircraft dives from above. In the lower foreground are 3 helmeted soldiers with backpacks and rifles. The reverse side is identical to the American and AP Campaign Medals. All 3 show a left profile of a bald eagle perched on a rock. At the upper right are the words UNITED STATES OF AMERICA; at the lower left are the dates 1941–1945. The campaign medal is worn with a suspension ribbon, although a ribbon bar may be worn instead. On the ribbon's left edge is a brown band and inside that band are 3 stripes of green, white, and red, the colors of Italy. In the center, 3 narrow stripes—blue, white, and red, the colors of the U.S.—separate 2 broad green bands that represent the fields of Europe. Between the green and brown bands on the right side appear 3 stripes of white, black, and white, the colors of Germany.

Executive Order No. 9265, November 6, 1942, established the EAME Campaign Medal. A service member earned it if at any time between December 7, 1941, and November 8, 1945, he or she served within the theater in a permanent assignment or on temporary duty for at least 30 consecutive or 60 nonconsecutive days, or participated in combat. The member also received a Bronze Service Star for each campaign credit, or a Silver Service Star in place of 5 Bronze Stars. These stars are worn on the suspension ribbon or the ribbon bar. Participants in at least 1 airborne or amphibious assault landing wear an arrowhead on the ribbon or ribbon bar.

EAME Theater Streamers

The EAME Theater Service Streamer is identical to the ribbon in design and color. A unit received the award if at any time between December 7, 1941, and November 8, 1945, it was based in or traveled for at least 30 days through the EAME Theater. A campaign streamer is a service streamer with the campaign's name and dates embroidered on it. A unit received a campaign streamer instead of a service streamer if it served within or flew combat missions into the campaign's combat zone. A unit participating in an amphibious or airborne assault landing received the campaign streamer with an embroidered arrowhead preceding the name and dates.

131

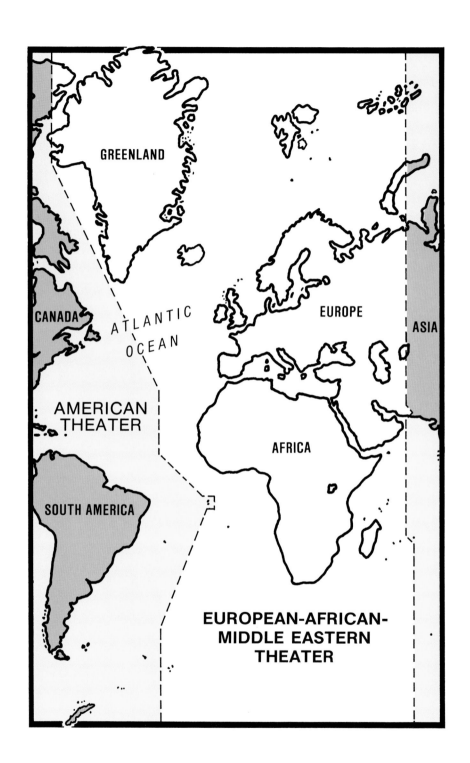

GREENLAND

CANADA

ATLANTIC OCEAN

EUROPE

ASIA

AMERICAN THEATER

AFRICA

SOUTH AMERICA

EUROPEAN-AFRICAN-
MIDDLE EASTERN
THEATER

132

European–African–Middle Eastern Theater Campaigns: December 7, 1941–September 2, 1945

Designated Campaigns in the EAME Theater

War Department General Order No. 24, March 4, 1947, designated 17 campaigns for the EAME Theater. Each campaign had a combat zone and specific dates for campaign credit; with 2 exceptions, campaign dates extended from December 7, 1941, the date of the Japanese attack on Pearl Harbor, to May 11, 1945, the date that marked the end of hostilities in Europe. The general order designated the end of the Air Combat and Antisubmarine Campaigns as September 2, 1945. But no unit or individual received campaign credit in the EAME Theater after May 11, 1945. The War Department extended the EAME Theater Service for 6 months to November 8, 1945, well beyond the date of Germany's unconditional surrender. During this time units that had not previously earned campaign streamers for service within the theater received the EAME Service Streamer; individuals with no previous award for service in the theater received the EAME Campaign Medal and Ribbon. The first campaign summarized for this theater is Air Combat.

Air Combat, EAME Theater:
December 7, 1941–September 2, 1945*

Air operations that occurred outside of the combat zones and times established for other campaigns in the European–African–Middle Eastern Theater are credited to the Air Combat Campaign, EAME Theater. Personnel and units participating in combat operations that did not come under other EAME Theater Campaigns received credit for this campaign.

Among the operations of the Air Combat Campaign is the aerial bombardment of Pantelleria Island, which is located in the Mediterranean about halfway between Tunisia and Sicily. In June 1943 the Northwest African Air Force bombed Pantelleria incessantly for over a week, as British naval forces shelled the island. The Italian garrison surrendered on June 11 as an Allied amphibious landing force approached.

Several important air operations in the Balkans also fall under this campaign. On June 11, 1942, thirteen B–24s of the HALPRO Detachment,† originally enroute to India and diverted to supplement the Royal Air Force's efforts in North Africa and the Middle East, took off from Fayid, Egypt, 60 miles east of Cairo. Twelve of these aircraft bombed an oil field near Ploesti, Rumania, at dawn on June 12, inflicting slight damage. This marked the first AAF bombardment attack in the EAME Theater and the first of 27 missions against the oil fields and refineries at Ploesti. A year later, on August 1, 1943, the Ninth Air Force launched a massive raid on the Ploesti refineries. In an experimental low-level attack, 177 B–24 heavy bombers, including aircraft from 3 Eighth Air Force bombardment groups, took off at dawn from airfields near Benghazi, Libya. About 42 percent of Ploesti's refining capacity was destroyed, at a cost of 54 aircraft and 532 airmen. The AAF subsequently restricted its heavy bombers to high-altitude operations. The Fifteenth Air Force flew the last mission against Ploesti on August 19, 1944.

---

*See Theater Map.

†See Egypt–Libya Campaign, pp. 139–140.

Many operations over the Balkans during the war consisted of airlift flights to support partisan operations behind enemy lines and evacuate downed airmen to Italy. Beginning in September 1943, the Fifteenth Air Force used C–47s to transport supplies to the partisan forces in the Balkan countries. In February 1944 the Fifteenth assigned the first of 5 troop carrier squadrons to this activity. The C–47s often airdropped supplies, but more frequently landed at primitive airstrips to unload guns, ammunition, food, clothing, and medical supplies, then returned to Italy with partisan families and wounded. Later, heavy bombers were also used for airlift, and gasoline, jeeps, mail, and even mules appeared on the cargo manifests.

Between September 1943 and April 30, 1945, the Fifteenth Air Force also transported some 3,000 Allied prisoners of war (POWs) and downed airmen evading enemy capture out of the Balkans into Italy. For example, on August 31, 1944—1 week after Rumania capitulated—Fifteenth Air Force B–17s were sent to retrieve AAF flyers released from POW camps near Bucharest. Over the next 3 days, during OPERATION REUNION, the B–17 aircrews airlifted 1,162 POWs from Rumania to Italy.

All these missions, as well as other military aerial operations in the Balkans, Central Europe, and Iceland, comprise the Air Combat Campaign, EAME Theater.

Antisubmarine, EAME Theater: December 7, 1941–September 2, 1945[*]

U.S. Army Air Forces units received credit for the Antisubmarine Campaign, EAME Theater, if they engaged in antisubmarine operations outside the designated campaign areas of the EAME Theater. In October 1942 the AAF activated the Army Air Forces Antisubmarine Command and the next month sent a radar-equipped B–24 squadron to St. Eval, Cornwall, England, 300 miles southwest of London. A second squadron of B–24s arrived in January 1943. Flying from St. Eval in February, the RAF and AAF antisubmarine squadrons conducted numerous patrols over the Bay of Biscay on the southwest coast of France and the north coast of Spain to intercept German submarines returning to French ports. The 2 AAF squadrons sighted 15 enemy submarines that month and attacked 5. An AAF B–24 on patrol in the North Atlantic sank a German submarine on February 10.

In March the Antisubmarine Command transferred 2 squadrons from St. Eval to French Morocco in northwest Africa. There, these units were organized into the 480th Antisubmarine Group, under the operational control of the U.S. Navy. Because its B–24 aircraft had a range of about 1,000 miles, the 480th was assigned the task of patroling the approaches to the Straits of Gibraltar. From March to April 1943 the pilots spotted 15 German submarines, attacked 13, and sank or probably sank 4 operating in the mid-Atlantic and off the coast of Portugal. In these waters the German Navy had established a screen of submarines to harass convoys on their way from the United Kingdom to the Mediterranean Sea. By August 1943 the efforts of the RAF, U.S. Navy, and AAF Antisubmarine Command permitted Allied ships to ply the eastern Atlantic Ocean without serious resistance from enemy submarines.

In late June the Antisubmarine Command sent 2 B–24 squadrons from Newfoundland, where they had operated in the North Atlantic, to England. Organized into the 479th Antisubmarine Group, the units were based first in St. Eval and later in Dunkeswell, England. Under the operational control of the RAF Coastal Command, the 479th began flying patrols over the Bay of Biscay and the eastern reaches of the North Atlantic on July 13. That month patrol aircraft sighted 12,

---

*See Theater Map.

attacked 7, and sank 3 enemy submarines. The Germans soon changed their tactics to avoid surfacing in daylight. Aircrews sighted only 1 more U–boat before ending operations on October 31, 1943.

The AAF Antisubmarine Command inactivated on August 24, and its aerial resources and missions were transferred to the U.S. Navy. AAF units flew few antisubmarine missions after October 1943, although some Twelfth Air Force units occasionally conducted antisubmarine missions in the Mediterranean Sea in support of the Allied operations in Sicily and Italy. With the U–boat threat for the most part eliminated, the 479th Antisubmarine Group disbanded in England in November 1943; the 480th Antisubmarine Group returned from Morocco to the United States late in 1943 and disbanded in January 1944.

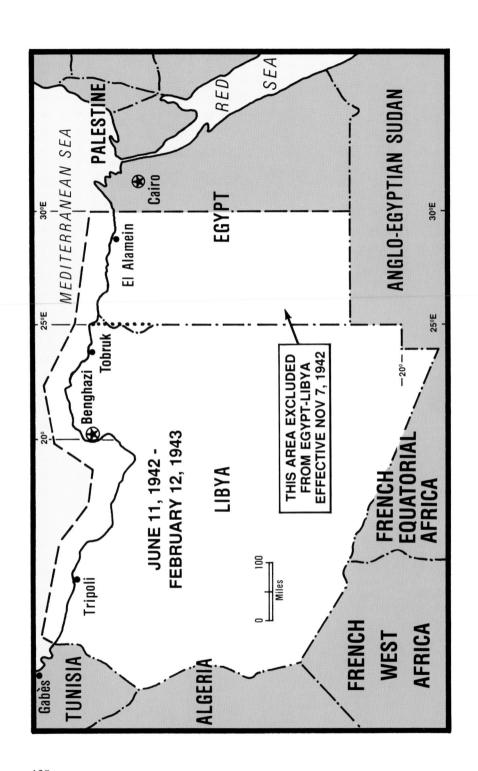

MEDITERRANEAN SEA

RED SEA

PALESTINE

Cairo

EGYPT

El Alamein

30°E

25°E

Tobruk

Benghazi

20°

LIBYA

JUNE 11, 1942 -
FEBRUARY 12, 1943

THIS AREA EXCLUDED
FROM EGYPT-LIBYA
EFFECTIVE NOV 7, 1942

—20°—

ANGLO-EGYPTIAN SUDAN

30°E

25°E

FRENCH
EQUATORIAL
AFRICA

100

Miles

0

Tripoli

Gabès

TUNISIA

ALGERIA

FRENCH
WEST
AFRICA

Egypt–Libya:
June 11, 1942–February 12, 1943

British forces in the Middle East fought German and Italian armies in Libya for nearly 3 years. The greatest penetration of Axis armies came in mid-1942, when Axis forces, led by Field Marshal Erwin Rommel, in an effort to reach the Suez Canal, drove the British back into Egypt. On June 21 Rommel captured Tobruk, a British stronghold on the north coast of Libya, then pressed eastward until halted on July 7 by British defenses at El Alamein, about 150 miles from Cairo and only 210 miles west of the Suez Canal.

The U.S. Army Air Forces entered the battle on June 10, 1942, when the U.S. War Department responded to a British request to employ in combat a special detachment of long-range B–24 bombers passing through Egypt on the way to India. The HALPRO Detachment* flew its first mission in the Mediterranean area on June 15 against an Italian fleet near the island of Malta. Agreeing to continuing British requests for aid, on June 28 the AAF activated the U.S. Army Middle East Air Force (USAMEAF). The new organization was based in Cairo and its personnel and aircraft were drawn initially from the Tenth Air Force in India. The USAMEAF's Commander was Maj. Gen. Lewis H. Brereton. Until August, the unit's striking power consisted of a few B–17s flown in from India and those B–24s already in the Middle East.

By July 11 British ground forces had established a defensive line from El Alamein on the Mediterranean coast in Egypt to the Qattara Depression, 30 miles south of El Alamein. The British held this position against repeated Axis attacks while the Allies reinforced their ground, sea, and air forces in the Middle East. The RAF flew tactical air support missions for the ground troops, and the AAF's heavy bombers struck enemy shipping and harbor facilities around the port of Tobruk, Libya. Other aerial targets included Matruh, a small Egyptian harbor 150 miles west of El Alamein, and Benghazi, Libya, 450 miles further west.

Germany, committed to an immense land war in the Soviet Union and with its supply lines across the Mediterranean Sea under constant

---

*So-called after its commander, Col. Harry A. Halverson.

attack, could not provide the men and equipment needed to overcome Allied resistance in North Africa. During the summer and fall of 1942, the USAMEAF contributed to the interdiction of Axis forces in the Mediterranean, operating its bombers from an airfield at Fayid, Egypt, near the Suez Canal. A P–40 fighter group and a medium bombardment group flying B–25s reinforced the USAMEAF by August 1. Other reinforcements followed, and the new AAF units joined the RAF in tactical air support of the British ground troops along the El Alamein line.

Augmented by New Zealand and Australian troops, British forces attacked the enemy's coastal positions near El Alamein on the night of October 23. With the ground troops locked in combat in the desert, the Allied air forces quickly gained air superiority over the battlefield and then were able to concentrate on close air support. Axis armored units suffered heavy losses from Allied air attacks; Allied fighters repulsed Axis aircraft that attempted to intervene; and on November 4 Allied troops broke through Axis lines. Eight days later, on the 12th, the AAF replaced the USAMEAF with the Ninth Air Force com- manded by General Brereton. During the next 3 months, as Allied ground forces pursued retreating Axis troops westward across Libya to Tunisia, the air echelons moved to new airfields, first in western Egypt, then in Libya.

Algeria–French Morocco: November 8–11, 1942

On November 8, 1942, while Axis forces were withdrawing from Egypt and Libya, the United States and Great Britain opened their first combined major offensive of World War II: OPERATION TORCH, the assault of French Vichy positions in northwestern Africa. Allied forces under Gen. Dwight D. Eisenhower, the Supreme Allied Commander in the theater, made 3 landings—1 at Oran on the north coast of Algeria, about 250 miles east of the Straits of Gibraltar; another at Algiers, the capital of Algeria, about 210 miles farther east along the coast; and a third at Casablanca, French Morocco, to the west on the Atlantic coast, almost 200 miles southwest of the Straits of Gibraltar. Maj. Gen. James H. Doolittle's Twelfth Air Force had been activated the previous summer, on August 20, 1942, in the United States and appointed the AAF organization for northwestern Africa; it now joined British Navy and RAF aircraft flying air cover to support the landings.

French forces in Algiers surrendered on November 8 with little resistance, but those at Oran, contrary to Allied expectations, opposed the landings of the U.S. 1st Infantry and 1st Armored Divisions. While the amphibious forces landed, the Twelfth Air Force dropped airborne troops near Oran. Twelfth Air Force C–47s flew to Oran from St. Eval and Predannack, 35 miles southwest of St. Eval and only 30 miles from Land's End, the southernmost tip of England. During the 1,100-mile flight, the transports became separated in bad weather over Spain. Late in the morning of November 8, most of the C–47s landed or dropped their paratroopers within a few miles of Tafaraoui, 15 miles south of Oran, but by the time the paratroopers reached Tafaraoui, other U.S. forces had seized it. An AAF fighter squadron flying Spitfires from Gibraltar landed at Tafaraoui shortly after its capture, and the next day the Spitfire pilots attacked and turned back a counterattacking column of French Legionnaires. After the French in Oran capitulated on November 10, the Spitfire pilots flew reconnaissance missions.

At Casablanca, meantime, the 3d Infantry and 2d Armored Divisions under Maj. Gen. George S. Patton, Jr., also met some opposition from French Vichy forces. On November 8 United States and British naval aircraft furnished air support for Patton's Casablanca landings. Two days later, the American forces captured Port Lyautey airfield, about 60 miles northeast of Casablanca, and Twelfth Air Force P–40s,

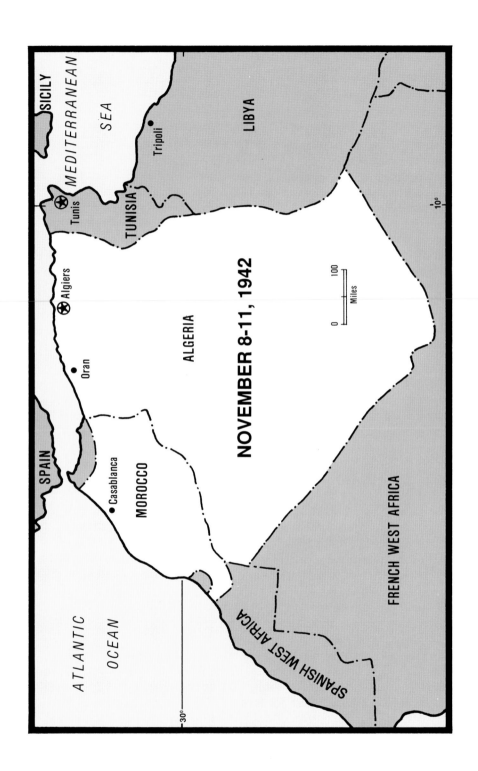

catapulted from a U.S. Navy carrier, immediately landed there. The XII Air Support Command moved its headquarters to Port Lyautey later in the day, and additional P–40s from a British carrier also landed there. However, on November 11, before these AAF aircraft could become operational, the French leaders surrendered.

The Allies were now posed to fight the Axis African armies on 2 fronts: 1 in the west from Algeria, and another in the east, from Egypt and Libya. The next objective for Eisenhower's command was Tunisia.

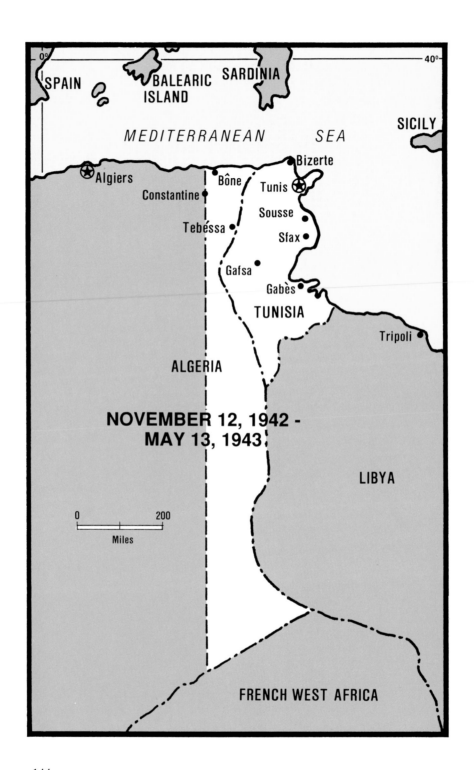

144

Tunisia:
November 12, 1942–May 13, 1943

In mid-November 1942, Field Marshal Erwin Rommel had just begun his retreat across Libya with British General Sir Bernard Montgomery in pursuit. Meanwhile, General Eisenhower's forces moved from Algeria eastward into Tunisia. AAF troop carriers, in 3 airborne missions conducted between November 12 and 17, dropped U.S. and British troops. These forces seized various forward airfields near Bône, Algeria, a Mediterranean port town 250 miles east of Algiers; at Souk-el-Arba, 60 miles southeast of Bône; and at Youks-les-Bain, about 100 miles south of Bône.

On November 15 Allied ground forces advancing eastward from Algiers made initial contact with German defenders dug in along the western dorsal of the Atlas Mountains, 60 to 80 miles east of the border between Algeria and Tunisia. Shortly afterward, on the 21st, the AAF moved fighter and light bombardment units from Algeria to the airfield at Youks-les-Bain to provide close air support for the Allied forces, which now included the recently converted French as well as British and American troops. The Twelfth Air Force, then operating from airfields in Algeria and Morocco, on November 16 began bombing raids against airfields in Tunisia. Action continued in the west as Allied forces pushed eastward against increasingly stiff Axis resistance. By mid-December the battle lines had stabilized in the Atlas Mountains near Medjez-el-Bab, 40 miles southwest of Tunis. The Luftwaffe fighters and dive bombers pummeled Allied ground troops along the front with low-level attacks.

In the east, on December 15, Ninth Air Force B–24s flew from bases in Libya to bomb Sfax, an east coast port 100 miles south of Tunis. During the rest of the campaign, both the Twelfth and Ninth Air Forces frequently bombed this area, which included Sousse, about halfway between Sfax and Tunis; Tunis Harbor; and Bizerte, 35 miles northwest of Tunis. These bombing raids, combined with other Allied naval and air attacks against enemy shipping in the Mediterranean Sea, further hindered Axis resupply attempts.

In southeastern Tunisia, Rommel's Italian troops were retreating westward from Libya, and in February 1943 they established a 20-mile defensive position extending from the Gulf of Gabès southward to the salt marshes of Shott Djerid. The position was based on the Mareth Line, a series of old French defenses near the border. Rommel's

Afrika Korps attacked westward on the 14th, in order to seize the passes in the eastern dorsal of the mountains and protect the Axis's western flank. The Allied forces, mostly elements of the 1st U.S. Armored Division, were driven back through the Kasserine Pass. The German attack forced the Twelfth Air Force to abandon several airfields near Tebéssa, disrupted Allied plans, and inflicted a major tactical defeat.

Before renewing the offensive in Tunisia, Great Britain and the United States reorganized their air forces, combining all air resources into the Mediterranean Air Command. On February 18, 1943, the Allies established the Northwest African Air Forces (NAAF) under the command of Lt. Gen. Carl Spaatz, who also took over the Twelfth Air Force on March 1. Consisting of the AAF Twelfth Air Force and the British Western Desert Air Force, the NAAF offered 2 advantages: unity of command within the theater and greater flexibility in employment of aerial forces.   The Ninth Air Force and the Eastern Desert Air Force remained in the Middle East Air Command.

Allied ground forces resumed the campaign on March 17–31, advancing, with tactical air support, in a pincer movement from the west and the southeast. Unfortunately, the Axis mounted a strong resistance while enemy ships moved as much of the German force as possible to Sicily. Allied air forces had gained virtual air superiority in Tunisia by April 22 and continued to choke the Axis supply lines across the Mediterranean Sea. On May 7 British troops entered Tunis and American units seized Bizerte. Then, having secured valuable air bases in North Africa, Allied air forces began the assault of enemy targets in the Mediterranean, Sicily, and Italy.

Sicily:
May 14–August 17, 1943

By May 1943 German and Italian installations on the island of Sicily had become frequent targets of the Northwest African Air Forces based in Algeria and the Ninth Air Force flying from Libya. After the surrender of Pantelleria Island,* located halfway between Sicily and Tunisia, British and U.S. air forces directed attacks against Sicilian airfields and the harbor at Messina, on the northeastern tip of Sicily. Allied pilots also bombed roads and attacked concentrations of troops and defensive installations. These operations and similar attacks on Italy and the island of Sardinia, coupled with aggressive air-to-air combat, by mid-July secured for the Allies air superiority over Sicily. Between mid-May and mid-July, aerial reconnaissance units photographed and furnished invasion planners the positions and strengths of the Axis forces.

The Allies launched the first large airborne operation of the war on July 9–10, 1943. During the Tunisia Campaign the Allies had employed a few dozen airplanes and a few hundred soldiers; the Sicilian airborne missions involved hundreds of airplanes and gliders and thousands of soldiers. Late on July 9 two troop carrier wings took off from airfields in northeast Tunisia. The 51st Troop Carrier Wing, whose C–47s towed gliders with British pilots, dropped 1,600 British troops south and west of Syracuse on Sicily's southeastern coast. But high winds, darkness, and enemy antiaircraft fire forced many C–47s off course; only 12 of 133 gliders came down near the designated landing zones. Sixty-five crashed in the sea. The 52d Troop Carrier Wing, meantime, carried 3,405 paratroopers of the U.S. Army's 82d Airborne Division, but the pilots, beset by high winds and darkness, widely scattered the soldiers east of the designated drop zones near Gela, on the southern coast 60 miles east of Syracuse.

Early on July 10, while the paratroopers disrupted enemy defenses and seized bridges and other objectives, the British Eighth Army under General Sir Bernard L. Montgomery landed at beaches around the southeastern area of Sicily and took Syracuse. Another amphibious force, the U.S. Seventh Army under Maj. Gen. George S. Patton Jr., landed simultaneously at Gela and Licata. NAAF aircraft flew aerial

---

*See Air Combat, EAME Theater, pp. 134–135.

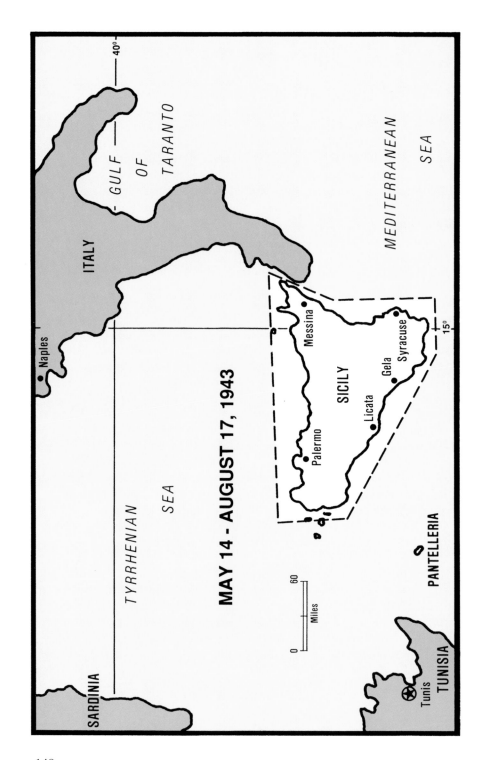

MAY 14 - AUGUST 17, 1943

148

cover for the naval craft and the ground troops, and by the end of the day Allied forces possessed secure beachheads. NAAF medium bombers and fighter-bombers then concentrated on attacking enemy troops and vehicles moving on the roads behind the battle lines.

The day after the amphibious landings, on the 11th, the 52d Troop Carrier Wing departed Tunisia to drop 2,000 American paratroopers near the Gela airfield. Unfortunately, U.S. Navy antiaircraft fire disrupted the C–47 formations, shooting down 23 of the 144 aircraft dispatched. The Allies nevertheless made another airdrop on the 13th, this time south of Catania, about 45 miles northwest of Syracuse. Once again the troop carriers received friendly antiaircraft fire as well as heavy enemy fire, and the British paratroopers were scattered over the countryside. Only 4 of the 11 gliders accompanying the paratroopers landed in the designated zone.

The airborne assaults sought to secure the flanks of the amphibious invasion forces. Although Allied leaders deemed 3 of the 4 operations a tactical success, 45 of 666 aircraft were lost, and less than 1/2 of the paratroopers and gliders landed near their assigned drop zones. It was a poor showing.

By July 23 the Seventh Army had moved northward and westward to capture Enna and Palermo and clear Axis forces from the western half of Sicily. Near Syracuse, the British Eighth Army encountered determined resistance from the Wehrmacht and made little headway until U.S. forces pressed eastward from Enna and Palermo toward Messina. Meanwhile, the Ninth and Twelfth Air Forces conducted air operations against transportation lines in Italy and between Italy and Sicily in order to limit Axis reinforcements reaching the island. During the first 2 weeks of August, the Axis conceded Sicily, and although under continuous air attack, withdrew considerable personnel and equipment across the Strait of Messina to Italy. By August 17 the Allies had secured the island and looked to the Italian mainland for the next offensive.

FRANCE

GERMANY

SWITZERLAND

HUNGARY

AUGUST 18, 1943 -
JANUARY 21, 1944

• Trieste

YUGOSLAVIA

Arno • Florence

River

LIGURIAN

SEA

ITALY

ADRIATIC

SEA

CORSICA

⊛Rome

Sangro
River

• Foggia

• Gaeta

SARDINIA

TYRRHENIAN

• Naples

• Salerno

Taranto

40°

SEA

0   75

Miles

IONIAN

SEA

MEDITERRANEAN

• Reggio Calabria

SICILY

• Tunis

SEA

TUNISIA

MALTA

15°

Naples–Foggia:
August 18, 1943–January 21, 1944

The Allied bombing campaign against enemy installations and communications in Italy began before the invasion of Sicily and gained momentum after August 18, 1943. Flying from North Africa, the XII Bomber Command, assisted by the IX Bomber Command, focused on marshaling yards and other transportation facilities near Rome, the capital; Naples, on Italy's west coast 120 miles to the southwest; and Foggia, across the Italian peninsula from Naples. The AAF also bombed roads and railway links between these cities and northern Italy. The Northwest African Air Forces (the combined Allied theater air force) asked for reinforcements to provide adequate air support for the invasion of Italy. In response to this request, between August 22 and 26, the AAF transferred most of the units, personnel, aircraft, and equipment of the Ninth Air Force to the Twelfth Air Force. Shortly thereafter, the Ninth Air Force moved to England.

On September 3 the British Eighth Army crossed the Strait of Messina and landed on the toe of Italy near Reggio Calabria. The Italian government signed a secret armistice on the same day, and formally surrendered 5 days later; however, German forces in Italy vigorously continued the battle. On September 9 the U.S. Fifth Army, composed of the British X Corps and the U.S. VI Corps, landed at Salerno, south of Naples, and in an ad hoc operation, a British division came ashore without opposition at Taranto in the Italian heel. Allied fighter aircraft based in Sicily provided close air support. During the next week the Wehrmacht delivered a determined counterattack, almost driving the Allies from their beachhead at Salerno. German aircraft pressed the attack on Allied ground forces in spite of the best efforts of Allied pilots. To reinforce the beachhead, AAF troop carriers dropped 2 battalions of airborne troops into Salerno on the night of September 13–14, and the NAAF committed most of its aircraft to close air support and battlefield interdiction. Allied bombers, meantime, destroyed German airfields within range of Salerno, and by September 22 the Luftwaffe could mount only "hit and run" bombing missions in the battle area.

In mid-September 1943 German troops began to withdraw from the vicinity. British Eighth Army forces joined American troops on September 16 near Salerno. Between September 13 and October 4, French forces, with the aid of local guerrilla units and frequent close air support from the NAAF, recaptured the island of Corsica. The

enemy, meanwhile, evacuated Sardinia. Allied forces seized the
Italian city of Foggia with its important airfields on October 1 as well
as the major port of Naples. By November 20 the Germans had
withdrawn behind fortifications of the Gustav Line, which ran from
the Gulf of Gaeta, on the west coast, across the Italian peninsula to
the mouth of the Sangro River on the Adriatic Sea and anchored in the
virtually impregnable country around Monte Cassino. From these
defensive positions, the enemy held Allied ground forces at bay for 6
months.

The capture of southern Italy gave the Allies bases, not only for
tactical air operations in Italy, but also for strategic bombing of
enemy targets in southern and eastern Europe. To take advantage of
this situation, the AAF on November 1, 1943, activated the Fifteenth
Air Force, with Maj. Gen. James H. Doolittle as Commander. The
Fifteenth's mission was to direct the long-range bombing of Axis
targets in northern Italy, Austria, and Germany. The new air force
inherited 6 heavy bomber groups, 5 medium bombardment groups,
and 4 long-range fighter escort groups from the Twelfth Air Force,
which remained responsible for tactical air support of Allied forces in
Italy. In December 1943 Lt. Gen. John K. Cannon assumed the
Twelfth Air Force command, and the Mediterranean Allied Air Forces
(MAAF) replaced the NAAF as the combined Allied Tactical Air
Force in the Mediterranean Theater.

Anzio:
January 22–May 24, 1944

To break the German defenses in central Italy and reach Rome quickly, the VI Corps, an Anglo-American combined force, landed on January 22, 1944, at Anzio on the Italian west coast, 30 miles south of Rome and 100 miles northwest of Naples. The enemy, taken by surprise, offered little resistance to the landing. The Mediterranean Allied Air Forces, operating from airfields around Naples, provided air cover for the invasion force. Unfortunately, the Allied Commander, U.S. Army Maj. Gen. John P. Lucas, devoted the first week to consolidating the beachhead at Anzio, allowing Field Marshal Albert Kesselring, the German commander in Italy, ample time to rush forward reinforcements to contain the Allied forces. MAAF aircraft attacked roads and railways near Anzio in an attempt to prevent German movements, but inclement weather hampered the effectiveness of aerial interdiction.

From January 23 to February 1, Allied aircraft provided close air support and fighter cover at Anzio, but the German Air Force mounted persistent attacks on Allied ships and beachhead positions. On February 1 the AAF's 307th Fighter Squadron moved to a reconstructed Anzio airstrip in order to respond quickly to enemy air attacks and afford better aerial protection for the beachhead. Although Luftwaffe losses increased, German aircraft continued effective attacks against Allied troops. The MAAF interdiction campaign on railroads and other transportation links in the Anzio region, meanwhile, helped delay a major German counterattack until mid-February.

On February 16 the Germans, under cover of perhaps their strongest air support of the Italian campaign, attacked Allied forces at Anzio. However, in 3 days of intense fighting the enemy failed to breach VI Corps's defensive positions. MAAF units contributed to the defense of the Anzio beachhead; on February 17, for example, 813 aircraft dropped 1,000 tons of bombs on German positions. During the 3-day battle the MAAF lost 13 aircraft over Anzio, while the Luftwaffe lost 41. Poor weather hindered flying operations during the next week, and the Germans reinforced their Anzio forces. Another determined counterattack between February 29 and March 3 also failed to dislodge the Allies, although the 307th Fighter Squadron abandoned the airstrip on the beach.

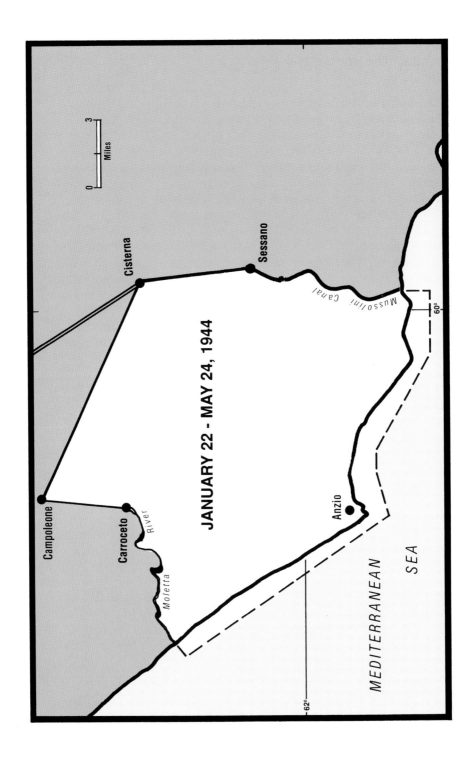

JANUARY 22 - MAY 24, 1944

Campoleone

Carroceto

River

Moletta

Cisterna

Sessano

Mussolini Canal

Anzio

60°

62°

MEDITERRANEAN

SEA

0 3 Miles

154

The MAAF continued to support the Anzio beachhead during the next 3 months. The landing failed in its primary objective but contributed to the gradual destruction of the enemy forces. The first real break in German defenses in Italy occurred instead at the Gustav Line in early May.

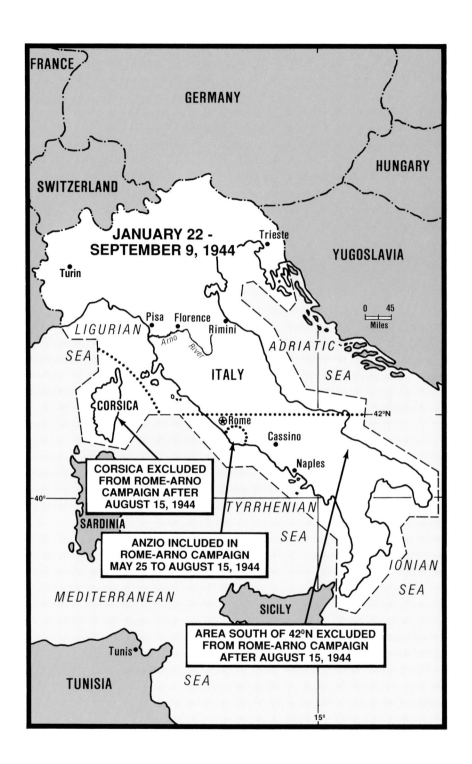

FRANCE

GERMANY

HUNGARY

SWITZERLAND

JANUARY 22 - SEPTEMBER 9, 1944

Trieste

YUGOSLAVIA

Turin

LIGURIAN

Pisa   Florence

Rimini

Arno *River*

SEA

ITALY

ADRIATIC

SEA

0   45
Miles

CORSICA

42°N

⊕ Rome

Cassino

CORSICA EXCLUDED FROM ROME-ARNO CAMPAIGN AFTER AUGUST 15, 1944

Naples

40°

TYRRHENIAN

SARDINIA

SEA

ANZIO INCLUDED IN ROME-ARNO CAMPAIGN MAY 25 TO AUGUST 15, 1944

IONIAN

SEA

MEDITERRANEAN

SICILY

Tunis

AREA SOUTH OF 42°N EXCLUDED FROM ROME-ARNO CAMPAIGN AFTER AUGUST 15, 1944

TUNISIA

SEA

15°

Rome–Arno:
January 22–September 9, 1944

Back on January 22, 1944, in conjunction with the Anzio landing, the Allies launched a futile attack against the Gustav Line.* Twelfth Air Force fighter pilots provided close air support between January 22 and February 1 as the weather permitted. From February 12 to March 23, on 3 different occasions, the Allies unsuccessfully renewed their assaults. In the First Battle of Cassino, the Germans repulsed on February 12 the U.S. 34th Infantry Division's attack on Cassino, a town on the Rapido River in central Italy, 80 miles southeast of Rome. The Second Battle of Cassino began on February 15, when Allied bombers destroyed the historic Benedictine Abbey of Monte Cassino atop a hill overlooking the town. The Allies, in the mistaken belief that the Germans were using the monastery to direct artillery fire, ordered it destroyed. The ground attack by New Zealand troops on February 16–17 failed. On March 15 Allied air forces bombed German positions in Cassino for more than 3 1/2 hours, destroying the town but leaving large craters in the streets that hindered the movement of Allied tanks. The Mediterranean Allied Air Forces continued its close air support of the ground forces and repulsed Luftwaffe aircraft attacks on Allied positions. By March 23, however, New Zealand troops had not dislodged the determined Germans who occupied the Cassino ruins.

Allied actions at Cassino were supported by interdiction efforts in central Italy. In January and February 1944, MAAF medium and heavy bombers attacked key roads and railroads to disrupt German resupply of the front lines. The bombing of the railway between Florence, located on the Arno River, and Rome, 140 miles to the southeast, temporarily interrupted the movement of supplies by rail. The MAAF also battered airfields from which German aircraft could attack Allied positions. Having gained air superiority over central Italy, the MAAF, beginning on March 19, increased its attacks on transportation lines and depot facilities as part of OPERATION STRANGLE. Fighter-bombers and medium bombers were also employed in the interdiction of bridges. Even the Fifteenth Air Force's heavy bombers, when not flying strategic bombing missions against targets in Eastern Europe, attacked Italian transportation installations. Allied

---

*See page 152.

interdiction of rail and highway bridges, marshaling yards, harbors, and intercoastal shipping hampered the flow of enemy supplies and reinforcements in central Italy, thus meeting the objective of OPERATION STRANGLE.

While the aerial interdiction campaign continued, on May 11, 1944, French, Canadian, Polish, British, and American troops attacked the Gustav Line along a 20-mile front between Cassino and the Gulf of Gaeta. The German forces, weakened by long months of battle and air interdiction, could not contain the assault. French troops made the initial breakthrough near the coast and outflanked Monte Cassino. Allied forces captured the town on May 17–18 and forced a general enemy withdrawal northward. The recently augmented Allied forces at Anzio broke out of the beachhead on May 23 and linked up with the rest of the Fifth Army 2 days later. The British Desert Air Force and the U.S. XII Tactical Air Command provided close air support for the advance on Rome, and Twelfth Air Force troop carriers evacuated the wounded. On June 4 the Fifth Army entered Rome. For the next 2 months Allied ground forces pushed northward to the Arno River. From August until September 1944, the Germans temporarily halted the Allied advance at the Arno Line, then withdrew slowly about 150 miles north of Rome to defenses blocking the Po River Valley.

North Apennines:
September 10, 1944–April 4, 1945

Early in September 1944, the U.S. Fifth and British Eighth Armies assaulted the Gothic Line in the North Apennines mountain range. Before the winter weather interfered with flying operations, Allied medium bombers and fighter-bombers attempted between September 9 and 20 to blast a path through the German defenses for the U.S. Fifth Army advancing slowly through central Italy, and the British Eighth Army moving northward up the coast of the Adriatic Sea. On the 21st the Eighth Army captured the city of Rimini, on the Adriatic Sea, 140 miles north of Rome. The Mediterranean Allied Air Forces were then knocking out bridges and ferries over the Po River in central and northeastern Italy, 70 to 90 miles north of the Gothic Line. Other MAAF targets in northern Italy included marshaling yards, crossroads, military camps, trucks, railroads, and rolling stock. By the end of the month, the MAAF could claim air superiority in northern Italy, and enemy aircraft rarely challenged Allied control of the skies. The Germans now moved supplies and troops at night and hid their vehicles during the day.

Weather over Italy in October restricted Allied flying operations primarily to close air support missions along the front lines. On the 20th the U.S. Fifth Army pushed on to the outskirts of Bologna, but failed to capture the city. Then on November 9 the British Eighth Army captured Forli, 30 miles northwest of Rimini, on the road to Bologna. Over the next 2 months, the MAAF shifted its interdiction priorities, downgrading activity in the Po Valley and giving first priority to bombing the Brenner Pass on the border between Germany and Italy. The combined air force also increased its attacks on transportation along the Brenta, Piave, and Tagliamento Rivers in northeastern Italy.

On December 26 elements of the Wehrmacht Fourteenth Army struck in the Bologna area, but Fifth Army troops contained the attack within 2 days and forced the Germans back into their defensive positions. The MAAF renewed attacks on German transportation in northeastern Italy on January 9, 1945, intending to disrupt further the resupply of German forces and hinder their withdrawal from Italy. On the 23rd the enemy began withdrawing a division from the Padua area, 65 miles northeast of Bologna; other units followed in February and March. Between December 1944 and April 1945, the front lines remained static, stretching from a point about 20 miles north of the

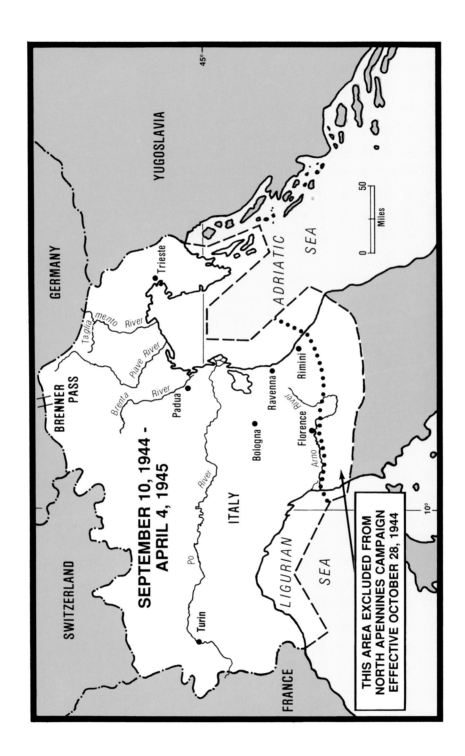

SEPTEMBER 10, 1944 -
APRIL 4, 1945

BRENNER
PASS

GERMANY

YUGOSLAVIA

SWITZERLAND

Tagliamento River

Piave River

Brenta River

Padua

Trieste

ADRIATIC SEA

Bologna

Ravenna

Rimini

Florence

Arno River

Po River

Turin

ITALY

LIGURIAN SEA

FRANCE

45°

10°

50
0
Miles

THIS AREA EXCLUDED FROM
NORTH APENNINES CAMPAIGN
EFFECTIVE OCTOBER 28, 1944

160

mouth of the Arno River, to 10 miles south of Bologna and to the coast on the south side of Lake Comacchio. The Allies then began preparing for a final offensive against the German forces remaining in Italy.

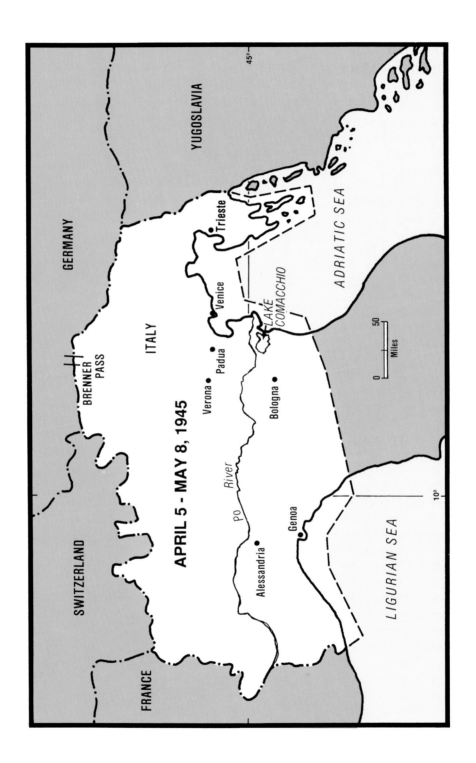

APRIL 5 - MAY 8, 1945

Po Valley:
April 5–May 8, 1945

In early April 1945, Allied aircraft attacked enemy positions in northern Italy, presaging a renewed offensive. On the 9th the British Eighth Army attacked the Germans southeast of Bologna, and other British units 40 miles east of Bologna made a successful amphibious assault across Lake Comacchio. Allied aircraft cut every major rail line north of the Po River to prevent the Germans from sustaining their defensive positions or withdrawing personnel to new positions. On April 9–10 Fifteenth Air Force heavy bombers struck enemy positions that blocked Allied troops, 20 to 30 miles southeast of Bologna, while fighter-bombers flew close air support missions. The pilots knocked out German artillery, permitting Allied ground forces to advance more rapidly than anticipated. The Allied air forces demonstrated overwhelming air superiority with as many as 15 aircraft attacking a single tank, and fighter-bombers strafing dispatch riders. By April 13 British forces had captured Argenta, 20 miles east of Bologna, and were advancing on Farrara, 25 miles northeast of Bologna.

The U.S. Fifth Army hit German positions southwest of Bologna on April 14. For 4 days AAF heavy bombers supplemented the close air support of XXII Tactical Air Command's fighter-bombers along the line of Allied advance. Meantime, Allied medium and heavy bombers continued to cut the railroads and bridges in the Brenner Pass, defeating German efforts to restore transportation between Austria and Italy. On April 20 the enemy withdrew from the Bologna area to the Po River, about 40 miles to the north; the next day the Allies occupied the city. The rapid Allied advance virtually split the German Tenth and Fourteenth Armies. Although the Wehrmacht tried to organize an orderly withdrawal, Allied aerial attacks on troops and transportation routes made this impossible. Because air operations had destroyed the bridges over the Po River, the Germans abandoned most of their heavy equipment and used ferries to carry personnel across the river, as they moved hurriedly north.

Enemy resistance in northern Italy had collapsed. The British Eighth Army crossed the Po River on April 25 and in the next 5 days advanced to Verona, almost 70 miles north of Bologna, then swung eastward to occupy Padua and Venice. Three days later, the U.S. Fifth Army seized the seaport of Genoa, 120 miles west of Bologna, while on the same day French troops moving east from Monaco captured Alessandria, 38 miles northwest of Genoa. German military leaders in Italy surrendered unconditionally on May 2.

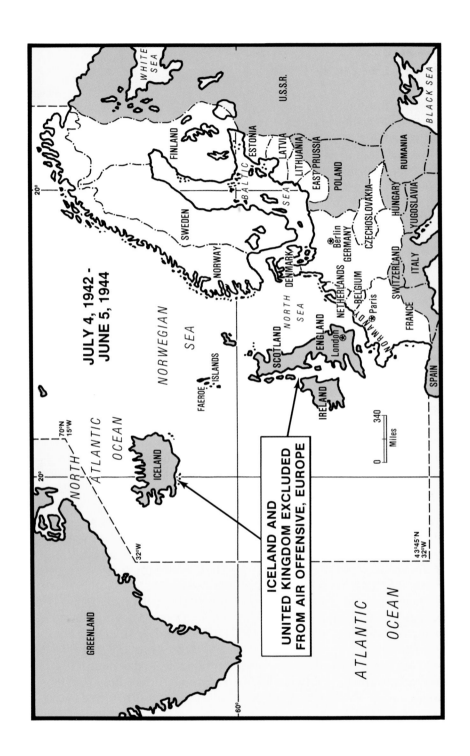

JULY 4, 1942 –
JUNE 5, 1944

ICELAND AND
UNITED KINGDOM EXCLUDED
FROM AIR OFFENSIVE, EUROPE

164

Air Offensive, Europe:
July 4, 1942–June 5, 1944

The Eighth Air Force, activated in January 1942 specifically for strategic bombardment missions, arrived in England in May and June 1942 under the command of Maj. Gen. Carl A. Spaatz. Lacking aircraft, members of the Eighth's 15th Bombardment Squadron borrowed 6 American-built medium bombers from the RAF and on July 4 flew on a low-level RAF raid against airfields in The Netherlands. The Eighth Air Force did not begin strategic bombardment operations until August 17, when heavy bombers struck marshaling yards at Rouen, France, 65 miles northwest of Paris. During the rest of the year, while awaiting the arrival of more bombers and air crews, small numbers (less than 100) of AAF heavy bombers made occasional daylight raids on the continent. On December 1 Maj. Gen. Ira C. Eaker took command of the Eighth.

In January 1943 U.S. President Franklin D. Roosevelt and British Prime Minister Winston Churchill met at Casablanca, Morocco. There General Eaker won Churchill's reluctant consent to continue the American concept of daylight precision bombing. The 2 allies agreed to pursue an around-the-clock combined bomber offensive against Germany. The British continued bombing targets at night while American bombers attacked enemy-held facilities during the day. On January 27 the Eighth Air Force flew its first mission against targets within Germany. Ninety-one heavy bombers bombed the port of Wilhelmshafen on the North Sea, 225 miles northwest of the capital city of Berlin. Throughout the year, as the Eighth built up its forces, it increased the tempo and intensity of the bombing operations— attacking factories, shipyards, submarine pens, transportation centers, airfields, oil refineries, and other targets on the continent.

Unfortunately, when the daylight bombers penetrated Europe beyond the range of fighter escorts, they sustained unacceptably heavy losses to German fighters. The raids on Regensburg and Schweinfurt, Germany, on August 17 had a high cost; of 315 bombers participating, 60 were shot down. The Eighth Air Force lost 60 more bombers against Schweinfurt on October 14. To provide the necessary fighter cover, the Eighth modified P–47s and P–38s with drop fuel tanks for long-range escort operations. All long-range P–51s manufactured in the last quarter of 1943 went directly to England and the Eighth Air Force. The range-extended fighters, though small in numbers, escorted bomber formations into Germany as early as November 3,

1943. They quickly proved their value, reducing bomber losses and taking a toll of the defending German fighter aircraft.

The Eighth did not operate alone in the Air Offensive, Europe, Campaign. In October 1943 the Ninth Air Force moved from the Mediterranean theater to England to provide tactical air support for the planned invasion of France. Ninth Air Force medium bombers and fighter-bombers subsequently struck airfields, defensive positions, and the V–weapon missile sites in France and Belgium. Activated on November 1, 1943, the Fifteenth Air Force, flying heavy bombers from Italy, joined the strategic air offensive with attacks on targets in France and Germany. To coordinate the operations of all 3 air forces, the AAF created the U.S. Strategic Air Forces in Europe on February 22, 1944, and named General Spaatz Commander. On January 15, 1944, Lt. Gen. Ira C. Eaker was named Commander-in-Chief, Mediterranean Allied Air Forces, consisting of the AAF's Twelfth and Fifteenth Air Forces and the British Desert and Balkan Air Forces.

In early 1944 the Allies increased attacks on the German aircraft industry seeking to reduce the threat of the Luftwaffe while preparing for the Normandy landings. Between February 20 and 25, Allied strategic bombers focused their attacks on 12 airframe factories. In just these 6 days, the RAF and the U.S. Eighth and Fifteenth Air Forces flew over 6,000 sorties. The combined forces lost 383 bombers, 28 fighters, and 2,600 airmen, but destroyed more than 500 enemy fighter aircraft.

Second in importance to the attrition of the German air forces and industry in the plans for OPERATION OVERLORD was the destruction by airpower of railroads and other lines of transportation in Belgium, The Netherlands, and France. In April and May the Allied air forces attacked railroad marshaling yards, repair facilities, bridges, and rolling stock. The Ninth Air Force's medium bombers proved especially effective in knocking out bridges with low-altitude bombing attacks. Thus, by D–Day Normandy was virtually isolated.

Normandy:
June 6–July 24, 1944

On June 6, 1944, the Allies invaded "Fortress Europe" at Normandy, a northwestern province of France on the English Channel. Throughout OPERATION OVERLORD, the AAF flew airborne assault missions, bombed enemy positions near the beaches, interdicted lines of supply, and contributed numerous close air support missions. The Luftwaffe, having sustained heavy losses throughout the spring, mounted limited attacks on the invasion force, but could provide little tactical air support to German ground troops opposing the invasion.

The evening before the invasion, on June 5, the Ninth Air Force began moving troops and equipment of the 82d and 101st Airborne Divisions to Normandy in gliders and transport airplanes. Nine hundred airplanes and 100 gliders took off from airfields in southern England and shortly after midnight, flying through intense flak, dropped the paratroopers. Most of the gliders landed in or near their appointed drop zones, although many paratroopers missed their zones. In spite of somewhat dispersed drops, the paratroopers seized most of their military objectives, thereby securing beach exits for and anchoring the right flank of the amphibious forces. The Allied military leaders judged the airborne portion of the Normandy invasion a success.

Immediately before the amphibious landings that began at daybreak on June 6, bombers of the Eighth and Ninth Air Forces struck key targets ashore, complementing naval gunfire. Medium and heavy bomber crews flew battlefield interdiction missions throughout D–Day, hitting roads, railroads, and bridges in Normandy and hindering German efforts to move reinforcements toward the beaches. Medium bombers made low-level bombing attacks on German artillery positions near the beaches and occasionally joined the fighter-bombers in close air support of Allied landing forces. On June 7 the AAF established a tactical air control detachment on the Utah beachhead to direct aircraft in attacks against specific targets. Two days later Ninth Air Force engineers established a transport airfield on Omaha Beach in order to deliver supplies and evacuate the wounded; fighter-bombers began operations from a Normandy airfield on June 19.

The tactical surprise, air superiority, and strong landing forces permitted the Allies to secure their beachheads quickly. The Allied command saw its "transportation plan" of isolating Normandy vindicated, since meager German reinforcements advanced to the front only with

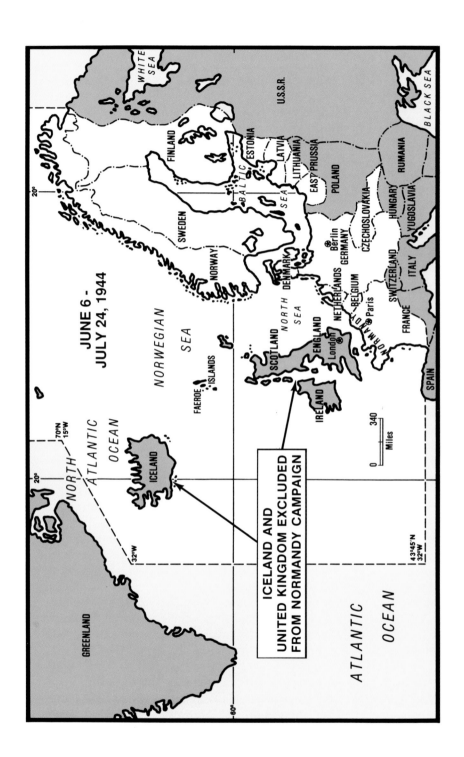

JUNE 6 –
JULY 24, 1944

ICELAND AND
UNITED KINGDOM EXCLUDED
FROM NORMANDY CAMPAIGN

168

great difficulty. But strong enemy opposition in the highly defensible Norman hedgerows, made expansion slow and difficult. Three weeks later, on June 27, the U.S. VII Corps took the port city of Cherbourg, on the tip of the Cotentin Peninsula. British troops by July 13 had captured most of Caen, inland of the British invasion beaches to the east. On July 18 the U.S. First Army seized St. Lo, 40 miles south of Cherbourg. Meanwhile, the British had advanced beyond Caen, and the Allies were now ready to attempt a breakout from the invasion beachhead.

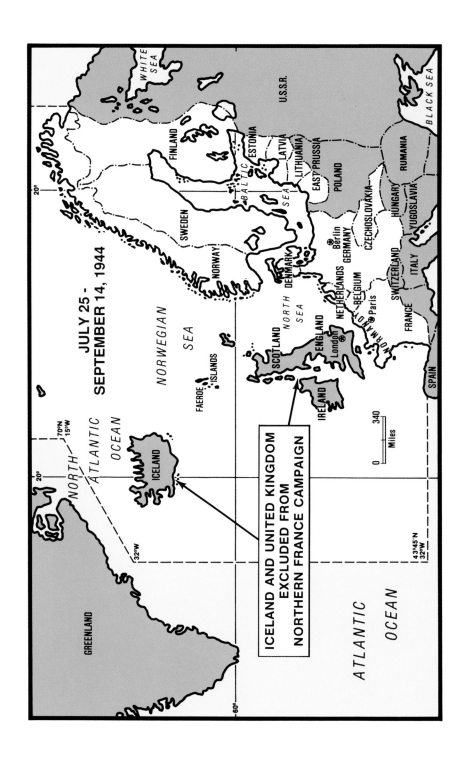

JULY 25 –
SEPTEMBER 14, 1944

ICELAND AND UNITED KINGDOM
EXCLUDED FROM
NORTHERN FRANCE CAMPAIGN

ATLANTIC OCEAN

GREENLAND

NORTH ATLANTIC OCEAN

ICELAND

NORWEGIAN SEA

FAEROE ISLANDS

SCOTLAND

NORTH SEA

ENGLAND
London

IRELAND

NORMANDY

Paris

FRANCE

SPAIN

BELGIUM
NETHERLANDS

SWITZERLAND

ITALY

DENMARK

Berlin
GERMANY

BALTIC SEA

SWEDEN

NORWAY

FINLAND

WHITE SEA

U.S.S.R.

ESTONIA
LATVIA
LITHUANIA
EAST PRUSSIA
POLAND

CZECHOSLOVAKIA
HUNGARY
YUGOSLAVIA
RUMANIA

BLACK SEA

0   340
Miles

70°N
15°W

20°

32°W

20°

60°

43°45'N
32°W

Northern France:
July 25–September 14, 1944

On July 25, 1944, American forces in Normandy, just west of St. Lo, began an offensive to break out of the invasion beachhead with a massive air attack. Altogether, 2,446 heavy, medium, and light bombers saturated a target area about 5 miles long by 1 mile wide. Although some bombs fell short into American positions and caused about 500 casualties, U.S. First Army infantry and armored forces advanced through the bombed area and successfully breached the German defenses.

During this campaign the Allies adopted a new tactic in close air support. Radios installed in fighter-bombers and in tanks permitted direct communication between pilots and tankers. Fighter-bomber groups operating from airstrips in Normandy provided continuous air cover for advancing armored forces, attacked targets in the path of the columns, and radioed useful reconnaissance information to tank commanders. As Allied armies advanced, aviation engineers built airfields in the rear areas, and by July 31 sixteen fighter-bomber groups had moved from England to the continent. On August 6 the Ninth Air Force, which had operated since D–Day with a forward and a rear headquarters, moved from England to the continent and reestablished a single headquarters. Two days later, Lt. Gen. Hoyt S. Vandenberg succeeded General Brereton as Ninth Air Force Commander.

Following the St. Lo breakout, on July 31, U.S. armor reached Avranches, 70 miles south of Cherbourg. From Avranches, Allied ground forces drove westward into Brittany, southward to the Loire River, and eastward toward the Seine River. A German counterattack at Mortain between August 6 and 10 came to nothing. During the first 2 weeks of August, the Luftwaffe made a determined effort to attack Allied positions and troops, but most of these air strikes came at night, involved small numbers of aircraft, and had little detrimental effect on Allied operations.

By August 13 U.S. forces had advanced to Nantes, almost 170 miles south of Cherbourg, and eastward to Argentan, about 100 miles southeast of Cherbourg. With British and Canadian armies pushing steadily south from Caen, the Allies captured 50,000 German troops at Falaise, near Argentan. While enemy forces fled over the Seine River, French and American troops liberated Paris on August 25. A week later, on September 4, British troops took Antwerp in The Netherlands, with its port facilities intact; however, the Germans held the Scheldt Estuary from the sea to Antwerp and blocked Allied use of the port until late November. Although transport aircraft helped carry supplies to forward airfields, the Allied advance slowed in September because of extended supply lines, shortages of gasoline, and stiffening enemy defenses. Nevertheless, by September 14, 1944, the Allies had taken much of Belgium, France, Luxembourg, and a small part of The Netherlands. The Germans halted the Allies along a fortified line that ran from Switzerland northward through France, Luxembourg, and Belgium to a point opposite Aachen, Germany, then westward through Maastricht, The Netherlands, along the Albert Canal to the English Channel at Ostend.

Southern France:
August 15–September 14, 1944

While the Germans retreated from Normandy and withdrew northward in Italy during the summer of 1944, the Allies invaded southern France on August 15 in an operation codenamed ANVIL, later DRAGOON. In July the Mediterranean Allied Air Forces, including the U.S. Twelfth and Fifteenth Air Forces, had prepared for the landings by conducting an air campaign against German transportation, airfields, and coastal installations in southern France. D–Day began with a paratroop drop of the 1st Airborne Task Force near Le Muy, France, about 10 miles inland from the Mediterranean coast and 60 miles northeast of Marseilles. A few hours later MAAF glider pilots landed more American and British troops near Le Muy. These 2 airborne operations, plus several diversionary tactics such as dropping dummy paratroops at various locations along the coast, helped make the amphibious assault a success. The U.S. Seventh Army, under Lt. Gen. Alexander Patch, and the French II Corps met little resistance on the Riviera beaches between Cannes, 25 miles east of Le Muy, and Hyeres, 50 miles southwest of Cannes.

As French forces pushed westward, the MAAF repeatedly bombed German coastal guns and other defenses near Marseilles until August 28, when the French took the port. Meanwhile, the U.S. Army's VI Corps, under the command of Maj. Gen. Lucian K. Truscott, Jr., thrust north from the beachhead in pursuit of retreating armies and arrived on August 22 at Montelimar, on the east bank of the Rhone River, 85 miles northwest of Marseilles. Allied, particularly Twelfth Air Force, tactical air attacks on German columns between Montelimar and Valence, 25 miles further north, destroyed more than 4,000 tanks, guns, and trucks.

The Twelfth Air Force provided advancing Allied troops with continuous close air support and battlefield interdiction. With most German aircraft committed to the defense of the homeland, air activity over southern France was extremely light, and between August 10 and September 11, Twelfth Air Force pilots could claim only 10 aircraft destroyed in aerial combat. Allied ground forces, meanwhile, advanced so rapidly that they outran supply lines, and the MAAF dropped rations, ammunition, and gasoline to the troops. Possessing complete air superiority in southern France, the Allies could operate freely behind the front lines and harass the enemy's attempts to marshal reinforcements or to shift forces from 1 area of the front to

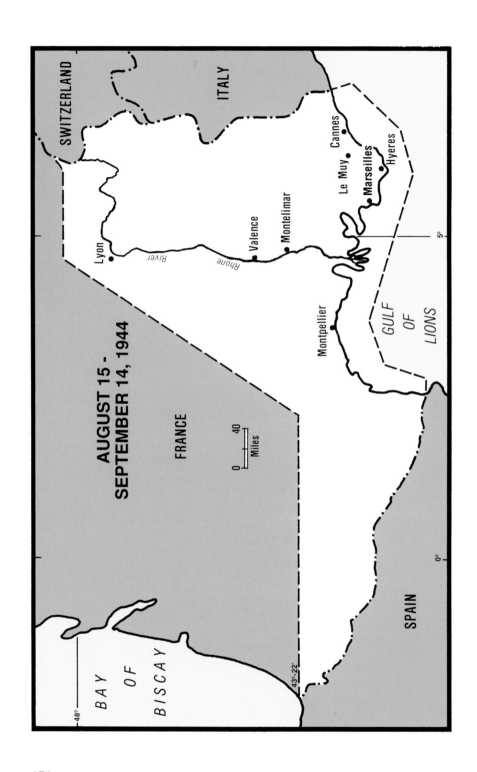

AUGUST 15 -
SEPTEMBER 14, 1944

FRANCE

0   40
Miles

SWITZERLAND

ITALY

Cannes
Le Muy
Marseilles
Hyeres

Lyon

Valence
Montelimar

Rhone   River

Montpellier

GULF
OF
LIONS

5°

0°

SPAIN

BAY
OF
BISCAY

48°

43°-22'

174

another. On September 11 the Allied armies that had invaded the French Riviera less than a month earlier made contact with Lt. Gen. George S. Patton, Jr.'s Third Army west of Dijon, almost 280 miles north of Marseilles and 160 miles southeast of Paris. During 4 weeks of battle, the Allies had captured almost 80,000 prisoners, destroyed most of the enemy's guns and other heavy equipment, and driven the Germans from southern France.

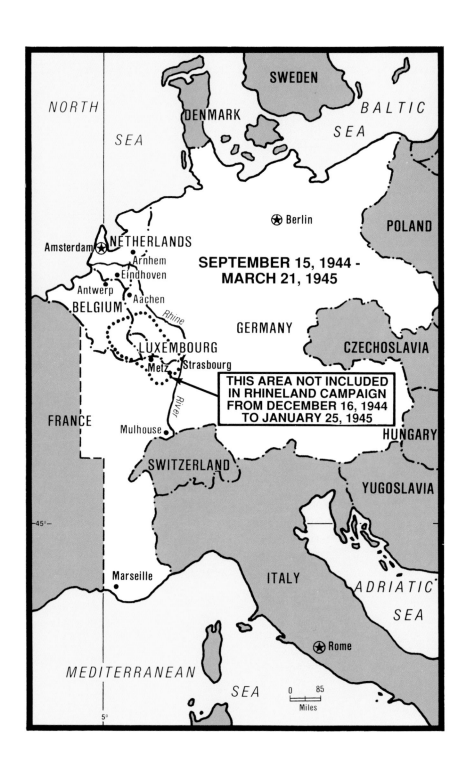

SEPTEMBER 15, 1944 -
MARCH 21, 1945

THIS AREA NOT INCLUDED
IN RHINELAND CAMPAIGN
FROM DECEMBER 16, 1944
TO JANUARY 25, 1945

Rhineland:
September 15, 1944–March 21, 1945

Between September 17 and 20, 1944, Army Air Forces and Royal Air Force troop carriers and gliders opened the Rhineland Campaign with OPERATION MARKET, one of the largest airborne operations of the war. They dropped 2 U.S. and 1 British airborne divisions, a Polish parachute brigade, and several small specialized units into The Netherlands, along a 60-mile corridor from Eindhoven, just north of the Belgian border, through Nijmegen to Arnhem, on the lower Rhine River. Troop carriers and B–24s airdropped supplies to the isolated paratroopers. The Allies lost 34 gliders and 102 aircraft to German flak, but the Luftwaffe posed little threat to the operation. British ground forces moving northward linked up with airborne troops in Eindhoven and Nijmegen, but failed to reach Arnhem, where the isolated British paratroopers surrendered on September 21.* On the 25th the Allies decided to postpone the attempt to capture the city.

To open the port at Antwerp and relieve growing logistical problems, on October 10 Canadian forces attacked German strongholds along the Scheldt Estuary leading from the sea to Antwerp. Allied air forces bombed sea dikes to flood enemy defenses and gave close air support. On November 8, after furious fighting, Allied troops overran the last German position. Ships swept mines from the estuary, and on November 28 the first Allied ship docked at Antwerp.

Elsewhere the Allied armies were advancing, and on October 21, 1944, they captured Aachen on the Belgian-German border, the first German city taken. During these operations the tactical air forces concentrated on battlefield interdiction and close air support, while reconnaissance flights reported on enemy fortifications and troop movements. The Eighth and Fifteenth Air Forces, meantime, continued strategic bombardment missions against German industry, petroleum production facilities, and railways. The Luftwaffe continued to threaten the heavy bombers, especially when new jet fighters became operational. Still, Allied bomber attacks on petroleum production and distribution facilities, aircraft factories, and airfields further eroded German air power, and Allied fighter escorts took a heavy toll of enemy aircraft, including the jet fighters. In September and Octo-

---

*This offensive, involving both airborne and ground forces, was known in its entirety as OPERATION MARKET GARDEN.

ber 1944 the Ninth Air Force sent medium bombers and fighter-bombers from airfields in France to bomb railroads 40 to 50 miles east of the Rhine River, as well as bridges, marshaling yards, fuel and ammunition dumps, and shipping canals.

The Allies again tried to drive the Germans across the Rhine River in November. On the 16th, with considerable close air support in spite of bad weather, the U.S. First and Ninth Armies renewed the attack near Aachen, and the U.S. Third Army began an offensive that on December 13 resulted in the capture of Metz, France, 115 miles south of Aachen (although German strongpoints in the area held out until December 31). Also on November 16, American and French forces penetrated German lines in the Vosges Mountains of northeastern France. French troops on November 23 captured Mulhouse, France, on the Rhine River, 17 miles from the border juncture of France, Germany, and Switzerland, and Strasbourg, almost 60 miles north of Mulhouse. Allied forces contained a major German counteroffensive, the Battle of the Bulge, in the Ardennes during December 1944 and January 1945. On January 17 they resumed the offensive. Six weeks later, on March 7, the U.S. 9th Armored Division seized a railroad bridge over the Rhine River at Remagen, 50 miles southeast of Aachen, and quickly established the first Allied bridgehead east of the Rhine. By March 15, 1945, Allied troops had driven the last of the German forces across the Rhine all along the front from the North Sea to the Swiss border.

Ardennes–Alsace:
December 16, 1944–January 25, 1945

On December 16, 1944, the Germans mounted a surprise counteroffensive in the Ardennes along a 60-mile front between Monschau, on
the German-Belgian border 40 miles southwest of Bonn, Germany,
and Echternach, on the Luxembourg-German border, about 20 miles
northeast of the city of Luxembourg. Driving a wedge between the
U.S. First Army to the north and the U.S. Third Army to the south,
the Germans created a large western salient, thus the name, Battle of
the Bulge. Their immediate objective was the Meuse River; their
ultimate goal, the port of Antwerp. Aided by a failure of Allied
intelligence to detect preparations for the offensive, and by inclement
weather that hindered Allied fighter-bomber attacks on advancing
columns, enemy forces pushed westward by December 26 to Celles,
about 3 miles short of the Meuse River but over 70 miles southeast of
Antwerp.

The Allied reaction was quick. On December 18 the Third Army
halted its offensive in the area of Saarbrücken, 100 miles south of
Bonn, and turned 90 degrees to the north to attack the German southern flank. On the northern flank, the U.S. 7th Armored Division
delayed the offensive at St. Vith, 20 miles southwest of Monschau.
Encircled American airborne troops at Bastogne, Belgium, 34 miles
northwest of Echternach, held up the Germans in the south, and by
December 26 American troops, with help from the British, had
blunted the enemy's drive.

The Germans had collected a sizable air force to support their drive,
but during the first few days, from December 16 through 24, cloudy,
snowy weather prevented much flying by either the Luftwaffe or the
Allies. Many of the best German pilots had been lost in combat, and
the more experienced Allied pilots held the upper hand in aerial
encounters. On December 17, for example, Army Air Forces fighters
claimed 68 enemy aircraft shot down, while only losing 16 aircraft.
The weather cleared on the 24th, permitting Allied air forces to fly
extensive close air support and battlefield interdiction missions over
the next few days. From December 23 to 27, Allied transports also
dropped supplies to the besieged 101st Airborne Division at Bastogne.
The weather deteriorated once again on the 28th and neither the
Axis nor the Allies flew missions, but as the weather improved, on
January 1, 1945, the Luftwaffe made one of its last determined
offensive strikes of the war, destroying 156 Allied aircraft on the

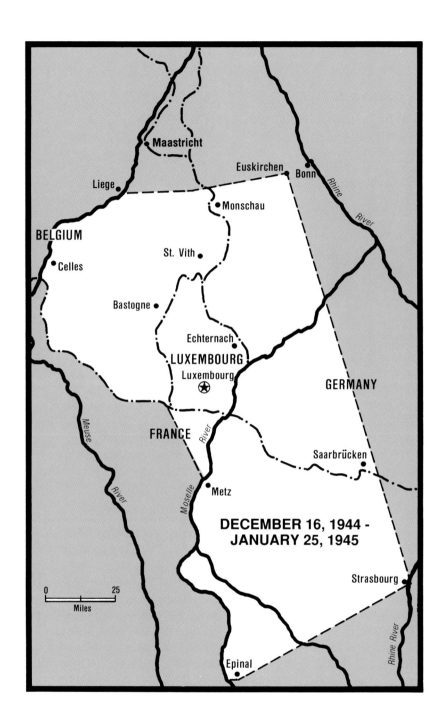

DECEMBER 16, 1944 -
JANUARY 25, 1945

180

ground in attacks on airfields in France, Belgium, and The Netherlands.

On December 29, 1944, after the 101st Airborne Division rejected German demands for the surrender of Bastogne, the U.S. 4th Armored Division opened a corridor to the beleaguered town. The Allies on January 3 counterattacked on the southern flank of the bulge. Now facing numerically superior forces on the ground and in the air, the Germans began a general retreat on January 8, and within 8 days U.S. troops had eliminated the Ardennes salient.

Meanwhile, on January 1, 1945, enemy forces attacked the U.S. Seventh Army along the Rhine River in the northeast region of France, to the east of Saarbrücken. The American forces withdrew southward, but at the behest of French authorities made a stand at Strasbourg. The German offensive failed to block the passes over the Vosges Mountains, and by January 25 the Wehrmacht was once again in retreat out of France.

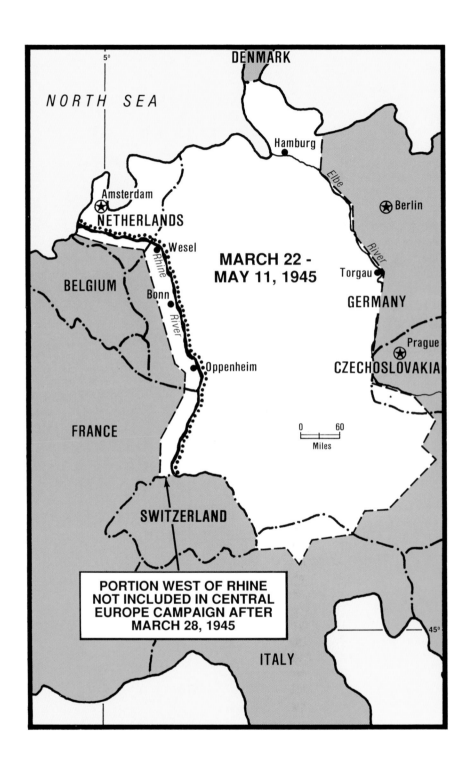

NORTH SEA

DENMARK

Hamburg

Amsterdam

Berlin

NETHERLANDS

Elbe

Wesel

Rhine

MARCH 22 -
MAY 11, 1945

River

BELGIUM

Torgau

Bonn

River

GERMANY

Oppenheim

Prague

CZECHOSLOVAKIA

FRANCE

0   60
Miles

SWITZERLAND

PORTION WEST OF RHINE
NOT INCLUDED IN CENTRAL
EUROPE CAMPAIGN AFTER
MARCH 28, 1945

ITALY

5°

45°

Central Europe: March 22–May 11, 1945

On March 22, 1945, the U.S. Third Army established a second salient, in addition to the one at Remagen, across the Rhine River at Oppenheim, 288 miles southwest of Berlin. The next day its troops also crossed the river at Boppard, 40 miles northwest of Oppenheim. Farther north, British and Canadian forces went across near Wesel, 65 miles northwest of Bonn. Ninth Air Force and Royal Air Force troop carriers and gliders dropped an American and a British airborne division north of Wesel on March 24, while the U.S. Ninth Army crossed the river 10 miles southeast of Wesel. The next day the U.S. First Army began an advance into Germany from Remagen, just south of Bonn, and on March 26 the Seventh Army crossed the Rhine River north of Mannheim, about 25 miles south of Oppenheim. Five days later, on March 31, French troops crossed the Rhine 10 miles south of Mannheim.

Before the Allied armies began crossing the Rhine in force, Allied air forces bombed and strafed German positions in the contested areas along the river. Heavy bombers also flew battlefield interdiction missions between March 21 and 24, before returning to strategic bombardment missions against targets in Germany. Although little of strategic value remained because of the destruction wrought by the combined bomber offensive, oil refineries and fuel depots remained primary targets.

The Luftwaffe could no longer effectively oppose the heavy bombers nor could it provide close air support for retreating German troops. When fuel was available, the enemy continued to intercept Allied bomber formations with a few fighter aircraft. On the battle front, AAF fighter-bombers flew close air support and tactical reconnaissance missions for Allied forces, while medium bombers attacked bridges, trucks, troop concentrations, railroads, and airfields. Troop carrier and transport aircraft flew critically needed supplies to forward airfields that had been rebuilt by aviation engineers behind the advancing Allied armies. After delivering supplies, the pilots loaded wounded soldiers and liberated prisoners of war and returned them to the rear areas. The last mission of the AAF's heavy bombers in Europe involved flying supplies to the starving population in The Netherlands.

WORLD WAR II SERVICE

Once across the Rhine River, Allied troops drove quickly toward the Ruhr. On April 1 United States forces reached Paderborn, a little over 200 miles west of Berlin, and on 11th they arrived at Magdeburg, only 85 miles west of Berlin. By the 18th the Allies had encircled the German armies in the Ruhr, capturing over 300,000 enemy soldiers. A week later American troops met Soviet forces on the Elbe River at Torgau, 65 miles south of Berlin. The Allied Supreme Commander, Gen. Dwight D. Eisenhower, ordered the Allied advance halted at the Elbe River, and Soviet troops captured Berlin on May 2. The next day the Allies took Hamburg, a key northern seaport 160 miles northeast of Berlin, and by May 5 all organized German resistance collapsed. A few days earlier, on April 30, Adolf Hitler had committed suicide, and on May 7 German leaders signed an unconditional surrender. Officially, World War II ended in Europe in the early minutes of May 9, 1945.

At the end of the Second World War, United States leaders looked forward to peace, which proved to be elusive. Less than 5 years later, in 1950, the country once again became engaged in military combat, this time in Korea, in an undeclared and limited war.

Korean
Service

1950-1954

Korean Service Medal

A gateway encircled with the inscription KOREAN SERVICE is embossed in the center of the obverse side of the Korean Service Medal. Centered on the reverse side is the Korean symbol that represents the unity of all beings, as it appears on the national flag of the Republic of Korea. Encircling this symbol is the inscription UNITED STATES OF AMERICA. A spray of oak and laurel graces the bottom edge. The medal is worn with a suspension ribbon, although a ribbon bar may be worn instead. Both the suspension ribbon and ribbon bar are blue, representing the United Nations, with a narrow, white stripe on each edge and a white band in the center.

Executive Order No. 10179, November 8, 1950, established the Korean Service Medal. A member of the U.S. Armed Forces earned the medal if he or she participated in combat or served with a combat or service unit in the Korean Theater on permanent assignment or on temporary duty for 30 consecutive or 60 nonconsecutive days anytime between June 27, 1950, and July 27, 1954. Service with a unit or headquarters stationed outside the theater but directly supporting Korean military operations also entitled a person to this medal. An individual also received a Bronze Service Star for each campaign in which he or she participated, or a Silver Service Star in place of 5 Bronze Stars. These stars are worn on the suspension ribbon or the ribbon bar. Service members who participated in at least 1 airborne or amphibious assault landings are entitled to wear an arrowhead on the ribbon or ribbon bar.

Korean Service Streamer

The Korean Service Streamer is identical to the ribbon in design and color. Air Force units received a service streamer if they were based in Korea between June 27, 1950 and July 27, 1954, or based in adjacent areas of Japan and Okinawa, where they actively supported other units engaged in combat operations. A campaign streamer is a service streamer with the name and dates of the campaign embroidered on it. A unit received a campaign streamer instead of a service streamer if it served in, or flew combat missions into, the combat zone during a particular campaign. Units participating in amphibious or airborne assault landings received the campaign streamer with an embroidered arrowhead preceding the name and dates.

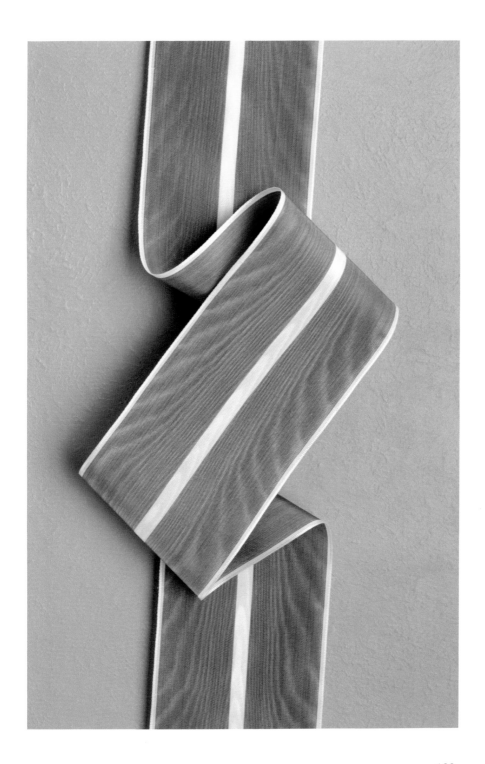

189

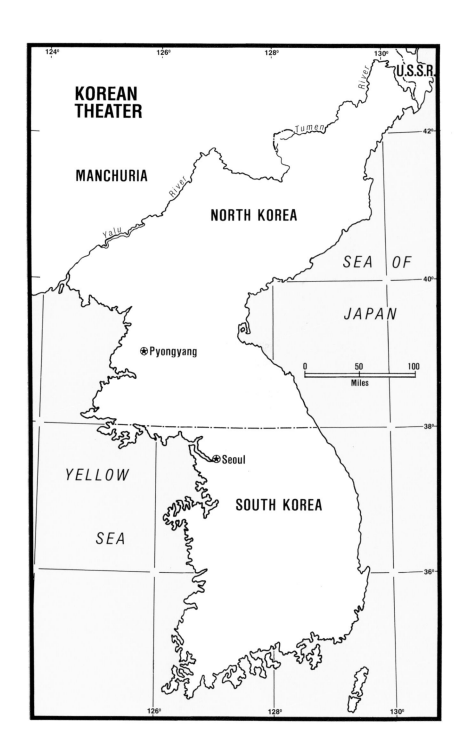

KOREAN THEATER

MANCHURIA

U.S.S.R.

NORTH KOREA

Tumen River

Yalu River

SEA OF JAPAN

⊕Pyongyang

0   50   100
Miles

YELLOW

SEA

⊕Seoul

SOUTH KOREA

124° 126° 128° 130°

42°

40°

38°

36°

126° 128° 130°

Korean Campaigns
June 27, 1950–July 27, 1953

Designated Campaigns of Korean Service

The U.S. Army designated 10 campaigns, adopted by the U.S. Air Force, for Korean Service. The first campaign began on June 27, 1950, when elements of the U.S. Air Force first countered North Korea's invasion of South Korea, and the last one ended on July 27, 1953, when the Korean Armistice cease-fire became effective. In all designated campaigns, the combat zone for campaign credit is the Korean Theater of Operations, which encompassed North and South Korea, Korean waters, and the airspace over these areas. The Secretary of Defense extended the period of Korean Service by 1 year from the date of the cease-fire. During this time, units and individuals earned no campaign credits, but received the Korean Service Streamer or the Korean Service Medal and Ribbon if stationed in Korea. The first campaign for Korean service is the UN Defensive.

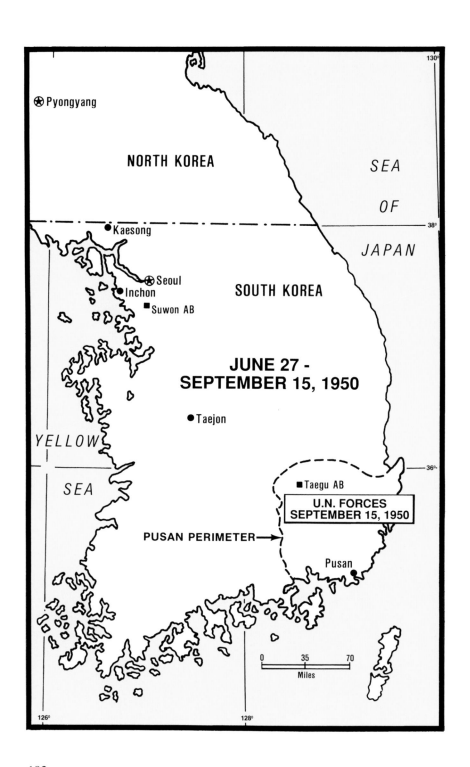

⊛ Pyongyang

NORTH KOREA

SEA

OF

JAPAN

● Kaesong

⊛ Seoul

● Inchon

■ Suwon AB

SOUTH KOREA

JUNE 27 - SEPTEMBER 15, 1950

● Taejon

YELLOW

SEA

■ Taegu AB

U.N. FORCES SEPTEMBER 15, 1950

PUSAN PERIMETER ➔

● Pusan

```
0        35        70
|____|____|____|____|
       Miles
```

130°

38°

36°

126°

128°

UN Defensive:
June 27–September 15, 1950

Early on June 25, 1950, North Korean forces crossed the 38th parallel near Kaesong to invade the Republic of Korea (ROK).* During the afternoon, North Korean fighter aircraft attacked South Korean and U.S. Air Force (USAF) aircraft and facilities at Seoul airfield and Kimpo Air Base, just south of Seoul. The next day, Far East Air Forces (FEAF) fighters flew protective cover while ships evacuated American citizens from Inchon, a seaport on the Yellow Sea, 20 miles west of Seoul.

With the Communists at the gates of Seoul, on June 27 FEAF transport aircraft evacuated Americans from the area. Fifth Air Force fighters escorting the transports destroyed 3 North Korean fighters to score the first aerial victories of the war. Meanwhile, in New York the United Nations (UN) Security Council, with the Soviet Union's delegate absent and unable to veto the resolution, recommended that UN members assist the Republic of Korea. President Harry S. Truman then ordered the use of U.S. air and naval forces to help counter the invasion.

The Far East Air Forces, commanded by Lt. Gen. George E. Stratemeyer, responded immediately. On June 28 FEAF began flying interdiction missions between Seoul and the 38th parallel, photo-reconnaissance and weather missions over South Korea, airlift missions from Japan to Korea, and close air support missions for the ROK troops. North Korean fighters attacked FEAF aircraft that were using Suwon airfield, 15 miles south of Seoul, as a transport terminal and an emergency airstrip. The next day the 3d Bombardment Group made the first American air raid on North Korea, bombing the airfield at Pyongyang. The FEAF Bomber Command followed this raid with sporadic B–29 missions against North Korean targets through July. Then in August the B–29s made concerted and continuous attacks on North Korean marshaling yards, railroad bridges, and supply dumps. These raids made it difficult for the enemy to resupply, reinforce, and move its front-line troops.

---

*The Republic of Korea, was established by the United Nations on August 15, 1948, with Seoul as the capital city. North Korea, the Democratic Republic of Korea, was established on September 9, 1948, under a Communist regime, with its capital at Pyongyang. In June 1950 the boundary between North and South Korea was the 38th degree, North latitude; i.e., the 38th parallel.

As Communist troops pushed southward, on June 30, 1950, President Truman committed U.S. ground forces to the battle. Shortly afterward, on July 7, the UN established an allied command under President Truman, who promptly named U.S. Army Gen. Douglas MacArthur as UN Commander. A few weeks later, on July 24, General MacArthur established the United Nations Command. Meantime, the Fifth Air Force, commanded by USAF Maj. Gen. Earl E. Partridge, established an advanced headquarters in Taegu, South Korea, 140 miles southeast of Seoul. Headquarters, Eighth U.S. Army in Korea, under U.S. Army Lt. Gen. Walton H. Walker, was also set up at Taegu.

During July 1950, as UN forces continued to fall back, most FEAF bombers and fighters operated from bases in Japan, over 150 miles from the battle front. This distance severely handicapped F–80 jet aircraft because of their very short range, even when equipped with wing fuel tanks. After only a short time over Korean targets, the F–80s had to return to Japan to refuel and replenish munitions. Cooperating with naval aviators, the USAF pilots bombed and strafed enemy airfields, destroying much of the small North Korean Air Force on the ground. During June and July, Fifth Air Force fighter pilots shot down 20 North Korean aircraft. Before the end of July, the U.S. Air Force and the Navy and Marine air forces could claim air superiority over North and South Korea.

UN ground forces, driven far to the south, had checked the advance of North Korean armies by August 5. A combination of factors—air support from the Far East Air Forces, strong defenses by UN ground forces, and lengthening North Korean supply lines—brought the Communist offensive to a halt. The UN troops held a defensive perimeter in the southeastern corner of the peninsula, in a 40- to 60-mile arc about the seaport of Pusan. American, South Korean, and British troops, under extensive and effective close air support, held the perimeter against repeated attacks as the United Nations Command built its combat forces and made plans to counterattack.

UN Offensive:
September 16–November 2, 1950

The first UN offensive against North Korean forces began on September 15, 1950, with the U.S. X Corps, under Army Maj. Gen. Edward M. Almond, making an amphibious assault at Inchon, 150 miles north of the battle front. In the south the Eighth U.S. Army, made up of U.S., ROK, and British forces, counterattacked the next day. The 1st Marine Air Wing provided air support for the landing at Inchon while the Fifth Air Force likewise supported the Eighth Army. On September 16, as part of a strategic bombing campaign, the FEAF bombed Pyongyang, the capital of North Korea, and Wonsan, an east coast port 80 miles north of the 38th parallel.

U.S. Marines attached to X Corps captured Kimpo Air Base near Seoul on September 17. Two days later the first FEAF cargo carrier landed there, inaugurating an around-the-clock airlift of supplies, fuel, and troops. C–54s returned wounded personnel to hospitals in Japan, and C–119s airdropped supplies to front-line forces. Bad weather hindered close air support of the Eighth Army, but on the 26th the U.S. 1st Cavalry Division forged out of the Pusan Perimeter north of Taegu and within a day thrust northward to link up with 7th Infantry Division forces near Osan, 25 miles south of Seoul. Air controllers, using tactics similar to those developed in France during World War II, accompanied the advancing tank columns, supported tank commanders with aerial reconnaissance, and called in close air support missions as needed. On September 26 General MacArthur announced the recapture of Seoul, but street fighting continued for several more days.

For a time in August and September 1950, before the recapture of Kimpo, all FEAF flying units had to fly from bases in Japan. The only continuously usable tactical base in Korea was Taegu, which the FEAF used as a staging field to refuel and arm tactical aircraft. On September 28 fighter-bombers returned permanently to Taegu. As UN forces swept North Korean troops from South Korea, aviation engineers rebuilt the airfields, beginning with Pohang, on the east coast 50 miles northeast of Taegu. USAF flying units returned on October 7 to Pohang and to other rebuilt airfields at Kimpo, near Seoul, and at Suwon, 20 miles south of Seoul.

Supported by a UN resolution, President Truman directed the U.S. Joint Chiefs of Staff to authorize pursuit of the retreating North

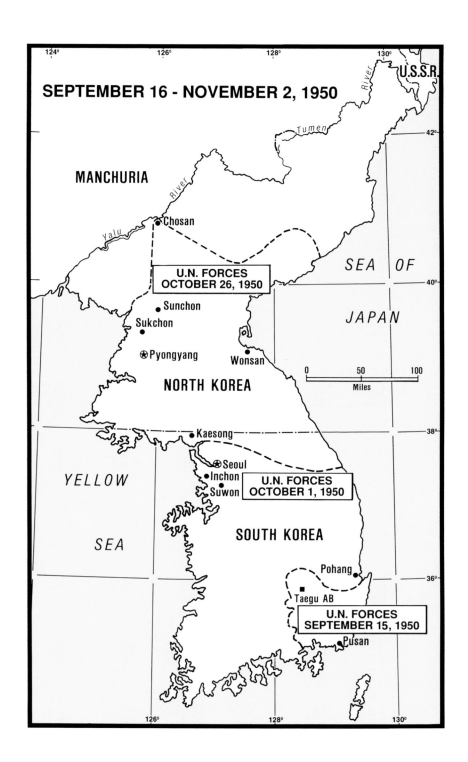

SEPTEMBER 16 - NOVEMBER 2, 1950

U.S.S.R.

Tumen River

MANCHURIA

Yalu River

● Chosan

**U.N. FORCES
OCTOBER 26, 1950**

● Sunchon

● Sukchon

⊛ Pyongyang

● Wonsan

SEA OF

JAPAN

NORTH KOREA

0   50   100
Miles

● Kaesong

⊛ Seoul
● Inchon
● Suwon

**U.N. FORCES
OCTOBER 1, 1950**

YELLOW

SOUTH KOREA

SEA

● Pohang

■ Taegu AB

**U.N. FORCES
SEPTEMBER 15, 1950**

● Pusan

196

Korean forces, and on October 9 the Eighth Army crossed the 38th parallel near Kaesong. American and South Korean forces entered the North Korean capital of Pyongyang on October 19. FEAF B–29s and B–26s continued to bomb surface transport lines and military targets in North Korea, while B–26s, F–51s, and F–80s provided close air support to ground troops. FEAF also furnished photographic reconnaissance, airlift, and air medical evacuation. For example, on October 20 the air force's troop carriers delivered 2,860 paratroopers and more than 301 tons of equipment and supplies to drop zones near Sukchon and Sunchon, 30 miles northeast of Pyongyang. The airborne troops by-passed strong defenses established by the North Koreans, and taken by surprise, the enemy troops abandoned their positions to retreat further northward.

Meantime, on the east coast of Korea, the ROK forces crossed the 38th parallel on October 1 and 10 days later captured Wonsan. On October 26 South Korean forces reached the Yalu River at Chosan, 120 miles north of Pyongyang. Communist forces counterattacked within 2 days along the ROK lines near Chosan, forcing the South Koreans to retreat. The People's Republic of China had entered the conflict against the Eighth U.S. Army in Korea in the west, and the U.S. X Corps in the east. At this point, the war in Korea took on an entirely different character as the tide turned against the UN forces.

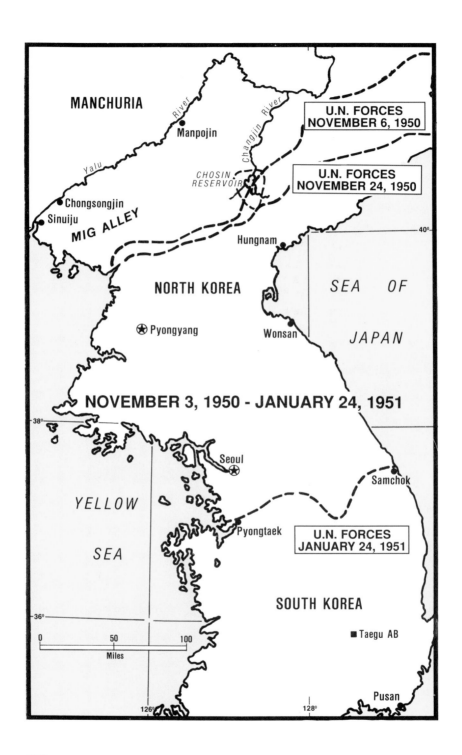

MANCHURIA

River

● Manpojin

Yalu

Changjin River

CHOSIN
RESERVOIR

● Chongsongjin
● Sinuiju

MIG ALLEY

U.N. FORCES
NOVEMBER 6, 1950

U.N. FORCES
NOVEMBER 24, 1950

● Hungnam

40°

NORTH KOREA

SEA   OF

JAPAN

⊛ Pyongyang

● Wonsan

NOVEMBER 3, 1950 - JANUARY 24, 1951

38°

⊛ Seoul

● Samchok

YELLOW

● Pyongtaek

U.N. FORCES
JANUARY 24, 1951

SEA

SOUTH KOREA

36°

0   50   100
Miles

■ Taegu AB

126°

128°

● Pusan

198

CCF* Intervention:
November 3, 1950–January 24, 1951

With Chinese troops fighting in North Korea against UN forces, on November 3, 1950, UN troops, under the protection of Fifth Air Force close air support, began to withdraw to the Chongchon River in northwest Korea. On November 8 FEAF bombed the city of Sinuiju, the gateway from Korea to Manchuria on the Yalu River. Chinese MiG–15 jet aircraft engaged the F–80 jets flying cover for the U.S. bombers, and in the first all-jet aerial combat, an American pilot scored a victory against a MiG.

During the rest of November, FEAF medium and light bombers, along with U.S. Navy aircraft, attacked bridges over the Yalu River and supply centers along the Korean side of the river. The operations against bridges were usually unsuccessful because the bombers had to fly parallel to the river to avoid violating Chinese air space. B–29s also dropped their bombs from at least 20,000 feet to avoid flak. Nevertheless on November 25 the bombers destroyed a span of a railroad bridge at Manpojin, 150 miles north of Pyongyang, and on November 26 two spans of a highway bridge at Chongsongjin, 110 miles northwest of Pyongyang. The Communists simply built pontoon bridges or, as winter set in, crossed the Yalu on the ice. The B–29s did destroy North Korean supply centers, thus forcing the enemy to disperse its supplies or to hold them in Manchuria until needed.

The United Nations Command planned a new offensive, unaware of the extent of the Chinese involvement. Even as General MacArthur kicked off the offensive on November 25–26, 1950, the Communist forces also launched a major attack, driving both the Eighth Army in northwest Korea and the X Corps in northeast Korea southward. In the Chosin Reservoir area, the U.S. 1st Marine Division was surrounded. Between December 1 and 11, the FEAF Combat Cargo Command, commanded by Maj. Gen. William H. Tunner, airlifted over 1,500 tons of supplies to the embattled Marines. FEAF pilots even dropped 8 bridge spans so that the Marines could build a bridge across a gorge. The division finally broke through the Chinese troops to UN lines near Hungnam, an east coast seaport 100 miles northeast of Pyongyang. The U.S. Navy, with some assistance from FEAF

---

*Chinese Communist Forces

airlifters, evacuated the X Corps from Wonsan on December 5–15 and from Hungnam on December 15–24, leaving northeast Korea to the Communist forces. On the 27th the X Corps passed to the control of the Eighth Army, and by the end of the month, Gen. Douglas MacArthur, UN Commander, had placed Lt. Gen. Matthew B. Ridgway, who had just arrived in Korea to replace General Walker, in control of all UN ground forces in Korea.

Meanwhile, the FEAF had brought additional C–54s to Korea to meet the demands of the ground forces for theater airlift, and the air force began moving its fighter units, including a squadron of South African Air Force fighters, to airfields in North Korea, in order to meet the close air support needs of UN troops. The appearance of the MiG–15 jet fighter in November 1950 threatened UN air superiority over Korea because the MiG outperformed available U.S. aircraft. The FEAF requested the newest and best jet fighters, and on December 6, less than a month later, the 27th Fighter-Escort Wing, flying F–84 Thunderjets, arrived at Taegu. Then on December 15 the 4th Fighter-Interceptor Wing flew its first mission in Korea in F–86 Sabrejets. Less than a week later, on the 22nd, the F–86 pilots shot down 6 MiG–15s, losing only 1 Sabrejet. The newer jet fighters permitted the UN Command to maintain air superiority.

During December 1950 the FEAF flew interdiction and armed recon-naissance missions that helped slow the advancing Chinese armies. B–29s and B–26s bombed bridges, tunnels, marshaling yards, and supply centers. When the Chinese troops resorted to daytime travel north of Pyongyang in pursuit of the Eighth Army, Fifth Air Force pilots killed or wounded an estimated 33,000 enemy troops within 2 weeks. By mid-December Communist forces were moving only at night, though still advancing.

On January 1, 1951, Communist forces crossed the 38th parallel and 3 days later entered Seoul behind retreating UN troops. Finally, on January 15 UN forces halted the Chinese and North Korean armies 50 miles south of the 38th parallel, on a line from Pyongtaek on the west coast to Samchok on the east coast.

1st UN Counteroffensive:
January 25–April 21, 1951

Taking the offensive on January 25, 1951, the UN Command began military operations directed toward wearing down the enemy rather than capturing territory. For 2 weeks UN forces, with close air support provided by Fifth Air Force fighter-bombers, advanced slowly northward against inconsistent but often stubborn resistance. On February 10 the troops captured Kimpo Air Base near Seoul. When thawing roads made ground transport virtually impossible, Brig. Gen. John P. Henebry's 315th Air Division airdropped supplies to the ground forces. For example, between February 23 and 28 the 314th Troop Carrier Group, flying C–119s, dropped 1,358 tons of supplies to troops north of Wonju, a town 50 miles southeast of Seoul. UN forces reoccupied Seoul on March 14.

A few days later, on March 23, the Far East Air Forces airdropped a reinforced regiment at Munsan, 25 miles north of Seoul. In preparation, fighter-bombers and medium bombers, under direction of airborne tactical controllers, bombed enemy troops and positions near the drop zones. The C–119s continued the airdrop of supplies until March 27, as the paratroopers advanced from Munsan to Yonchon, 35 miles north of Seoul.

By this time, Communist forces had established such a strong air presence between the Chongchon and Yalu Rivers in northwestern Korea that Fifth Air Force pilots began to refer to this region as "MiG Alley." The Fifth, unable to challenge the enemy's temporary air superiority in northwestern Korea from bases in Japan, returned its tactical fighter units to Korean airfields recently wrested from Communist control. By March 10, F–86 Sabrejets were once again battling Chinese and North Korean pilots in MiG Alley while flying cover for FEAF Bomber Command's B–29s against targets in the area. Through the rest of March and April, FEAF bombed bridges over the Yalu River and other targets under the protection of escorting jet fighters. In spite of the escorts, MiG pilots on April 12 destroyed 3 of 38 B–29s attacking bridges at Sinuiju, causing the FEAF Bomber Command to put Sinuiju temporarily off-limits to B–29s.

On the eastern side of the peninsula, the Bomber Command carried on an interdiction campaign against railroads, tunnels, and bridges. U.S. naval aviators also were conducting missions against targets in the northeastern section of Korea between Wonsan and the Siberian

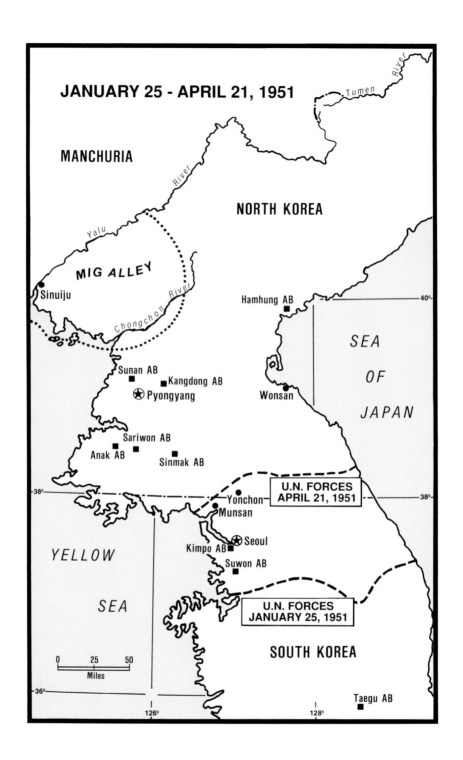

JANUARY 25 - APRIL 21, 1951

MANCHURIA

NORTH KOREA

Tumen River

Yalu River

MIG ALLEY

Sinuiju

Chongchon River

Hamhung AB

40°

Sunan AB
Kangdong AB
⊛ Pyongyang

Wonsan

SEA

OF

JAPAN

Sariwon AB
Anak AB
Sinmak AB

38°

U.N. FORCES
APRIL 21, 1951

38°

Yonchon
Munsan

YELLOW

Kimpo AB ⊕ Seoul
Suwon AB

SEA

U.N. FORCES
JANUARY 25, 1951

0   25   50
Miles

SOUTH KOREA

36°

Taegu AB

126°

128°

border. From April 12 to 23 the FEAF Bomber Command attacked rebuilt airfields on the outskirts of Pyongyang, at Sariwon, 40 miles south of Pyongyang, and at Hamhung, on the east coast 110 miles northeast of Pyongyang.

On the ground, the Eighth Army pushed north of Seoul to reach the 38th parallel on March 31. Soon after, on April 11, President Harry S. Truman removed the UN Commander, General Douglas MacArthur, because of his outspoken criticism of the President's prosecution of the war. Gen. Matthew B. Ridgway replaced General MacArthur, and Lt. Gen. James A. Van Fleet inherited the Eighth Army command. With close air support from the Fifth Air Force, UN ground forces pushed north beyond the 38th parallel between April 17 and 21, until halted by a North Korean and Chinese counterattack.

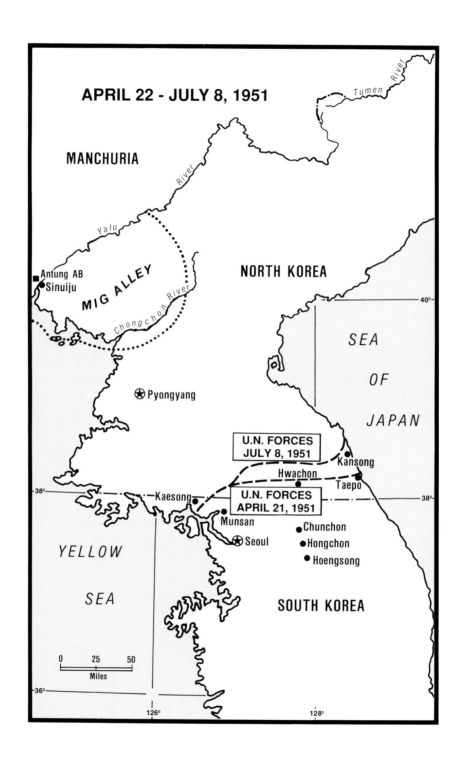

APRIL 22 - JULY 8, 1951

Tumen River

MANCHURIA

Yalu River

NORTH KOREA

MIG ALLEY

Antung AB
Sinuiju

Chongchon River

40°

SEA

OF

JAPAN

⊛ Pyongyang

U.N. FORCES
JULY 8, 1951

Kansong

Hwachon

Taepo

38°

Kaesong

U.N. FORCES
APRIL 21, 1951

38°

Munsan

⊛ Seoul

• Chunchon

• Hongchon

• Hoengsong

YELLOW

SEA

SOUTH KOREA

0   25   50
Miles

36°

126°

128°

CCF Spring Offensive:
April 22–July 8, 1951

The Chinese Communist Forces' spring offensive began on April 22, 1951, with an assault on Republic of Korea Army positions 40 to 55 miles northeast of Seoul. United States Army and Marine forces joined a United Kingdom brigade to plug the gap opened in UN lines north of Seoul, and by May 1 the Communist drive had lost momentum. For the next 2 weeks the Chinese and North Koreans built their strength before attacking in the vicinity of Taepo, between the east coast and Chunchon, 45 miles northeast of Seoul. By May 20 Eighth Army forces had stopped the Communist troops just north of Hongchon, 50 miles east of Seoul.

The UN Command launched a counterattack 2 days later, on the 22nd, along most of the battle line, except for a holding action just north of Munsan. ROK forces on the east coast quickly advanced northward to Kansong, 25 miles north of the 38th parallel. Advance in the center of the peninsula was slower, but by May 31 the Communist forces had their backs to Hwachon, 65 miles northeast of Seoul. Further west, UN troops had pushed the enemy troops to Yonchon, 40 miles north of Seoul.

During the CCF Spring Offensive, the Far East Air Forces and the U.S. Navy maintained air superiority over Korea through aerial combat and continued bombing of North Korean airfields. The Fifth Air Force and a U.S. Marine air wing extended airfield attacks on May 9 to include Sinuiju airfield in the northwest corner of Korea. MiG fighters from Antung airfield just across the Yalu River in Manchuria offered little resistance to the American raid. Jet fighter-bombers destroyed antiaircraft positions, followed by Marine Corsairs and Air Force Mustangs that bombed and rocketed targets around Sinuiju airfield. F–86s protected the attack aircraft from MiGs. This mission destroyed all North Korean aircraft on the field, most buildings, and several fuel, supply, and ammunition dumps. All U.S. aircraft returned safely from the Sinuiju raid.

General Stratemeyer, Commander of FEAF, suffered a heart attack in May 1951, and General Partridge became Acting Commander while Gen. Edward J. Timberlake temporarily took over the Fifth Air Force. Maj. Gen. Frank F. Everest succeeded to the command of the Fifth Air Force on June 1, and 10 days later, Lt. Gen. O. P. Weyland took over FEAF.

Through most of May the Chinese pilots stayed on the Manchurian side of the Yalu River, but on the 20th 50 MiGs engaged 36 Sabres in aerial combat. During this fight Capt. James Jabara destroyed 2 MiGs. Added to his 4 previous victories, these credits made him the first jet ace in aviation history. MiG pilots again challenged Sabre flights escorting B–29 bombers on May 31 and June 1, but the Communists lost 6 more aircraft.

FEAF, Marine, and Navy close air support of the UN ground forces, coupled with extensive artillery fire, forced the North Korean and Chinese forces during the spring of 1951 to restrict their movements and attacks to periods of darkness and bad weather. In addition, the air force used ground-based radar with considerable success to direct B–29 and B–26 night attacks against Communist positions and troop concentrations. The FEAF also supplemented sealift with its cargo aircraft by flying supplies, mostly artillery ammunition and petroleum products, from Japan to Korea. Transports usually landed at Seoul or Hoengsong, 55 miles southeast of Seoul; the 315th Air Division delivered 15,900 tons in April, 21,300 tons in May, and 22,472 tons in June 1951. Also, whenever rains slowed overland transport to the front lines, C–119s airdropped supplies to UN troops. In late May FEAF initiated OPERATION STRANGLE, an interdiction campaign aimed at highways south of the 39th parallel. The next month the campaign was extended, with somewhat greater success, to railroads.

On June 23, 1951, the North Koreans, through the Soviet Union, proposed a cease-fire, and in July delegations began negotiations at Kaesong, North Korea, on the 38th parallel 35 miles northwest of Seoul. UN forces continued pushing the Communist troops northward until by July 8 the front line correlated closely with the armistice line established 2 years later.

UN Summer–Fall Offensive:
July 9–November 27, 1951

Although truce negotiations began on July 10, 1951, hostilities continued. When the parties suspended negotiations on August 23, the UN Command conducted an offensive in central Korea, to gain an important tactical position. But overall the UN ground forces fought a war of attrition. When the ground action subsided, the Far East Air Forces began to improve its Korean airfields.

The Allies distributed their air power on the improved airfields throughout South Korea. In July 1951 the Royal Australian Air Force sent a squadron of jet fighters to Kimpo airfield, on the western outskirts of Seoul. U.S. Air Force units assigned to Kimpo included a fighter-interceptor group and a tactical reconnaissance group. A South African Air Force fighter-bomber squadron, flying Mustangs, operated from Chinhae airfield on the south coast, 10 miles west of Pusan. The USAF also stationed a fighter-bomber group at Chinhae. Other major UN airfields in Korea included 2 at Pusan, 1 with a Marine air wing assigned and the other hosting a USAF light bomber group. The USAF had stationed 2 fighter-bomber groups at Taegu, 140 miles southeast of Seoul; a fighter-bomber group and a fighter-interceptor group at Suwon, 15 miles south of Seoul; and a light bomber group at Kunsan, on the west coast 110 miles south of Seoul. The FEAF and Fifth Air Force used other airfields in South Korea primarily as staging bases from which to rearm and refuel aircraft, make emergency landings, and fly in supplies for front-line troops. The B–29s and cargo carriers operated from bases in Japan.

The Chinese Air Force implemented an air campaign in late July to test UN air superiority. Through August the Communist pilots tried their tactics in scattered air battles, then in September they challenged Fifth Air Force pilots in earnest. During the month UN pilots engaged 911 Communist aircraft in aerial combat and shot down 14 MiGs, while suffering 6 losses. Aggressive Communist pilots nonetheless forced the Fifth Air Force to suspend fighter-bomber interdiction attacks in MiG Alley until the winter, and on October 28 FEAF Bomber Command restricted the vulnerable B–29s to night operations.

UN fighter-bombers, no longer able to attack targets in MiG Alley, turned to the destruction of railway lines in the area between Pyongyang and the Chongchon River. On August 18 the UN Command expanded its railway interdiction campaign. The Fifth Air Force

JULY 9 - NOVEMBER 27, 1951

MANCHURIA

NORTH KOREA

U.S.S.R.

Tumen River

MIG ALLEY

Yalu River

Sinuiju

Taechen AB

Namsi AB

Chongchon River

Saamcham AB

Pyongyang

SEA OF

JAPAN

0   50   100
Miles

Panmunjom

U.N. FORCES
NOVEMBER 27, 1951

Seoul
Kimpo AB
Suwon AB

YELLOW

SEA

SOUTH KOREA

Kunsan AB

Taegu AB

Chinhae AB   Pusan

208

attacked railroads and bridges in the northwest but outside MiG Alley; FEAF Bomber Command hit transportation targets, especially bridges, in the center of North Korea; and U.S. Navy aerial units bombed railroads and bridges on the northeast coast. This campaign forced the Communists to resort to motor vehicles and to move supplies and troops at night. Thus, in August and September night-flying B–26s found lucrative targets on the roads of North Korea. Stronger flak defenses and worsening weather in October and November permitted the Communists to repair damaged railroads.

Meantime, in October 1951, the North Koreans began to construct 3 new airfields within a few miles of each other at Saamcham, Taechon, and Namsi, all 50 to 70 miles north and northwest of Pyongyang. American B–29s attempted to destroy the newly constructed airfields. During the night of October 13 FEAF Bomber Command unsuccessfully raided the field at Saamcham. The Bomber Command staff subsequently planned daytime raids under the escort of F–84s and F–86s. The B–29s made successful raids on October 18, 21, and 22, damaging the landing strips and other facilities at all 3 airfields. However, on the 23rd MiG interceptors attacked the bombers and their escorts, shooting down 3 B–29s and an F–84, while losing 4 MiGs. The B–29s returned to night raids but failed to destroy the North Korean airfields, and the MiG pilots flying from these fields continued to intercept and shoot down UN aircraft.

On November 12, 1951, truce negotiations resumed at a new site—Panmunjom—and UN ground forces ceased all offensive action. By November 27 the UN had established defensive positions, and the Allies settled into a war of containment, although the Communists still pursued their effective air offensive.

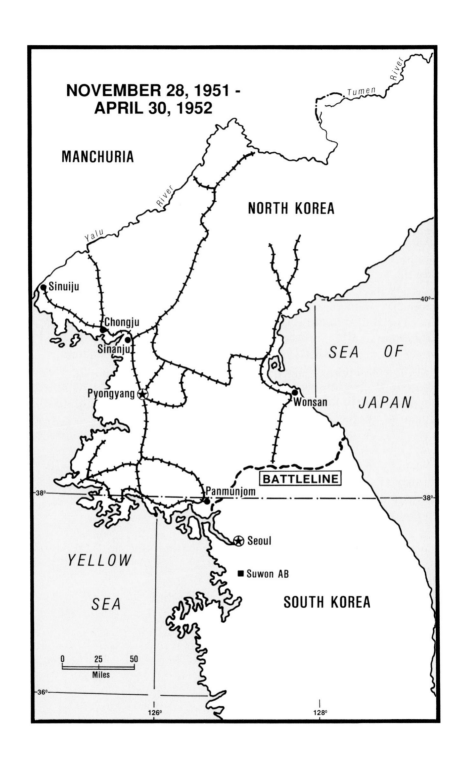

NOVEMBER 28, 1951 -
APRIL 30, 1952

MANCHURIA

NORTH KOREA

Tumen River

Yalu River

Sinuiju

Chongju

Sinanju

Pyongyang

Wonsan

SEA OF JAPAN

BATTLELINE

Panmunjom

Seoul

Suwon AB

SOUTH KOREA

YELLOW SEA

40°

38°

36°

126°

128°

0   25   50
Miles

210

Second Korean Winter: November 28, 1951–April 30, 1952

USAF officials recognized the need for more F–86s to counter the Chinese Air Force in Korea. The 51st Fighter-Interceptor Wing at Suwon Airfield, 15 miles south of Seoul, consequently received F–86s from the United States to replace its F–80s. On December 1, 1951, the wing flew its first combat missions in the new Sabrejets. Members of the 51st and 4th Fighter-Interceptor Wings shattered the Communists' air offensive, downing 26 MiGs in 2 weeks, while losing only 6 F–86s. The Sabrejets achieved in the air the results that eluded the B–29s that bombed the enemy airfields near Pyongyang. For the rest of the winter, the MiG pilots generally avoided aerial combat; nevertheless, Fifth Air Force pilots between January and April 1952 destroyed 127 Communist aircraft while losing only 9 in aerial combat.

In spite of increasing vulnerability to flak damage, the Fifth Air Force continued its raids against railways. In January 1952 the FEAF Bomber Command's B–29s joined this interdiction campaign. Although the Communists managed to build up supply dumps in forward areas, the UN air forces damaged the railways enough to prevent the enemy from supporting a sustained major offensive. The interdiction missions also forced the North Koreans and Chinese to divert materiel and troops from the front lines to protect and repair the railways. As the ground began to thaw, between March 3 and 25, the Fifth Air Force bombed key railways, but with limited success. For example, on the 25th fighter-bombers attacked the railway between Chongju, on the west coast 60 miles northeast of Pyongyang, the North Korean capital, and Sinanju, 20 miles further to the southeast. This strike closed the railway line for only 5 days before the Communists repaired it. The B–29s were somewhat more successful during the last week in March, knocking out bridges at Pyongyang and Sinanju. Fifth Air Force continued the interdiction campaign through April while looking for more effective means to block North Korean transport systems.

In the winter of 1951–1952, with the establishment of static battle lines, the need for close air support declined drastically. To use the potential fire power of the fighter-bombers, in January 1952 the UN commander alternated aerial bombardment of enemy positions on 1 day with artillery attacks of the same positions on the next day. The Chinese and North Korean troops merely dug deeper trenches and tunnels that were generally invulnerable to either air or artillery strikes. After a month the UN Commander, General Ridgway, ordered the strikes stopped.

With peace talks at Panmunjom stalemated and ground battle lines static, on April 30 UN air commanders prepared a new strategy of military pressure against the enemy by attacking targets previously exempted or underexploited.

Korea, Summer–Fall 1952:
May 1–November 30, 1952

The new UN strategy sought to increase military pressure on North Korea and thus force the Communist negotiators to temper their demands. In May 1952 the Fifth Air Force shifted from interdiction missions against transportation networks to attacks on North Korean supply depots and industrial targets. On May 8 UN fighter-bombers blasted a supply depot and a week later destroyed a vehicle repair factory at Tang-dong, a few miles north of Pyongyang. The Fifth Air Force, under a new Commander, Maj. Gen. Glenn O. Barcus, also destroyed munitions factories and a steel-fabricating plant during May and June. Meanwhile, Gen. Mark W. Clark took over the United Nations Command. Beginning on June 23, U.S. Navy and Fifth Air Force units made coordinated attacks on the electric power complex at Sui-ho Dam, on the Yalu River near Sinuiju, followed by strikes against the Chosin, Fusen, and Kyosen power plants, all located midway between the Sea of Japan and the Manchurian border in northeastern Korea.

The aerial reconnaissance function, always important in target selection, became indispensable to the strategy of increased aerial bombardment, since target planners sought the most lucrative targets. One inviting target was the capital city of Pyongyang. It remained unscathed until July 11, when aircraft of the Seventh Fleet, the 1st Marine Air Wing, the Fifth Air Force, the British Navy, and the Republic of Korea Air Force struck military targets there. That night, following day-long attacks, the Far East Air Forces Bomber Command sent a flight of B–29s to bomb 8 targets. Post-strike assessments of Pyongyang showed considerable damage inflicted to command posts, supply dumps, factories, barracks, antiaircraft gun sites, and railroad facilities. The North Koreans subsequently upgraded their antiaircraft defenses, forcing UN fighter-bombers and light bombers (B–26s) to sacrifice accuracy and bomb from higher altitudes. Allied air forces returned to Pyongyang again on August 29 and 30, destroying most of their assigned targets. In September the Fifth Air Force sent its aircraft against troop concentrations and barracks in northwest Korea while Bomber Command bombed similar targets near Hamhung in northeast Korea.

Along the front lines, throughout the summer and fall of 1952, the FEAF joined the U.S. Navy and Marines to provide between 2,000 and 4,000 close air support sorties each month. For example, FEAF

MAY 1 - NOVEMBER 30, 1952

Tumen River

MANCHURIA

Kyosen
Power
Plant

Yalu River

Chosen
Power
Plant

Fusen
Power
Plant

Suiho
Power
Plant

MIG ALLEY

Sinuiju

Chongchon River

40°

Hamhung

NORTH KOREA

SEA OF

JAPAN

Pyongyang

BATTLELINE

38°   Panmunjom   38°

Seoul

YELLOW

SEA

SOUTH KOREA

0   25   50
Miles

36°

126°

128°

Taegu AB

214

Bomber Command not only flew nighttime interdiction missions but also gave radar-directed close air support (10,000 or more meters from friendly positions) at night to front-line troops under Communist attack. During the daytime the Mustang (F–51) pilots flew preplanned and immediate close air support missions.

The 315th Air Division also supported the ground forces, flying supplies and personnel into Korea and returning wounded, reassigned, and furloughed personnel to Japan. C–124s, more efficient on the long haul, carried personnel and cargo. C–47s provided tactical airlift to airfields near the front lines, and C–119s handled bulky cargo and airborne and airdrop operations.

During the summer of 1952, the 4th and 51st Fighter-Interceptor Wings replaced many of their F–86Es with modified F–86Fs. The new Sabre aircraft had more powerful engines and improved leading wing edges which allowed them to match the aerial combat performance of the MiG–15 jet fighters of the North Korean and Chinese air forces. Even though the Communists had built up their air order of battle, they still tended to restrict their flights to MiG Alley and often avoided aerial combat with the F–86 pilots. By August and September, however, MiG pilots showed more initiative, and aerial engagements occurred almost daily. Even though the Communist pilots improved their tactics and proficiency, U.S. pilots destroyed many more MiGs, achieving at the end of October a ratio of 8 enemy losses to every U.S. loss.

The Communists, in spite of the pressure of the air campaign, remained stubborn in the truce talks. On October 8, 1952, the UN negotiators at Panmunjom recessed the talks because the Chinese would not agree to nonforced* repatriation of prisoners of war. As winter set in, UN forces in Korea remained mired in the stalemated conflict.

---

*Only those POWs who wanted repatriation would return to Communist control. Many enemy POWs preferred to remain in South Korea, but the Communist authorities insisted that these POWs also be returned.

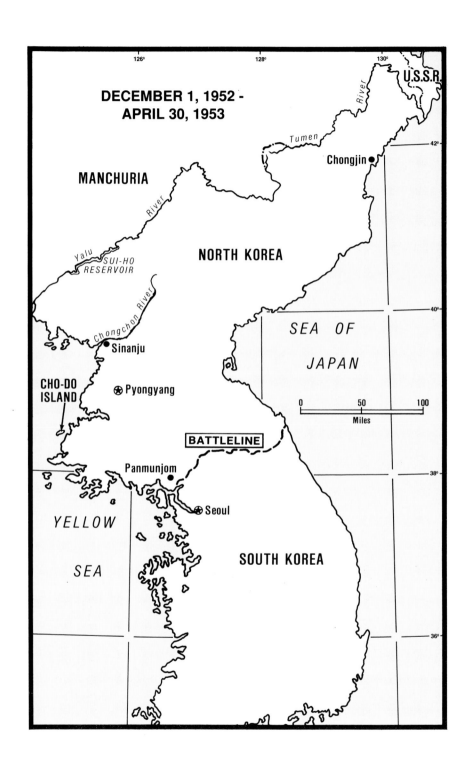

DECEMBER 1, 1952 -
APRIL 30, 1953

U.S.S.R.

MANCHURIA

Tumen *River*

River

Chongjin●

NORTH KOREA

Yalu

SUI-HO
RESERVOIR

Chongchon River

●Sinanju

SEA OF

JAPAN

CHO-DO
ISLAND

⊛ Pyongyang

0   50   100

Miles

BATTLELINE

Panmunjom
●

⊛ Seoul

YELLOW

SEA

SOUTH KOREA

216

Third Korean Winter:
December 1, 1952–April 30, 1953

The military stalemate continued throughout the winter of 1952–1953. Allied Sabrejet pilots, meantime, persisted in destroying MiGs at a decidedly favorable ratio. In December the Communists developed an ambush tactic against F–86 pilots patroling along the Yalu River: MiG pilots would catch the UN aircraft as they ran short of fuel and headed south to return to base. During these engagements, some of the F–86 pilots exhausted their fuel and had to bail out over Cho-do Island, 60 miles southwest of Pyongyang. United Nations forces held the island and maintained an air rescue detachment there for such emergencies. To avoid combat while low on fuel, Sabre pilots began to fly home over the Yellow Sea. MiG pilots at this time generally sought the advantages of altitude, speed, position, and numbers before engaging in aerial combat. The UN pilots, on the other hand, relied on their skills to achieve aerial victories, even though they were outnumbered and flying aircraft that did not quite match the flight capabilities of the MiG–15s. One memorable battle occurred on February 18, 1953, near the Sui-ho Reservoir on the Yalu River, 110 miles north of Pyongyang; 4 F–86Fs attacked 48 MiGs, shot down 2, and caused 2 others to crash while taking evasive action. All 4 U.S. aircraft returned safely to their base.

While the Fifth Air Force maintained air superiority over North Korea during daylight hours, the Far East Air Forces Bomber Command on nighttime missions ran afoul of increasingly effective Communist interceptors. The aging B–29s relied on darkness and electronic jamming for protection from both interceptors and antiaircraft gunfire, but the Communists used spotter aircraft and searchlights to reveal bombers to enemy gun crews and fighter-interceptor pilots. As B–29 losses mounted in late 1952, the Bomber Command compressed bomber formations to shorten the time over targets and increase the effectiveness of electronic countermeasures. The Fifth Air Force joined the Navy and Marines to provide fighter escorts to intercept enemy aircraft before they could attack the B–29s. Bomber Command also restricted missions along the Yalu to cloudy, dark nights because on clear nights contrails gave away the bombers' positions. FEAF lost no more B–29s after January 1953, although it continued its missions against industrial targets. On March 5 the B–29s penetrated deep into enemy territory to bomb a target at Chongjin in northeastern Korea, only 63 miles from the Soviet border.

While Bomber Command struck industrial targets throughout North Korea during the winter of 1952–1953, the Fifth Air Force cooperated with the U.S. Navy's airmen in attacks on supplies, equipment, and troops near the front lines. In December 1952 the Eighth Army moved its bombline from 10,000 to 3,000 meters from the front lines, enabling Fifth Air Force and naval fighter-bombers to target areas closer to American positions. Beyond the front lines, the Fifth Air Force focused on destroying railroads and bridges, allowing B–26s to bomb stalled vehicles. In January 1953 the Fifth Air Force attempted to cut the 5 railroad bridges over the Chongchon Estuary near Sinanju, 40 miles north of Pyongyang. Expecting trains to back up in marshaling yards at Sinanju, Bomber Command sent B–29s at night to bomb them, but these operations hindered enemy transportation only briefly. As the ground thawed in the spring, however, the Communist forces had greater difficulty moving supplies and reinforcements in the face of the Fifth Air Force's relentless attacks on transportation.

At the end of March 1953, the Chinese Communist government indicated its willingness to exchange injured and ill prisoners of war and discuss terms for a cease-fire in Korea. On April 20 Communist and United Nations officials began an exchange of POWs, and 6 days later, resumed the sessions at Panmunjom.

Korea, Summer 1953:
May 1–July 27, 1953

Although Communist leaders showed a desire to negotiate an armistice, they would not do so before trying to improve their military positions. During May 1953 Fifth Air Force reconnaissance revealed that the Chinese and North Koreans were regrouping their front-line forces. On the last day of the month, Lt. Gen. Samuel E. Anderson took command of the Fifth Air Force.

Communist forces directed a major assault on June 10 against the Republic of Korea's II Corps near Kumsong, a small town in central Korea, 110 miles southeast of Pyongyang. With American aid, the South Koreans stopped the Communist drive by June 19 with little loss of territory. During the enemy offensive, UN pilots broke previous records in flying close air support sorties, with Far East Air Forces flying 7,032, the Marines, 1,348, and other UN air forces, 537. Also during June FEAF devoted about 1/2 of its combat sorties to close air support. Communist troops attacked again in central Korea on July 13, forcing the ROK II Corps to retreat once more. But by the 20th Allied ground forces had stopped the foe's advance only a few miles south of previous battle lines. Once again, during July, FEAF devoted more than 40 percent of its 12,000 combat sorties to close air support missions.

During the Communist offensives, the 315th Air Division responded to demands of the Eighth Army and between June 21 and 23 airlifted an Army regiment (3,252 soldiers and 1,770 tons of cargo) from Japan to Korea. From June 28 through July 2, the airlifters flew almost 4,000 more troops and over 1,200 tons of cargo from Misawa and Tachikawa Air Bases in Japan to Pusan and Taegu airfields in Korea. These proved to be the last major airlift operations of the Korean conflict.

In aerial combat, meanwhile, Fifth Air Force interceptors set new records. Sabrejet pilots fought most aerial battles in May, June, and July 1953 at 20,000–40,000 feet in altitude, where the F–86F was most lethal, and during these 3 months, claimed 165 aerial victories against only 3 losses—the best quarterly victory-loss ratio of the war.

Fifth Air Force and FEAF Bomber Command also continued to punish the enemy through air interdiction, making attacks on the Sui-ho power complex and other industrial and military targets along the

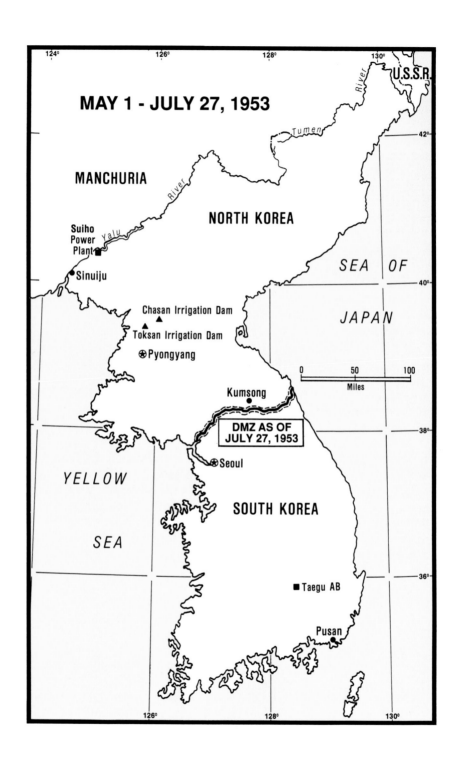

MAY 1 - JULY 27, 1953

U.S.S.R.

MANCHURIA

NORTH KOREA

Suiho
Power
Plant

Sinuiju

Chasan Irrigation Dam

Toksan Irrigation Dam

Pyongyang

Kumsong

DMZ AS OF
JULY 27, 1953

Seoul

SOUTH KOREA

SEA OF

JAPAN

0   50   100
Miles

YELLOW

SEA

Taegu AB

Pusan

220

Yalu River. In addition, the Fifth Air Force in May attacked irrigation dams that had previously been excluded from the list of approved targets. On May 13 U.S. fighter-bombers broke the Toksan Dam about 20 miles north of Pyongyang, and on the 16th they bombed the Chasan Dam, a few miles to the east of Toksan Dam. The resulting floods extensively damaged rice fields, buildings, bridges, and roads. Most importantly, 2 main rail lines were disabled for several days. Between July 20 and 27 the UN Command bombed North Korean airfields to prevent extensive aerial reinforcement before the armistice ending the Korean conflict became effective on July 27, 1953.

Only 5 years had intervened between the end of World War II and the Korean War. Officially, only 5 years would separate the Korean War from the War in Southeast Asia: July 1, 1958, marked the beginning of Vietnam Service.

Vietnam Service

1958-1973

Vietnam Service Medal

On its obverse side, the Vietnam Service Medal (VSM) depicts an oriental dragon behind a grove of bamboo; the words REPUBLIC OF VIETNAM SERVICE appear below. On the reverse is a drawn crossbow surmounted by a blazing torch; the words UNITED STATES OF AMERICA are around the bottom edge. The VSM is worn with a suspension ribbon, although a ribbon bar may be worn instead. The ribbon is yellow, representing the color of Vietnam and the Buddhist belief, with 3 red center stripes, symbolizing the 3 ancient Vietnamese empires, Tonkin, Annam, and Cochin China. A green stripe on each edge represents the Vietnamese jungles.

Executive Order No. 11231, July 9, 1965, established the VSM. The period of service is July 4, 1965–March 28, 1973; however, a member awarded the Armed Forces Expeditionary Medal* for Vietnam service (July 1, 1958–July 3, 1965) can apply to have that medal converted to the VSM. Recipients served in combat or with a unit directly support- ing a military operation or combat in Southeast Asia; or they served in Vietnam on temporary duty for at least 30 consecutive or 60 noncon- secutive days. A person received a Bronze Service Star for each campaign credit, or Silver Service Star for every 5 campaigns.

Vietnam Service Streamer

The Vietnam Service Streamer is identical to the ribbon in design and color. A USAF unit qualified for the Vietnam Service Streamer if it was based in South Vietnam at any time between July 1, 1958, and November 14, 1961, or January 29 through March 28, 1973;† if it was based during these periods in Thailand and flying missions into or over Vietnam; or if it was based in Thailand, as a non-flying support unit, any time between July 1, 1958, and March 28, 1973. A cam- paign streamer is a service streamer with the campaign name and dates embroidered on it. With 1 exception (the Vietnam Air/Ground Campaign), a unit qualified for a campaign streamer if it was based in Vietnam or engaged in combat in Southeast Asia during a designated campaign.

---

*See Appendix 1 for a description of the Armed Forces Expeditionary Medal.

†Units earned the appropriate campaign streamers from November 15, 1961, to January 28, 1973.

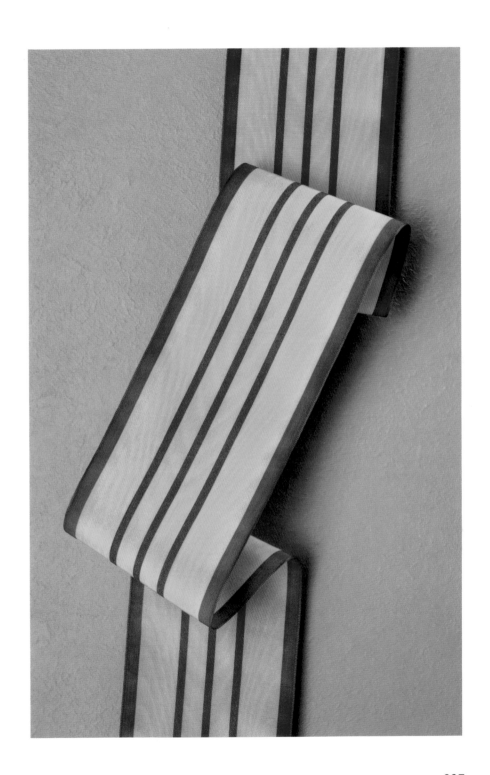

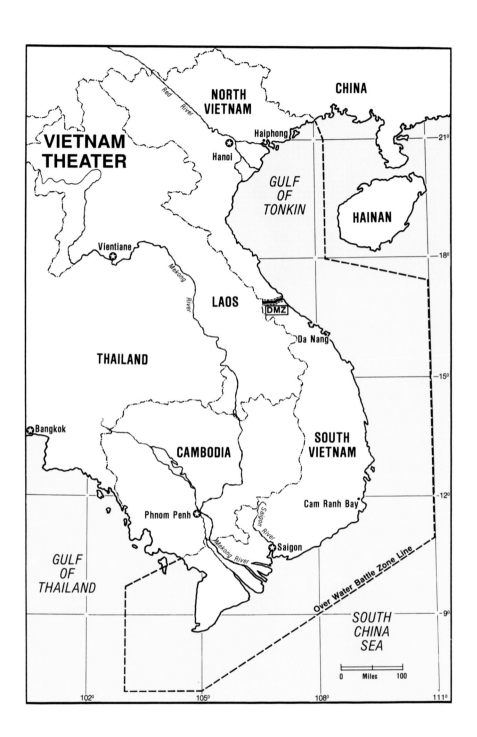

228

Vietnam Campaigns
November 15, 1961–January 28, 1973

Designated Campaigns of Vietnam Service

The USAF designated 17 campaigns for Vietnam Service. As explained in the Introduction, the USAF campaigns in this conflict differed in title and dates from those of the other services. The USAF campaigns appear in chronological sequence from November 15, 1961, through January 28, 1973, with 1 exception: the Vietnam Air/Ground Campaign overlaps in time the campaigns immediately preceding and following it, and its designated campaign area is limited exclusively to South Vietnam (Republic of Vietnam). The designated campaign area for the remaining 16 campaigns is Southeast Asia; that is, Cambodia, Laos, and Vietnam—the Theater of Operations for Vietnam Service. The first campaign summarized is the Vietnam Advisory Campaign.

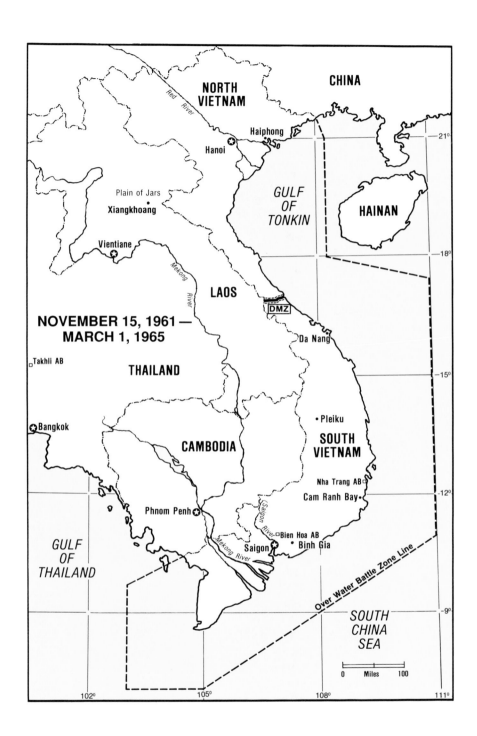

NORTH VIETNAM

CHINA

Red River

Haiphong

Hanoi

Plain of Jars

Xiangkhoang

GULF OF TONKIN

HAINAN

Vientiane

Mekong River

LAOS

DMZ

NOVEMBER 15, 1961 — MARCH 1, 1965

Da Nang

Takhli AB

THAILAND

Bangkok

CAMBODIA

Pleiku

SOUTH VIETNAM

Nha Trang AB

Cam Ranh Bay

Phnom Penh

GULF OF THAILAND

Saigon River

Bien Hoa AB

Saigon

Binh Gia

Mekong River

Over Water Battle Zone Line

SOUTH CHINA SEA

0   Miles   100

21°

18°

15°

12°

9°

102°   105°   108°   111°

230

Vietnam Advisory:
November 15, 1961–March 1, 1965

On November 15, 1961, the 2d Advanced Echelon (2d ADVON) was activated in Saigon, capital of the Republic of Vietnam (South Vietnam). The 2d ADVON, administratively part of the Thirteenth Air Force, controlled USAF units operating in Vietnam and reported to the Military Assistance Advisory Group, Vietnam. The 4400th Combat Crew Training Squadron's FARM GATE detachment arrived on November 16. The FARM GATE organization, although trained for counter insurgency combat, for about 2 months limited its mission to training Vietnamese aircrews and supporting with reconnaissance flights the operations of the Vietnamese Air Force (VNAF). Activation of the 2d ADVON and arrival of the FARM GATE detachment heralded the buildup of the United States Air Force presence in Vietnam.

Responding to the Republic of Vietnam's appeal in December 1961 for increased military aid to counter Communist (Viet Cong) insurgents, the United States gradually increased its forces. From January 2 to 5, 1962, for example, the USAF moved a tactical air control system to South Vietnam and landed equipment and personnel at Tan Son Nhut Air Base (AB) in Saigon; Bien Hoa AB, 15 miles north of Saigon; Da Nang AB, 375 miles northeast of Saigon; Pleiku AB, in the Central Highlands 230 miles northeast of Saigon; and Nha Trang AB, on the coast, a little less than 200 miles northeast of Saigon. Shortly afterwards, on January 7, a flight of C–123s equipped for aerial spray missions arrived at Tan Son Nhut. Code-named RANCH HAND, this USAF detachment 3 days later began defoliation operations that continued for 9 years.

To manage U.S. forces in Vietnam, the Commander in Chief, Pacific Command, at the direction of President John F. Kennedy and the Joint Chiefs of Staff, created Military Assistance Command, Vietnam (MACV) on February 8, 1962. Army Gen. Paul D. Harkins was named the first Commander of MACV. The 2d ADVON became the air component of the new command. A few months later, on October 8, the USAF activated the 2d Air Division, which replaced the 2d ADVON. In spite of increased U.S. aid, the Viet Cong insurgency grew, and the government of South Vietnam faced growing civil disorder. A year later, on November 1, 1963, a group of South Vietnamese military officers deposed President Ngo Dinh Diem in a coup d'état, and not until June 1965 would the South Vietnamese establish a reasonably stable government. Meanwhile, on June 20,

1964, Army Gen. William C. Westmoreland became Commander of MACV.

Communist insurgents also operated actively in Laos, and in May 1964 United States involvement in Southeast Asia expanded to include military aid to that country. On June 9, F–100s flying from Takhli Air Base, Thailand, about 110 miles north of Bangkok, made the first USAF strike in Laos. Air Force pilots bombed an antiaircraft installation at Xiangkhoang, on the Plain of Jars, about 100 miles northeast of Vientiane, the Laotian capital. In December 1964 the USAF launched an air interdiction campaign against the Ho Chi Minh Trail, a network of roads, trails, and waterways in the southern Laotian panhandle.

The nature of the conflict in Southeast Asia changed dramatically in late 1964. On August 2 and 4 torpedo boats from North Vietnam (Democratic Republic of Vietnam) attacked U.S. naval vessels in the Gulf of Tonkin. On the 5th, U.S. naval aircraft launched retaliatory air strikes against coastal targets in North Vietnam. That same day the USAF deployed B–57s to Bien Hoa AB and F–100s to Da Nang AB. Then in December 1964 the Viet Cong used conventional field rather than hit-and-run tactics to drive South Vietnamese forces temporarily from Binh Gia, near the coast, only 40 miles southeast of Saigon. For both North and South Vietnam governmental authorities this battle marked an escalation of the conflict. As the war rapidly intensified, on February 7, 1965, President Lyndon B. Johnson ordered American dependents evacuated from South Vietnam. The same day the Viet Cong shelled Pleiku Air Base. In retaliation, the USAF conducted its first raid against North Vietnam on the 8th, hitting a target just north of the 17th parallel.

Vietnam Defensive:
March 2, 1965–January 30, 1966

On March 2, 1965, the United States began an air campaign, known as ROLLING THUNDER, against North Vietnam. This campaign sought to discourage North Vietnamese aggression, reduce infiltration of men and supplies from the north to the south, and raise South Vietnamese morale. At first, the United States limited air strikes to military and transportation targets south of the 20th parallel. After May 18 the target list gradually expanded to include targets north of the 20th parallel. American pilots, however, had to observe a 30-mile buffer zone along the Chinese border; another 30-mile buffer around Hanoi, capital of North Vietnam; and a third buffer 10 miles wide around Haiphong, the country's chief seaport.

While the United States pursued ROLLING THUNDER, North Vietnam improved its air defenses, deploying more antiaircraft guns, jet fighters, and its first surface-to-air missiles. A month after the U.S. began the air campaign, on April 4, 1965, North Vietnamese MiG–17s shot down 2 USAF F–105s bombing a bridge near the coastal town of Thanh Hoa, 76 miles south of Hanoi. These represented the first USAF Southeast Asia losses in air-to-air combat. The Air Force subsequently sent EC–121 radar picket aircraft over the Gulf of Tonkin to warn U.S. strike aircraft of approaching MiGs. On June 17 Navy F–4 pilots shot down 2 MiG–17s, achieving the first American aerial victories of the war. USAF pilots scored their first victories a few weeks later, on July 10, when aircrews of the 45th Tactical Fighter Squadron destroyed 2 MiG–17s with Sidewinder (heat-seeking) missiles.

Throughout early 1965 the number of American air and ground forces in South Vietnam increased rapidly. The U.S. 9th Marine Brigade landed on March 8 at Da Nang, and, between May 5 and 8 USAF C–130s and C–123s airlifted the 173rd Airborne Brigade, the first Army unit sent to South Vietnam, from Okinawa to Bien Hoa Air Base and the village of Vung Tau, situated on a peninsula about 40 miles southeast of Saigon. Six weeks later, on June 18, B–52s from Andersen Air Force Base, Guam, bombed a Viet Cong troop concentration near Ben Cat, 30 miles north of Saigon. This mission marked the first use of the B–52 in a conventional role and the beginning of extensive B–52 operations in Southeast Asia.

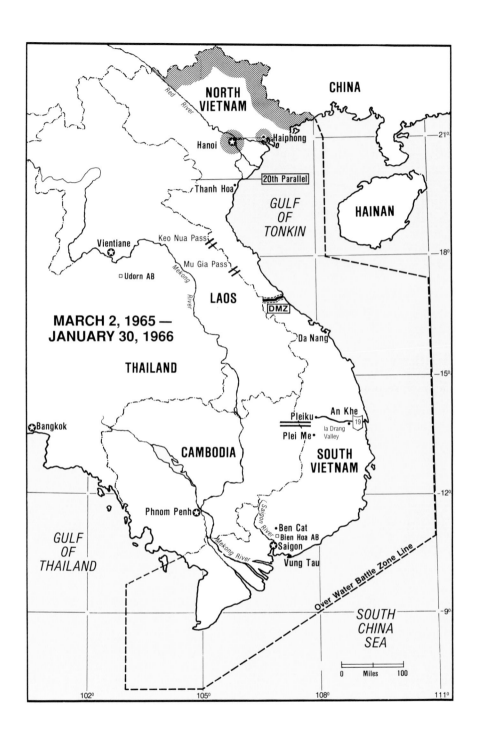

NORTH VIETNAM

CHINA

Red River

Hanoi

Haiphong

Thanh Hoa

20th Parallel

GULF OF TONKIN

HAINAN

21°

18°

Keo Nua Pass

Vientiane

Mu Gia Pass

Udorn AB

Mekong River

LAOS

DMZ

Da Nang

**MARCH 2, 1965 —
JANUARY 30, 1966**

THAILAND

15°

Pleiku

An Khe

19

Plei Me

Ia Drang Valley

Bangkok

CAMBODIA

SOUTH VIETNAM

12°

Phnom Penh

Saigon River

Ben Cat

Bien Hoa AB

Saigon

GULF OF THAILAND

Mekong River

Vung Tau

Over Water Battle Zone Line

9°

SOUTH CHINA SEA

0   Miles   100

102°   105°   108°   111°

234

On October 19, 1965, Viet Cong and North Vietnamese troops attacked an Army of the Republic of Vietnam (ARVN) camp at Plei Me,
30 miles south of Pleiku. The Communists blocked all land routes to
Plei Me, forcing the USAF to resupply defenders with parachute
drops. Air Force fighters, meantime, provided intensive close air
support. On October 23 the U.S. Army moved from An Khe, on the
highway and 30 miles east of Pleiku, to break the siege at Plei Me.
On November 14 American troops in pursuit of the retreating enemy
entered the Ia Drang Valley, immediately to the northwest of Plei Me.
The Communist forces fought fiercely to defend their supply base in
the valley, but with close air support and B–52 strikes, the Allies
drove the enemy across the border into Cambodia.

As the conflict expanded and intensified still further in late 1965,
North Vietnam increased the number of personnel and amount of
equipment and supplies moving south, primarily over the Ho Chi
Minh Trail. To slow this infiltration of men and supplies into South
Vietnam, reconnaissance aircraft located enemy trucks, bridges,
troops, and storage areas. Strike aircraft, refueled by KC–135 tankers,
later hit these targets on the Ho Chi Minh Trail and the Mu Gia and
Keo Nua (Nape) Passes, principal entry points on the Laotian/North
Vietnamese border. On Christmas Day 1965 the United States ceased
all bombing in North Vietnam for 37 days in an attempt to
promote peace negotiations. The North Vietnamese and Viet Cong,
however, used the interlude to rebuild their military forces.

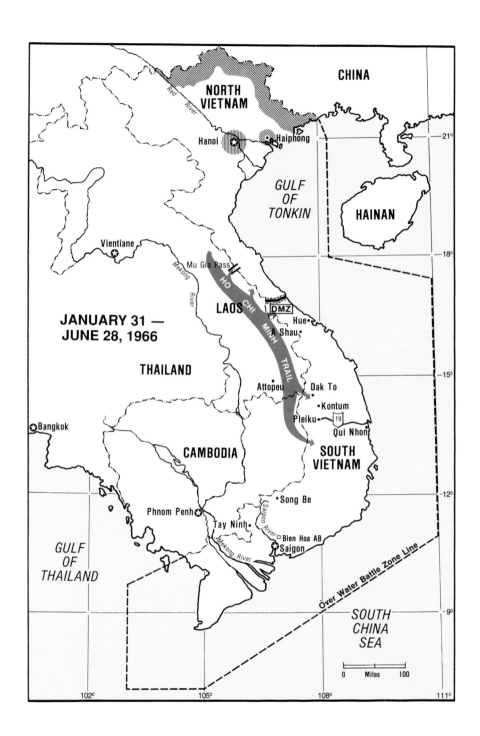

CHINA

NORTH VIETNAM

Red River

Hanoi ⊛ •Haiphong

GULF OF TONKIN

HAINAN

Vientiane ⊛

Mu Gia Pass

LAOS

HO CHI MINH TRAIL

DMZ

Hue•

A Shau•

JANUARY 31 — JUNE 28, 1966

THAILAND

Mekong River

Attopeu• •Dak To
•Kontum

Pleiku• 19

Qui Nhon•

⊕Bangkok

CAMBODIA

SOUTH VIETNAM

•Song Be

Phnom Penh⊛

Tay Ninh•

Saigon River

□ Bien Hoa AB
⊛Saigon

Mekong River

GULF OF THAILAND

Over Water Battle Zone Line

SOUTH CHINA SEA

0   Miles   100

102°   105°   108°   111°

—21°

—18°

—15°

—12°

—9°

236

Vietnam Air:
January 31–June 28, 1966

However intended, the 37-day bombing halt failed to prompt peace negotiations, and on January 31, 1966, the U.S. resumed aerial attacks against North Vietnam. USAF and U.S. Navy pilots soon brought practically all of North Vietnam under attack, even though targets in the restricted zones had to be approved in Washington—a procedure that greatly limited the number of strikes near Hanoi, Haiphong, and the Chinese border. On April 11 B–52s on their first raid over North Vietnam dropped 600 tons of munitions on the Mu Gia Pass to interdict forces and supplies on their way to the Ho Chi Minh Trail.

North Vietnam's air defenses continued to claim U.S. aircraft, although in air-to-air battles the victory-to-loss ratio favored the United States. To counter surface-to-air missiles (SAMs), the USAF deployed WILD WEASEL F–100Fs equipped with radar warning and homing sets to pinpoint SAM radars and mark them for F–105 IRON HAND strikes. After April 18, 1966, the WILD WEASELS also carried strike missiles that homed on radar signals to destroy the SAM sites. Between May and July, F–105s replaced F–100s as WILD WEASEL aircraft.

While the air war escalated in North Vietnam, Allied ground forces required increased air support in South Vietnam. During January and February 1966, the U.S. Army, in cooperation with the Army of the Republic of Vietnam and other Allied ground forces, engaged the Viet Cong in a series of attacks designed to drive them from long-held areas. The Allied ground forces operated in the Central Highlands near Dak To, a village and airfield about 280 miles northeast of Saigon; Kontum, the provincial capital 20 miles south of Dak To; and Pleiku. Allied forces also conducted operations along Highway 19 between Pleiku and Qui Nhon and near Saigon and Tay Ninh, 50 miles northwest of Saigon. These operations called for extensive airlift, aerial resupply, and close air support from the USAF.

To control the growing, diverse air operations in South Vietnam, the USAF on April 1, 1966, activated the Seventh Air Force in place of the 2d Air Division. Its former Commander, Lt. Gen. Joseph H. Moore, assumed command of the Seventh. A few days later, on the 10th, USAF C–130s flew 129 sorties to move an entire U.S. Army brigade from Bien Hoa to Song Be, 60 miles north. The brigade conducted search and destroy missions in the area before returning to Bien Hoa by air on April 22 and 23.

Although generally successful in search and destroy operations, the Allies did suffer some reverses. Perhaps the most significant was the loss of the South Vietnamese Special Forces Camp at A Shau, on the Laotian border some 30 miles southwest of the old Vietnamese imperial capital of Hue. In spite of USAF close air support with AC–47 gunships and A–1 fighters, the North Vietnamese overran the camp on March 9–10. The enemy subsequently developed the A Shau Valley as a major logistics base with a road network to the Ho Chi Minh Trail.

In Laos the USAF continued to bomb the Ho Chi Minh Trail and provide close air support for Laotian forces battling Communist Pathet Lao and North Vietnamese Army (NVA) troops. In one engagement, on March 4 and 5, the enemy attacked Royal Laotian forces at Attopeu in the panhandle of Laos, about 270 miles north of Saigon. Two USAF AC–47s provided close air support to help break the attack. The USAF also used B–52s extensively to fly more than 400 interdiction sorties over the Ho Chi Minh Trail in Laos during the first half of 1966.

Vietnam Air Offensive:
June 29, 1966–March 8, 1967

On June 29, 1966, the USAF bombed petroleum storage and distribution facilities for the first time in the immediate vicinity of Hanoi and Haiphong, after political leaders authorized limited and specific strikes within the buffer zones for these cities. Gen. William W. Momyer replaced General Moore as Seventh Air Force Commander on July 1. The United States expanded the ROLLING THUNDER campaign as of July 9 to include petroleum targets in the northeast and rail lines and highways between China and Hanoi, although the buffer zone on the border limited targets. American aircraft also flew armed reconnaissance over North Vietnam.

On July 30, 1966, the USAF bombed targets in the demilitarized zone (DMZ) to counter the build-up of North Vietnamese forces there. By September the U.S. air campaign against North Vietnam had destroyed or damaged two-thirds of the enemy's petroleum storage capacity, several thousand trucks and watercraft, hundreds of rail cars and bridges, and numerous ammunition and supply storage areas. Beginning on February 14, 1967, USAF aircraft hit additional strategic targets in North Vietnam, knocking out major power plants, and railyard repair facilities. But these results had little effect on the enemy's ability to carry on the war, because the country possessed only a small industrial base and imported most of its military materiel.

In the face of extensive air attacks, North Vietnam further strengthened its air defenses. By January 1967, the United States had lost 455 aircraft within 2 years. Antiaircraft guns and SAMs accounted for most of the losses, but MiGs continued to challenge U.S. air strikes. On January 2 the Seventh Air Force enticed a large MiG–21 force over North Vietnam into battle against F–4s. The USAF pilots destroyed 7 MiGs within 12 minutes without a loss. Four days later, on January 6, the Seventh destroyed 2 more MiGs, and the North Vietnamese temporarily abandoned aerial combat to regroup and retrain.

In South Vietnam Allied forces continued search and destroy operations, blunting new Viet Cong and North Vietnamese offensives. Between July 14 and August 4, 1966, U.S. Marines and South Vietnamese troops battled North Vietnam Army forces near Quang Tri, 20 miles south of the DMZ. Later, between October 15 and November 26, the Allies engaged in a major battle with Viet Cong and NVA

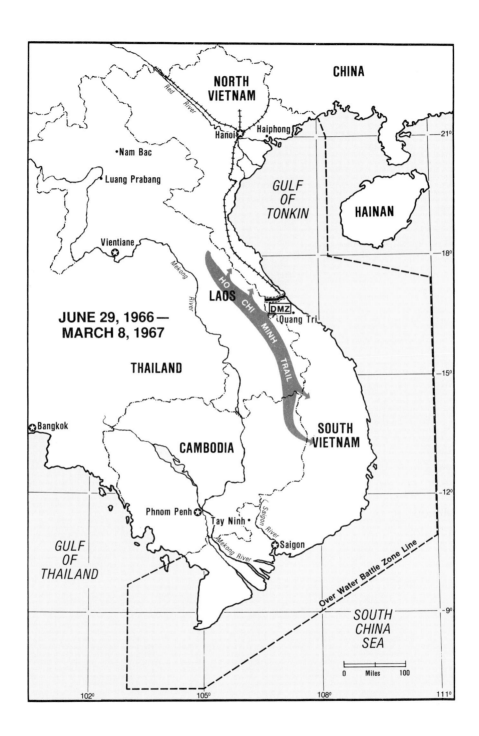

CHINA

NORTH
VIETNAM

Red River

Hanoi • Haiphong

•Nam Bac

Luang Prabang

*GULF
OF
TONKIN*

HAINAN

Vientiane

Mekong River

LAOS

**JUNE 29, 1966 —
MARCH 8, 1967**

DMZ
•Quang Tri

HO CHI MINH TRAIL

THAILAND

SOUTH
VIETNAM

CAMBODIA

•Bangkok

Phnom Penh

Tay Ninh •

Saigon River

Mekong River

• Saigon

*GULF
OF
THAILAND*

Over Water Battle Zone Line

*SOUTH
CHINA
SEA*

0   Miles   100

102°   105°   108°   111°

240

forces northwest of Tay Ninh, near the Cambodian border, 60 miles northwest of Saigon. Enemy resistance was light at first, but on November 4, as ARVN and U.S. troops approached storage areas, the Viet Cong and NVA counterattacked. The Allies responded by airlifting more troops, including elements of the U.S. Army's 1st, 4th, and 25th Infantry Divisions, and the 173rd Airborne Brigade. The USAF provided close air support, and between November 8 and 25, B–52s bombed targets in the area. The Allies drove the enemy from the region temporarily, seizing weapons, ammunition, food, and other supplies that the Communist forces left behind.

The next year, between February and May 1967, U.S. Army units joined ARVN forces to return to Tay Ninh Province, about 50 miles north of Saigon and 15 miles northeast of Tay Ninh. Seventh Air Force C–130s dropped American paratroopers near the Cambodian border to cut off the Viet Cong retreat. The airlifters also flew reinforcements and supplies to the ground troops during this operation. With the help of forward air controllers flying O–1s, Air Force F–100 and F–4 pilots provided close air support, and AC–47 gunship crews illuminated targets and conducted air strikes at night. Again, the enemy withdrew into Cambodia, leaving behind weapons, supplies, and ammunition.

In the panhandle of Laos, the USAF pounded enemy forces on the Ho Chi Minh Trail, while in northern Laos U.S. pilots supported Allied forces under attack. By August 1966 Laotian troops fighting Pathet Lao insurgents had advanced, with the aid of U.S. close air support, to Nam Bac, only 45 miles west of the North Vietnamese border and about 55 miles northeast of Luang Prabang, an ancient city on the Mekong River some 130 miles north of Vientiane. The Laotian gains were short lived, however, and by February 2, 1967, the insurgents had regained lost territory and were in a position to attack the airfield at Luang Prabang.

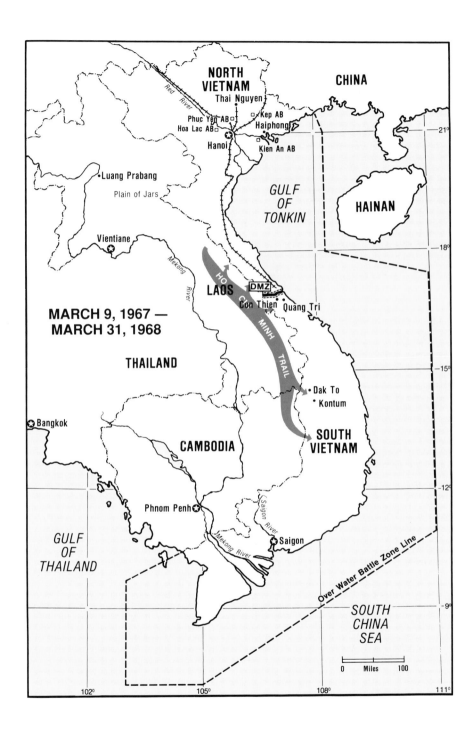

NORTH
VIETNAM

CHINA

Thai Nguyen

Kep AB
Phuc Yen AB
Hoa Lac AB
Haiphong

Hanoi
Kien An AB

Luang Prabang

Plain of Jars

GULF
OF
TONKIN

HAINAN

Red River

Vientiane

Mekong River

LAOS

DMZ
Con Thien
Quang Tri

MARCH 9, 1967 —
MARCH 31, 1968

HO CHI MINH TRAIL

THAILAND

Dak To
Kontum

Bangkok

CAMBODIA

SOUTH
VIETNAM

Phnom Penh

Saigon River

Mekong River

Saigon

GULF
OF
THAILAND

Over Water Battle Zone Line

SOUTH
CHINA
SEA

0   Miles   100

21°

18°

15°

12°

9°

102°   105°   108°   111°

242

Vietnam Air Offensive, Phase II: March 9, 1967–March 31, 1968

On March 10, 1967, Seventh Air Force F–105s and F–4s bombed a new target, the Thai Nguyen iron and steel plant, 30 miles north of Hanoi. The ROLLING THUNDER bombing campaign continued with strikes against bridges, petroleum storage, cement plants, and power transformer stations near Hanoi. USAF and naval aircraft also conducted armed reconnaissance over most of North Vietnam. Missions against major supply routes from China targeted railroad yards, repair facilities, bridges, and support areas. Early in August 1967 American air attacks against the Paul Doumer Bridge in Hanoi knocked out the center span. Poor weather in the first 3 months of 1968 forced U.S. aircraft to rely almost exclusively on all-weather bombing techniques in North Vietnam; nevertheless, the Paul Doumer Bridge remained unusable most of the time. While overland routes might be interdicted, Haiphong harbor and docks still remained off limits to U.S. pilots. A continuous flow of supplies moved through the port from the People's Republic of China and the Soviet Union, which largely offset North Vietnam's losses.

U.S. aircraft used electronic countermeasures and other techniques to limit the effectiveness of North Vietnam's antiaircraft defenses. North Vietnamese forces fired 55 SAMs on the average for each U.S. aircraft destroyed. To reduce the threat of a resurgent North Vietnamese Air Force, in April 1967 the United States bombed MiG bases, destroying several jet aircraft on the ground. In aerial combat during the first 6 months of 1967 (primarily in April, May, and June), U.S. pilots destroyed 54 MiGs while losing 11 aircraft. But between August 1967 and February 1968, the United States lost 18 aircraft to MiGs while destroying only 5 enemy aircraft. On January 14, 1968, two MiGs shot down an EB–66 that was jamming enemy radars from an orbit 90 miles from Hanoi. The USAF subsequently used the vulnerable EB–66s in already established orbits over Laos and the Gulf of Tonkin, accepting degradation of jamming to lessen the risks of aerial interception.

On April 6, 1967, the North Vietnam Army and Viet Cong forces attacked Quang Tri, the northernmost provincial capital, 20 miles south of the demilitarized zone. To counter the offensive, on May 18 South Vietnamese and U.S. troops entered the DMZ for the first time. USAF B–52s, tactical air forces, and naval and army artillery strikes combined with Allied ground forces to destroy temporarily NVA strength in the zone. The NVA then shifted its artillery positions north of the DMZ, rebuilt its forces in the area, and on September 1 renewed attacks on the U.S. Marine base at Con Thien, immediately south of the DMZ. With forward air controllers pinpointing artillery and other targets, the USAF began an aerial attempt to destroy enemy positions, and by October 4 the North Vietnam Army had been forced to withdraw once again.

Shortly afterward, in November 1967, U.S. forces conducting search and destroy operations in the Central Highlands encountered strong Viet Cong resistance near Dak To, 15 miles east of the border junction between Laos, Cambodia, and the Republic of Vietnam. Tactical aircraft and B–52s provided close air support while USAF C–130s flew supplies and reinforcements to the Dak To airstrip. U.S. airpower inflicted heavy casualties, and the enemy withdrew on November 24.

In the Laotian part of the conflict, during the summer of 1967, Seventh Air Force provided extensive air support to Laotian troops battling the Pathet Lao and North Vietnamese forces on the Plain of Jars near Luang Prabang. The Ho Chi Minh Trail in the Laotian panhandle also came under constant attack. Between December 1967 and February 1968, Seventh Air Force pilots flew over 20,000 sorties against transportation lines in Laos and claimed destruction of more than 3,000 trucks. But the Communists continued to build up forces in Laos and Cambodia in preparation for a major offensive that began on January 21, 1968, when the NVA surrounded and laid siege to Khe Sanh, a U.S. Marine base in a valley 7 miles east of the Laotian border and 15 miles south of the demilitarized zone.

Vietnam Air/Ground:
January 22–July 7, 1968

The air campaign in defense of Khe Sanh, an outpost held by the U.S. 26th Marine Regiment, began on January 22, 1968. For 2 and 1/2 months Allied tactical air forces continuously attacked targets surrounding the base, and B–52s dropped bombs near Khe Sanh on an average of every 90 minutes. At night AC–47 gunships provided illumination and close air support. Air Force and Marine airlifters, mostly C–130s, frequently landed under fire at the Khe Sanh airstrip, bringing in supplies and reinforcements and flying out the wounded and refugees. When the transports could no longer land because of intense mortar and artillery fire, their crews used parachutes and arrester cables to extract cargo from the aircraft as they flew a few feet above the ground over the airstrip. Beginning on March 6 the Seventh Air Force provided fighter escorts to suppress enemy fire and lay down smoke screens until the C–130s dropped their cargoes. Gen. William C. Westmoreland, MACV Commander, encountered difficulties coordinating the air resources of the USAF and U.S. Marines to meet both the military demands at Khe Sanh and the requirements introduced by the Tet Offensive that the North Vietnamese and Viet Cong launched on January 30, 1968. On March 8 he appointed the Seventh Air Force Commander, Gen. William W. Momyer, as Deputy Commander for Air Operations, MACV, to manage all tactical air resources in South Vietnam.

Late in March 1968 the North Vietnamese surrounding Khe Sanh withdrew, leaving only a single NVA division to oppose the Allied advance. On April 1 the 1st Marine regiment and the Army's 1st Cavalry Division moved along Route 9, relieving Khe Sanh 5 days later. On April 10, for the first time in 48 days, no shells fell on the base.

A week later, on April 19, the Allies mounted a helicopter-borne attack against A Shau Valley on the Laotian border, 30 miles southwest of Hue. The Viet Cong and NVA had built a vast stores and logistical base in this area since 1966. Preliminary USAF and Allied air strikes, including B–52 bombings between April 8 and 13, 1968, failed to clear the enemy from landing zones. In spite of the heavy resistance, on April 24 the U.S. Army seized the A Luoi airstrip at the northwest end of the valley. USAF transports airdropped supplies, often during bad weather and without tactical air support, because intense ground fire prevented the landing of C–130s until May 4. The

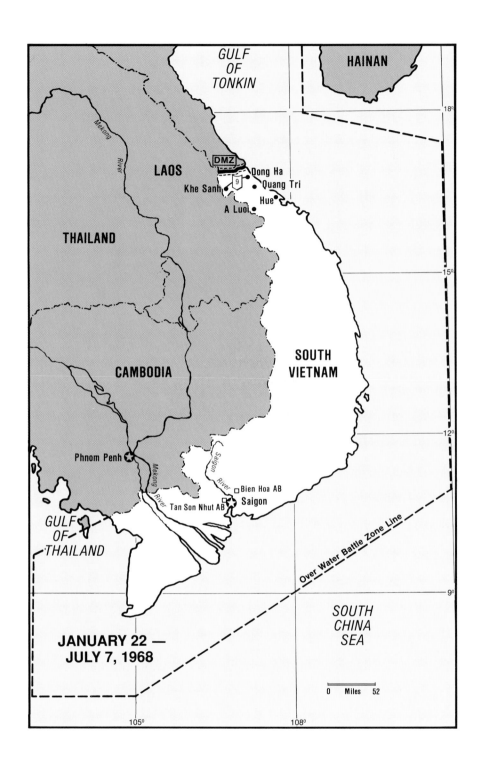

GULF OF TONKIN

HAINAN

18°

LAOS

DMZ

Dong Ha

Khe Sanh 9 Quang Tri

Hue

A Luoi

THAILAND

15°

Mekong River

CAMBODIA

SOUTH VIETNAM

12°

Phnom Penh

Saigon River

Bien Hoa AB

Mekong River

Tan Son Nhut AB Saigon

GULF OF THAILAND

Over Water Battle Zone Line

9°

SOUTH CHINA SEA

JANUARY 22 —
JULY 7, 1968

0   Miles   52

105°   108°

Viet Cong and North Vietnamese withdrew into Laos in mid-May, leaving behind large caches of weapons and supplies.

Earlier in the year, on January 30, the Viet Cong and North Vietnamese launched the Tet (Buddhist New Year) Offensive throughout South Vietnam in an effort to regain the political and military initiative that they had held 2 years previously. At Bien Hoa and Tan Son Nhut Air Bases, alert base defenders successfully repulsed initial attacks, but in the next 2 weeks the air bases came under frequent mortar and rocket attacks; in all, the USAF lost 14 aircraft on the ground and another 114 damaged. During the Tet Offensive, Seventh Air Force pilots provided close air support for Allied troops, and C–7s and C–130s hauled ammunition, supplies, and reinforcements to isolated areas. Within 2 or 3 days Allied forces cleared the Viet Cong troops from all cities except Saigon and Hue. By February 5 the Allies had driven the Viet Cong from Saigon, although a large force remained in the vicinity. North Vietnamese forces that had taken the old imperial city of Hue were more difficult to dislodge. The Seventh Air Force used close air support carefully to avoid indiscriminate and unwanted damage in Hue; AC–130 gunships that could deliver precise fire day or night provided the most effective support. On February 25 Allied forces succeeded in driving the enemy from the city. Although the Allies successfully and rapidly countered the Tet Offensive, the Communists gained a significant propaganda victory. Many Americans believed that a failure of U.S. military policy had permitted the Communists to mount so extensive a battle throughout South Vietnam.

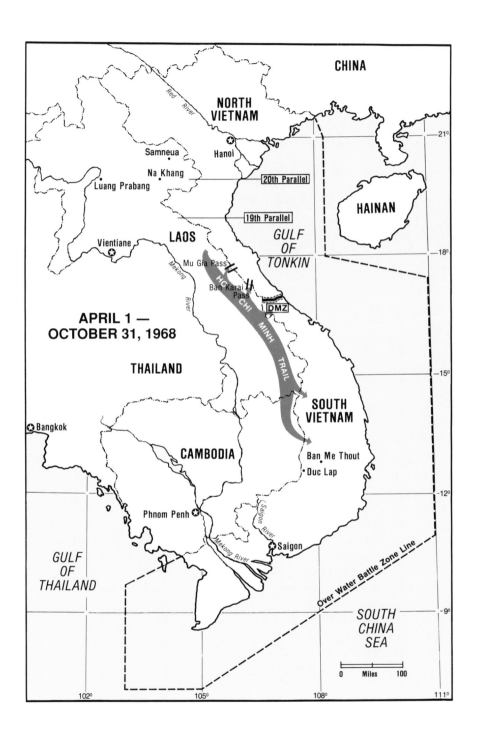

CHINA

NORTH
VIETNAM

Red River

Samneua

Hanoi

Na Khang

20th Parallel

HAINAN

Luang Prabang

19th Parallel

LAOS

GULF
OF
TONKIN

Vientiane

Mekong River

Mu Gia Pass

HO CHI MINH TRAIL

APRIL 1 —
OCTOBER 31, 1968

Ban Karai
Pass

DMZ

THAILAND

SOUTH
VIETNAM

Bangkok

CAMBODIA

Ban Me Thout

Duc Lap

Phnom Penh

Saigon River

GULF
OF
THAILAND

Mekong River

Saigon

Over Water Battle Zone Line

SOUTH
CHINA
SEA

0   Miles   100

21°

18°

15°

12°

9°

102°   105°   108°   111°

248

Vietnam Air Offensive, Phase III:
April 1–October 31, 1968

On April 1, 1968, the United States suspended bombing in North Vietnam north of the 20th parallel to encourage North Vietnam to agree to peace negotiations, which it did 2 days later. At that time, President Lyndon B. Johnson moved the bombing ban farther south to the 19th parallel. U.S. and North Vietnamese diplomats met in Vientiane, Laos, on April 25 to choose a site for the peace talks, and on May 3 they agreed to meet in Paris, France. Preliminary discussions between representatives of the United States and the Democratic Republic of Vietnam began in Paris on May 10. A month later, on June 11, Gen. Creighton Abrams, USA, became Commander of MACV. Then, on August 1, Gen. George S. Brown replaced General Momyer as Commander, Seventh Air Force.

On July 14, 1968, the U.S. began another interdiction campaign between the 19th parallel and the DMZ. American pilots struck rail cars, watercraft, trucks, and storage areas. They also bombed roads leading to Mu Gia and Ban Karai Passes on the Laotian border to disrupt movement of North Vietnamese supplies and personnel into Laos, destined for South Vietnam. Following the cessation of bombing north of the 19th parallel, North Vietnam began to rebuild its industry, transportation network, stores of war materiel, and air defenses. It also moved its MiGs, most of which had been based in China, back into the country. Still, North Vietnamese pilots generally avoided the panhandle south of the 19th parallel. Attempting to encourage progress in the Paris peace negotiations, President Johnson on October 31, 1968, ordered a halt to all bombing in North Vietnam.

The conflict in Laos became more active in 1968, as the Communists increased their efforts during April to send supplies, equipment, and personnel down the Ho Chi Minh Trail before the impending monsoon wet season (mid-May to early October) made the roads impassable. To counter this infiltration, between April 19 and June 10, B–52 crews, flying up to 30 sorties each day, bombed truck parks and storage areas along the trail. The Seventh Air Force, meantime, used its tactical assets to hit small targets, such as trucks and other surface traffic on the move, and to make follow-up raids on the B–52 targets along the Ho Chi Minh Trail. In northern Laos the USAF continued to provide close air support to Laotian troops battling the Pathet Lao and North Vietnamese forces. In May 1968 the enemy massed forces at Na Khang, 150 miles northeast of Vientiane and 100 miles east of

Luang Prabang. The USAF increased its close air support in the face of this threat, and by the end of October, the Laotians had driven the Communist forces back to Samneua, about 35 miles northeast of Na Khang.

In South Vietnam, during the summer of 1968, the USAF flew close air support, interdiction, and airlift missions in support of Allied forces, while the Communists launched another offensive. A typical Communist attack occurred on August 23 against Duc Lap, a border camp 3 miles east of Cambodia and 35 miles southwest of Ban Me Thuot, a town 160 miles northeast of Saigon. The next day the 483rd Tactical Airlift Wing's C–7s joined U.S. Army helicopters in resupplying and reinforcing Duc Lap. Heavy tactical air strikes drove the enemy from the camp's perimeter and suppressed enemy fire, permitting aerial resupply. To help check similar attacks, USAF tactical aircraft and B–52s provided close air support while airlifters flew in or airdropped supplies to several other Army Special Forces camps. The Viet Cong and North Vietnamese were not nearly as well equipped as they had been during the Tet Offensive, and by mid-September the Allies had blunted this offensive.

Vietnam Air Offensive, Phase IV: November 1, 1968–February 22, 1969

Following the cessation of bombing on October 31, 1968, the United States for the next 4 years restricted flights over North Vietnam primarily to reconnaissance missions. The Air Force diverted airpower resources committed to the campaign over North Vietnam to the air campaign in Laos, in an attempt to slow the flow of supplies from North Vietnam down the Ho Chi Minh Trail. This interdiction effort covered an area in the Laotian panhandle from about the 16th to the 18th parallel and focused on the Laotian/North Vietnamese border near the Keo Nua, Mu Gia, and Ban Karai Passes. Much information about targets on the Ho Chi Minh Trail came from air-dropped electronic sensors. When American bombing choked the major transportation arteries, the North Vietnamese directed truck convoys along secondary roads where they became more vulnerable to tactical air strikes. Throughout November and December 1968 U.S. tactical aircraft and B–52s attacked targets in the Laotian panhandle; AC–130 gunships, flying at night and relying on infrared, radar, and other sensors, proved especially effective in destroying trucks. To counter the intense air attacks, the North Vietnamese quadrupled the number of antiaircraft guns along the Ho Chi Minh Trail, while adding logistical personnel in Laos for repair work and transport duties.

The USAF also provided close air support to hard-pressed Royal and irregular Laotian forces in northern Laos, where, on December 25, North Vietnamese and Pathet Lao troops launched a strong offensive. By late February 1969 the enemy had driven the Laotian forces back across the Plain of Jars to Na Khang.

In South Vietnam, meanwhile, the Viet Cong suffered temporary setbacks under Allied air and ground attacks. On November 1, 1968, the Republic of Vietnam began a military and civic pacification program intended to bring most of the country quickly under government control. Two operations underscored Allied military approaches to pacification.

In the first, the Allies learned of a large enemy force moving into the Savy Rieng Province, Cambodia, the so-called "Parrot's Beak" that jutted deep into South Vietnam northwest of Saigon. To thwart this penetration, between October 18 and November 11, 1968, the U.S. Air Force airlifted 11,500 men of the U.S. 1st Cavalry Division and 3,400 tons of cargo in C–130s over 500 miles from Quang Tri Prov-

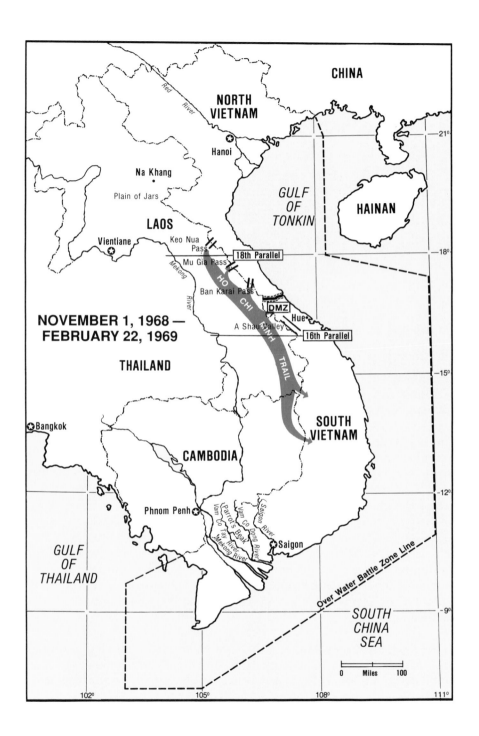

CHINA

NORTH
VIETNAM

Red River

Hanoi

Na Khang

Plain of Jars

LAOS

Vientiane

Keo Nua Pass

Mu Gia Pass

18th Parallel

GULF
OF
TONKIN

HAINAN

21°

18°

Ban Karai Pass

Mekong River

HO CHI MINH TRAIL

DMZ

Hue

16th Parallel

NOVEMBER 1, 1968 —
FEBRUARY 22, 1969

A Shau Valley

THAILAND

Bangkok

15°

CAMBODIA

SOUTH
VIETNAM

Phnom Penh

Vam Co Tay River

Parrot's Beak

Vam Co Dong River

Saigon River

Mekong River

Saigon

12°

GULF
OF
THAILAND

Over Water Battle Zone Line

SOUTH
CHINA
SEA

9°

0   Miles   100

102°   105°   108°   111°

ince in the north to Tay Ninh, Binh Long, and Phuoc Long Provinces, northwest of Saigon. Until the turn of the year, these U.S. Army forces, working with the South Vietnamese, conducted operations in the Cambodian/South Vietnamese border area along the Parrot's Beak, between the Vam Co Tay and Vam Co Dong Rivers. The USAF supported these operations with tactical aircraft and B–52s flying air support and interdiction missions against troop concentrations, base areas, logistics complexes, and transportation lines. In the second major winter operation, starting the first week of December, the Seventh Air Force launched another air campaign in the A Shau Valley, located near the Cambodian border some 30 miles southwest of Hue. Afterward, in January 1969, U.S. Marines entered the valley and found large amounts of materiel that the Communists had abandoned, unable to move it during the sustained air attacks.

After months of negotiations, on January 18, 1969, representatives of the government of South Vietnam and of the National Liberation Front, the Communist political branch in South Vietnam, joined the United States and North Vietnam in the Paris peace talks. While negotiations continued in France, the Communist forces in Vietnam launched their first offensive of the new year.

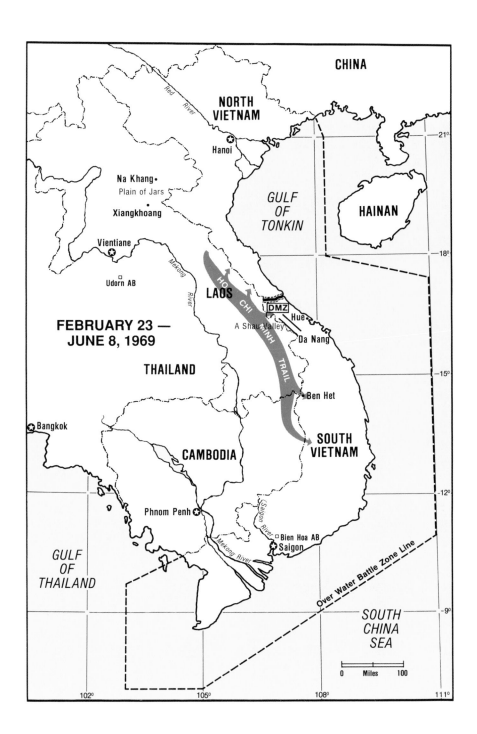

CHINA

NORTH
VIETNAM

Hanoi

Red River

Na Khang•
Plain of Jars
• Xiangkhoang

GULF
OF
TONKIN

HAINAN

Vientiane

Udorn AB

LAOS

Mekong River

DMZ

Hue

A Shau Valley

Da Nang

FEBRUARY 23 —
JUNE 8, 1969

THAILAND

HO CHI MINH TRAIL

Ben Het

Bangkok

CAMBODIA

SOUTH
VIETNAM

Phnom Penh

Saigon River

Bien Hoa AB
Saigon

Mekong River

GULF
OF
THAILAND

Over Water Battle Zone Line

SOUTH
CHINA
SEA

0   Miles   100

102°   105°   108°   111°

254

Tet 69/Counteroffensive:
February 23–June 8, 1969

On February 23, 1969, the Viet Cong and North Vietnamese launched mortar and rocket attacks on Saigon, Da Nang, Hue, Bien Hoa Air Base, and other key targets throughout South Vietnam. In this offensive, Communist forces relied heavily on the use of stand-off firepower in hit-and-run attacks, since, in the previous year's offensives, Allied ground operations and air interdiction efforts had countered the Communists' logistical capacity to wage conventional battles. By March 30 the Allies had blunted the hit-and-run attacks, and the enemy withdrew into Cambodian and Laotian sanctuaries to restock their munitions and weapons inventories.

Later in the spring, on May 12, the Viet Cong and North Vietnamese launched a second phase, consisting of more than 200 attacks in South Vietnam, the heaviest assault since the 1968 Tet Offensive. An intense battle in the A Shau Valley required USAF close air support and tactical airlift of supplies and reinforcements until May 20, when the U.S. Army captured Ap Bia Mountain, thus enabling Allied aircraft to land in the A Shau Valley without receiving mortar fire. Another significant battle occurred at Ben Het Defense Camp, located about 260 miles northeast of Saigon, where the Cambodian/Laotian borders join the boundary of South Vietnam. Here, the USAF employed AC–47 and AC–119 gunships at night and tactical air and B–52 strikes during the day in support of the defenders. Fighter aircraft laid down suppressive fire to permit C–7s to drop supplies to the besieged forces. By the end of June the Allies had forced the enemy's withdrawal.

Throughout this campaign, the USAF joined the Vietnamese Air Force and the other U.S. services in close air support of Allied forces throughout South Vietnam and in a continuing interdiction campaign, COMMANDO HUNT I, along South Vietnam's borders with Laos and Cambodia. In Laos Air Force pilots joined Navy aviators to hit targets along the Ho Chi Minh Trail, where North Vietnam, no longer having to protect its lines of communication and storage areas north of the demilitarized zone, had shifted more antiaircraft defenses. The USAF consequently relied heavily on high-flying B–52s and such fast tactical aircraft as F–4s and F–105s for most missions over the trail. AC–130 gunships, though flying less than 4 percent of the missions in Laos, nevertheless accounted in the spring of 1969 for 44 percent of the trucks claimed damaged or destroyed.

In northeastern Laos AC–47 gunships provided close air support to Royal Laotian and irregular forces battling North Vietnamese and Pathet Lao troops. On March 2, 1969, the Royal Laotian forces abandoned Na Khang under cover of USAF aircraft. Then on the 12th the USAF deployed AC–47s to Udorn, a Royal Thai Air Force Base 40 miles south of Vientiane, Laos, to defend forward Royal Laotian air bases. The USAF and the Royal Laotian Air Force on March 23 began a new Laotian counteroffensive with air attacks on targets in the Xiangkhoang area of the Plain of Jars, 100 miles northeast of Vientiane. Two weeks later, on April 7, Laotian troops entered Xiangkhoang virtually unopposed. With Laotian positions temporarily safe, the USAF AC–47s returned to South Vietnam on June 9.

American involvement in Southeast Asia expanded on March 18, 1969, when the United States began B–52 night attacks on Communist sanctuaries in Cambodia. About the same time, however, the U.S. began to reequip South Vietnam's forces in preparation for eventual withdrawal of all American forces. On April 19 the U.S. transferred to the VNAF its first jet aircraft. Shortly afterwards, on June 8, President Richard M. Nixon announced that during July and August 1969 the United States would withdraw 25,000 of its 540,000 troops in South Vietnam, even though no progress had been made in the Paris peace talks.

Vietnam Summer/Fall 1969:
June 9–October 31, 1969

In the summer of 1969 Communist military action in South Vietnam temporarily decreased. On July 2, following the siege on Ben Het, Viet Cong and North Vietnamese forces withdrew into Laos. Defenders at Ben Het credited air power, especially B–52s that bombed concentrations of troops, with preventing the enemy from capturing the camp. On August 12, however, a new enemy offensive began; Communist forces attacked over 100 cities, towns, and military installations in South Vietnam with mortars, rockets, and, in a few cases, infantry. During the next month, between September 15 and October 20, the Seventh Air Force flew close air support against Viet Cong and North Vietnamese forces that attempted unsuccessfully to take a camp near Duc Lap, about 160 miles northeast of Saigon and 3 miles east of the Cambodian border.

Meanwhile, South Vietnam intensified its pacification program, and the United States began withdrawing its military forces. The first U.S. troops left the country on July 8, 1969, and in August the USAF reduced the number of tactical air and B–52 sorties flown daily in South Vietnam. Two F–100 tactical fighter squadrons and a B–57 tactical bomber squadron left South Vietnam during October, and the United States transferred to the VNAF operation of the air base at Nha Trang, located on the coast about 200 miles northeast of Saigon.

During the summer and fall of 1969, on the Plain of Jars in Laos, the USAF provided close air support to Royal Laotian and irregular forces continuing to fight the Pathet Lao and North Vietnamese. On June 24 the Communists attacked Muong Soui, a town 110 miles north of Vientiane and about 45 miles southeast of Luang Prabang. U.S. Army helicopters, protected by tactical aircraft, evacuated the Laotian troops from Muong Soui on June 27, and 4 days later Laotian government forces counterattacked with the aid of USAF close air support. The advance stalled on July 8, however, when the weather deteriorated and few tactical fighter sorties could be flown. When the weather improved in late August, the Laotians renewed their offensive, supported by 200 USAF tactical air sorties daily. On September 12 Laotian forces captured Xiangkhoang and on September 27 they re-entered Muong Soui.

In the panhandle of Laos, the USAF continued its interdiction campaign, COMMANDO HUNT II, concentrating on an area near the Ban Hieng River

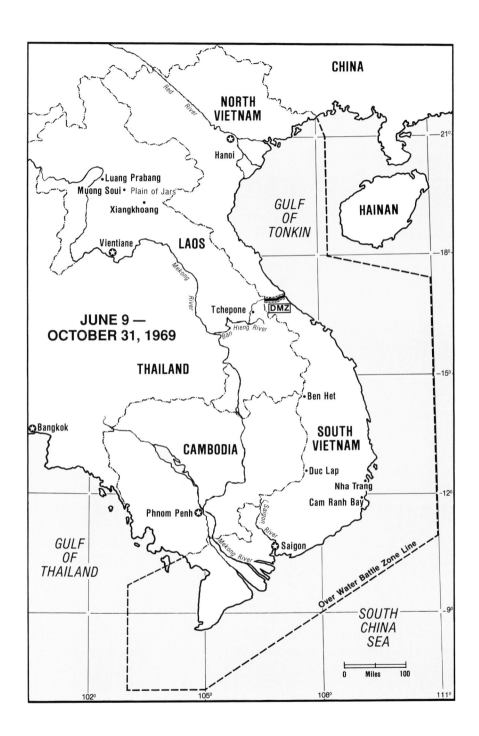

CHINA

NORTH
VIETNAM

Red River

Hanoi

Luang Prabang
Muong Soui · Plain of Jars
Xiangkhoang

Vientiane

LAOS

GULF
OF
TONKIN

HAINAN

Mekong River

JUNE 9 —
OCTOBER 31, 1969

Tchepone

DMZ

Ban Hieng River

THAILAND

Ben Het

Bangkok

CAMBODIA

SOUTH
VIETNAM

Duc Lap
Nha Trang
Cam Ranh Bay

Phnom Penh

Saigon River

Mekong River

Saigon

GULF
OF
THAILAND

Over Water Battle Zone Line

SOUTH
CHINA
SEA

0   Miles   100

21°

18°

15°

12°

9°

102°   105°   108°   111°

258

running from the DMZ in Vietnam southwest about 25 miles to Tchepone, Laos, 400 miles north of Saigon. The North Vietnamese used the river and its tributaries to transport supplies from the demilitarized zone into Laos. Strong antiaircraft batteries along the river protected storage and transshipment points, petroleum pipelines, and roads used to move supplies, personnel, and equipment into South Vietnam. The USAF flew tactical air and B–52 missions against this network during the day and gunship missions at night to destroy much of the materiel the enemy attempted to move.

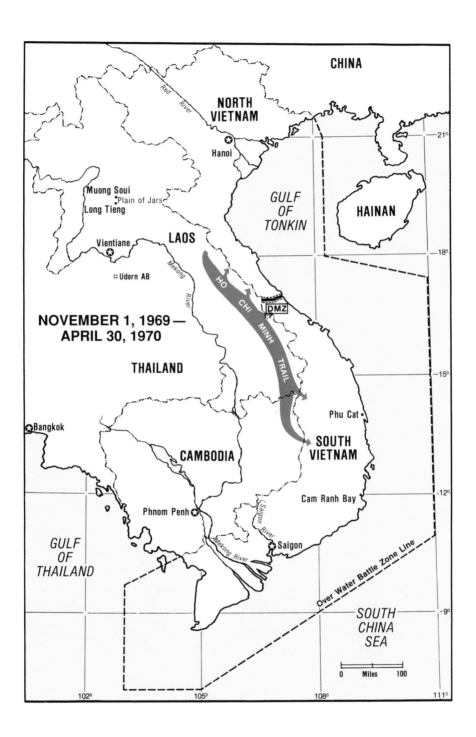

CHINA

NORTH
VIETNAM

Red River

Hanoi

Muong Soui
Plain of Jars
Long Tieng

GULF
OF
TONKIN

HAINAN

Vientiane

LAOS

□ Udorn AB

Mekong River

HO CHI MINH TRAIL

DMZ

**NOVEMBER 1, 1969 —
APRIL 30, 1970**

THAILAND

Phu Cat •

Bangkok

CAMBODIA

SOUTH
VIETNAM

Cam Ranh Bay

Phnom Penh

Saigon River

Mekong River

Saigon

GULF
OF
THAILAND

Over Water Battle Zone Line

SOUTH
CHINA
SEA

0   Miles   100

102°   105°   108°   111°

260

Vietnam Winter/Spring 1970: November 1, 1969–April 30, 1970

While Viet Cong and North Vietnamese military activity in South Vietnam continued at a low level and U.S. forces gradually withdrew, the Republic of Vietnam re-equipped and modernized its armed forces in a program called "Vietnamization." To meet the VNAF's needs for trained personnel, the USAF in the fall of 1969 began training programs both in South Vietnam and the United States. On December 1, 1969, the AC–47 gunships flew their last combat missions as U.S. aircraft; subsequently, the United States transferred the AC–47s to the VNAF and the Royal Laotian Air Force (RLAF). A few weeks later, on January 22, 1970, the U.S. Air Force began transferring to the VNAF the Tactical Air Control System that handled air defense, tactical attacks, and air traffic control in South Vietnam. On March 15 the USAF inactivated the 37th Tactical Fighter Wing at Phu Cat, an air base on the coast 250 miles northeast of Saigon, and the 12th Tactical Fighter Wing at Cam Ranh Bay, 180 miles northeast of Saigon. The USAF began withdrawing civil engineering units in April.

The USAF might reduce its forces and operations in South Vietnam, but other events prompted increased U.S. involvement in Laos. On November 1, 1969, with the onset of another dry season, the USAF began another intensive air campaign, COMMANDO HUNT III, in the Laotian panhandle to counter an increasing flow southwards of enemy troops and supplies. The 14th Special Operations Wing's AC–119 and AC–130 gunships, although only flying a small number of the total sorties along the Ho Chi Minh Trail, accounted for almost half of the destroyed or damaged trucks. Meanwhile, tactical air and B–52 aircrews focused on area targets and antiaircraft positions.

While the USAF effort in the Laotian panhandle focused on interdiction, aerial action in northern Laos involved close air support. In January 1970 the Pathet Lao and North Vietnamese mounted a major offensive against Royal Laotian forces. On January 4 the Seventh Air Force sent a helicopter squadron to Long Tieng, an airstrip 100 miles north of Vientiane, for operations around Muong Soui. It also dispatched AC–119K gunships to Udorn Air Base, Thailand, on February 15 to provide armed reconnaissance along major roads in northern Laos and close air support for Laotian forward bases. Two days later, in an effort to slow the enemy advance, the USAF used B–52s against North Vietnamese and Pathet Lao positions in northern Laos. Despite the intense air attacks, the Communist forces captured Muong Soui on February 24 and, advancing over the Plain of Jars, by March 17 threatened Long Tieng. The Seventh Air Force helped fly in reinforcements of Thai and Laotian troops to Long Tieng and evacuated refugees, while its tactical aircraft provided close air support to the beleaguered troops. By March 30 the Pathet Lao and North Vietnamese forces once again had retreated, and Long Tieng appeared safe, at least until the next dry season.

The North Vietnamese and Viet Cong for many years had used Cambodia as a sanctuary with relative impunity, although the USAF as early as March 1969 bombed targets in Cambodia with B–52s. Then, in March 1970, a new Cambodian government challenged the Communist military presence. The Communists reacted with a military campaign against Cambodian forces. As the conflict escalated, on April 20 Cambodian Premier Lon Nol formally sought U.S. aid. On the 24th the USAF began flying tactical missions against enemy targets in Cambodia, and 5 days later, the ARVN entered Cambodia to destroy enemy bases and supplies and assist Cambodian troops fighting the Communists.

Sanctuary Counteroffensive:
May 1–June 30, 1970

The U.S. Army 1st Cavalry Division, supported by USAF airlift and tactical air forces, on May 1, 1970, swept into the Parrot's Beak, the Cambodian salient west of Saigon. On May 6 U.S. troops also moved into the so-called Fishhook area of the Cambodian border, near the town of Phuoc Binh, about 75 miles north of Saigon.

During the incursion, the 834th Air Division delivered supplies initially at Katum, some 55 miles northwest of Saigon, at Loc Ninh, about 65 miles northwest of Saigon, and later at Bu Dop, 80 miles north of Saigon. When other landing sites were unavailable, the airlifters used Song Be, an all-weather strip 15 miles east of the border, on the outskirts of Phuoc Binh. USAF C–130 and C–7 transports also flew cargo and troops to the northern front, landing primarily at Plei Djereng, 10 miles from the border and about 15 miles west of Pleiku, a provincial capital 215 miles northeast of Saigon. From June 23 to 25, USAF C–123s evacuated civilian refugees from the Cambodian towns of Ba Kev, about 45 miles southwest of Pleiku, and Buong Long, 14 miles further west. The 834th Air Division, from May 1 to June 30, delivered 75,000 people and 49,600 tons of cargo to forward areas in support of the Cambodian Sanctuary Counteroffensive.

Meanwhile, Seventh Air Force provided close air support and flew river and road convoy escort to permit the reinforcement of troops in the field and the movement of supplies to the Cambodian capital of Phnom Penh. B–52s bombed enemy base sites and troop concentrations beyond the 18-mile limit inside the Cambodian border that restricted the deployment of ground forces and tactical aircraft. By June 30, 1970, B–52s had flown 763 sorties against enemy targets in Cambodia. During the Cambodian incursion, the Allies surprised the Viet Cong and North Vietnamese forces and destroyed or captured significant quantities of weapons, vehicles, and other supplies. Air power helped ensure the success of the campaign, and the USAF continued to fly missions over Cambodia after Allied ground forces withdrew on June 29, 1970.

Shortly after the Cambodian counteroffensive began, Communist forces sharply increased their attacks in South Vietnam. On May 8, 1970, the Viet Cong shelled 64 bases and towns, and North Vietnamese troops attacked several ARVN camps near the DMZ. The battle in Cambodia also spread into Laos, and on May 13 Pathet Lao and North Vietnamese troops attacked Royal Laotian forces on the Bolovens Plateau. On June

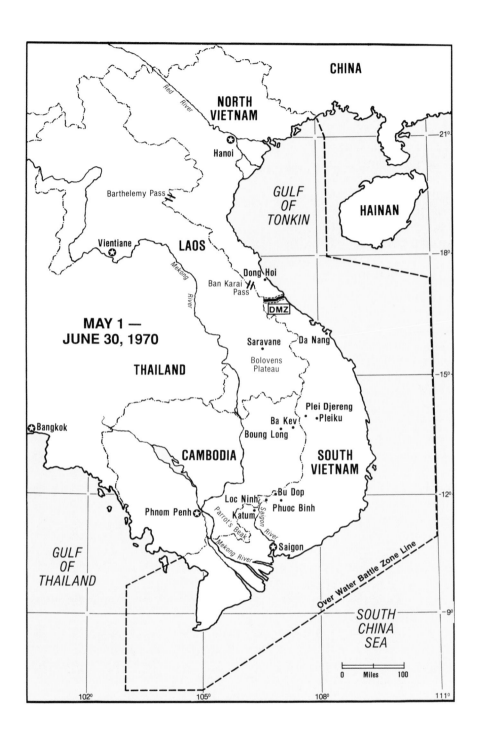

CHINA

NORTH
VIETNAM

Red River

⊛ Hanoi

GULF
OF
TONKIN

HAINAN

21°

Barthelemy Pass

Vientiane ✪

LAOS

Mekong River

Dong Hoi

Ban Karai
Pass

DMZ

18°

MAY 1 —
JUNE 30, 1970

Saravane

Da Nang

Bolovens
Plateau

THAILAND

15°

Plei Djereng
• Pleiku
Ba Kev •
Boung Long

✪ Bangkok

CAMBODIA

SOUTH
VIETNAM

• Bu Dop

Loc Ninh
Katum

Phuoc Binh

12°

Phnom Penh ✪

Parrot's Beak

Saigon River

Mekong River

✪ Saigon

GULF
OF
THAILAND

Over Water Battle Zone Line

SOUTH
CHINA
SEA

9°

0   Miles   100

102°   105°   108°   111°

264

9 the enemy captured the provincial capital of Saravane, in the Laotian panhandle, but withdrew 3 days later. Despite increasingly effective enemy antiaircraft fire, the USAF continued interdiction missions in southern Laos.

Although the United States had limited its flying activities over North Vietnam to reconnaissance after the bombing cessation of 1968, these missions resumed in 1970. Between May 1 and 4 almost 500 U.S. tactical aircraft attacked missile sites, antiaircraft guns, and logistics facilities near Barthelemy and Ban Karai Passes and Dong Hoi, a sea-coast town about 40 miles north of the DMZ.* In Paris, meanwhile, the peace talks continued intermittently; Communist delegates frequently boycotted sessions on various pretexts. For example, the Communists boycotted the session on May 6, 1970, protesting the renewed bombing of North Vietnam.

---

*These were the first aerial attacks against North Vietnam since the November 1968 bombing halt. The United States conducted such raids occasionally until, in April 1972, it resumed sustained and intensive bombing of North Vietnam.

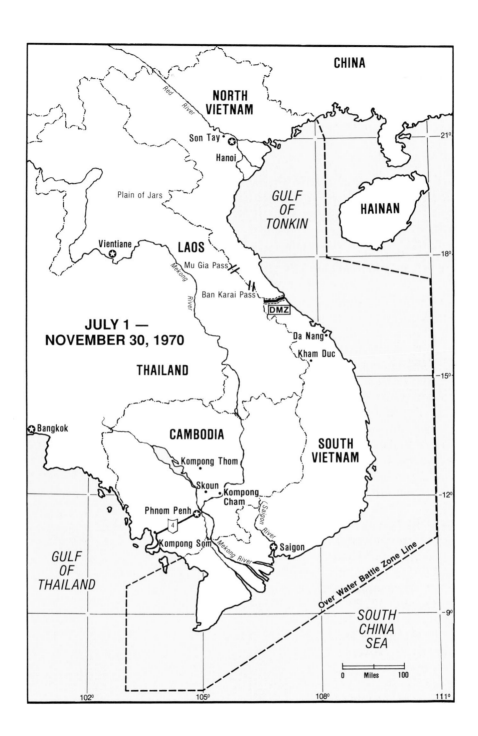

CHINA

NORTH
VIETNAM

Red River

Son Tay •
Hanoi

Plain of Jars

GULF
OF
TONKIN

HAINAN

Vientiane
LAOS

Mekong River

Mu Gia Pass

Ban Karai Pass

DMZ

Da Nang •
Kham Duc •

JULY 1 —
NOVEMBER 30, 1970

THAILAND

CAMBODIA

Bangkok

Kompong Thom

Skoun
Kompong
Cham

Phnom Penh

4

Kompong Som

Mekong River

Saigon River

Saigon

SOUTH
VIETNAM

Over Water Battle Zone Line

GULF
OF
THAILAND

SOUTH
CHINA
SEA

0   Miles   100

266

Southwest Monsoon:
July 1–November 30, 1970

Throughout the summer and fall of 1970, USAF aircraft flew interdiction and close air support missions in Cambodia to help ensure that the major towns and cities stayed in friendly hands. Gunships proved especially effective in defending Phnom Penh, the Cambodian capital; the town of Kompong Chom, 50 miles to the northeast; and Kompong Thom, about 65 miles north of the capital. On August 8 Cambodian troops, backed by USAF close air support, drove North Vietnamese forces from Skoun, an important highway junction between Kompong Thom and Phnom Penh. Despite these efforts, Communist forces controlled about half of Cambodia by November and kept the highway closed between Phnom Penh and the seaport of Kompong Som, 100 miles to the southwest. The Cambodians had to resupply Phnom Penh and their troops by transporting goods up the Mekong River, and Allied aircraft escorted the river convoys to protect the ships from attack.

The chaotic military situation in Cambodia during 1970 closely resembled the one to the north in Laos. With the coming of another wet season, Laotian forces began 2 new offensives in an effort to wrest control of the Plain of Jars from the Pathet Lao and the North Vietnamese. The first offensive occurred between August 2 and 23 and the second from August 31 to October 23. The Communist forces retreated slowly to the southeast rim of the plain, inflicting heavy losses on the Royal and irregular Laotian forces. During the Laotian offensives, the USAF provided close air support and continued to attack supply routes in both the northern and southern parts of the country.

In South Vietnam, the withdrawal of U.S. forces gained momentum. The USAF redeployed the 31st Tactical Fighter Wing to the United States in September 1970 and inactivated or redeployed several of its A–1, A–37, and F–105 squadrons. Meanwhile, on September 1, Gen. Lucius D. Clay, Jr., assumed command of the Seventh Air Force. Six weeks later, on October 12, President Richard M. Nixon announced that the U.S. would withdraw 40,000 more troops from South Vietnam by December 1, 1970, leaving about 335,000 military personnel in the country. Subsequently, in November, the USAF redeployed 2 tactical reconnaissance squadrons from South Vietnam to the United States.

Whatever the rate of U.S. disengagement, intense fighting continued. The Allies mounted a heliborne, multi-brigade operation between July 12 and August 26 to disrupt Communist transportation networks in the mountainous border area near the Kham Duc airstrip, only 55 miles southwest of Da Nang. Allied ground forces received extensive close air and airlift support from the Seventh Air Force, but reported few contacts with the enemy.

Later in the year, on November 21, the USAF and the U.S. Army attempted to rescue U.S. prisoners of war believed held at Son Tay, a prison camp 20 miles northwest of Hanoi. Two C–130s led a rescue force of helicopters and A–1 aircraft from bases in Thailand to Son Tay, while F–105Fs suppressed North Vietnamese surface-to-air missiles. The C–130s illuminated the prison compound and marked targets for the A-1s' suppressive fire while 1 helicopter crash landed in the compound and the rest landed outside. The raiders found no POWs and withdrew without loss of personnel, although the helicopter in the compound was blown up and 1 F–105F was destroyed by enemy fire.

A few hours after the Son Tay raid, some 200 U.S. tactical aircraft, sup–ported by 50 other airplanes, bombed SAM sites, antiaircraft gunsites, and supply and transport facilities in North Vietnam near the Mu Gia and the Ban Karai Passes, and in the DMZ. Within a few days, on November 25, 1970, the North Vietnamese and Viet Cong delegation again boycotted the Paris peace negotiations.

COMMANDO HUNT V: December 1, 1970–May 14, 1971

On December 1, 1970, the USAF began another interdiction campaign named COMMANDO HUNT V, the third so-named dry season campaign in as many years.* In Commando Hunt V, the USAF attacks focused on the Laotian panhandle, although tactical aircraft periodically struck targets in northern Laos and Cambodia. B–52s and fighter-bombers hit the passes between North Vietnam and Laos, creating chokepoints that forced the North Vietnamese to channel traffic and reinforcements moving southward so that gunships, B–57G bombers, and other tactical aircraft could more easily destroy them. The IGLOO WHITE automated system of sensors that the USAF airdropped along the Ho Chi Minh Trail was designed to aid in the location of trucks and other moving targets.

The South Vietnamese and U.S. military leaders intended this aerial campaign to prevent a sustained enemy offensive in South Vietnam, thus giving the Republic of Vietnam more time to equip with modern weapons and train its armed forces. To that end, between January 30 and March 24, 1971, the ARVN entered Laos near Khe Sanh, 15 miles south of the DMZ. The Allies in this operation, code-named LAM SON 719, hoped to cut a segment of the Ho Chi Minh Trail and capture Tchepone, the hub of the Communists' logistics system in Laos. From February 8 to March 24 the USAF supported Lam Son 719 by airlifting South Vietnamese troops and supplies into Khe Sanh, flying tactical air strikes in Laos, and furnishing forward air control (FAC) in the battle area.

On March 7, 1971, the Army of the Republic of Vietnam reached Tchepone; however, North Vietnamese forces inflicted such heavy casualties that South Vietnamese commanders were forced to withdraw 3 days later. The USAF then covered U.S. Army helicopters evacuating ARVN troops with heavy tactical air and B–52 attacks. By March 24 the last ARVN troops returned to South Vietnam, but they had abandoned large quantities of military hardware, including trucks and tanks, during the evacuation. In spite of the ARVN's chaotic withdrawal, the North Vietnamese army also suffered heavy losses and did not begin another major offensive in South Vietnam for almost a year.

---

*COMMANDO HUNT I and III were the previous dry season (October–May) interdiction campaigns. COMMANDO HUNT II and IV applied to operations during the rainy seasons (June–September).

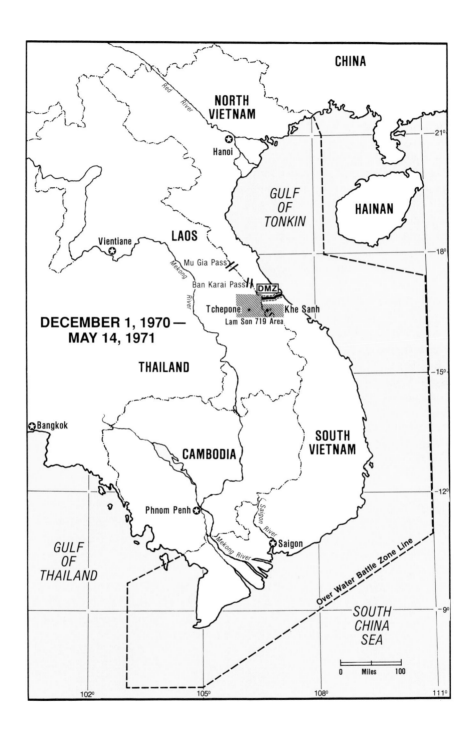

CHINA

NORTH VIETNAM

Red River

⊗ Hanoi

GULF
OF
TONKIN

HAINAN

LAOS

Vientiane ⊗

Mu Gia Pass

Mekong River

Ban Karai Pass

DMZ

Tchepone · · ⊛ Khe Sanh

Lam Son 719 Area

**DECEMBER 1, 1970 —
MAY 14, 1971**

THAILAND

21°

18°

15°

12°

9°

⊕ Bangkok

CAMBODIA

SOUTH
VIETNAM

Phnom Penh ⊕

Saigon River

Mekong River

⊕ Saigon

GULF
OF
THAILAND

Over Water Battle Zone Line

SOUTH
CHINA
SEA

0 Miles 100

102°   105°   108°   111°

270

The COMMANDO HUNT V campaign saw the first extensive use of 2 new USAF weapons: laser-guided bombs and "daisy cutter" bombs. On February 3, 1971, F–4s equipped with laser-seeker pods and laser-guided bombs destroyed a 37-mm antiaircraft site along the Ho Chi Minh Trail. Then, on February 19, F–4 pilots used this weapon to destroy 2 trucks. On March 3 the Seventh Air Force used laser-guided bombs to destroy tanks that had been spotted near Tchepone. The USAF now had the means to hit accurately small targets on the first try. During LAM SON 719, the USAF also used large, high-explosive "daisy cutter" bombs (up to 15,000 pounds) to clear landing zones for helicopters. These bombs, extracted by parachute from C–130s, exploded a few feet above the ground and cleared enough area in the jungle for 1 or 2 helicopters to land. The ordnance allowed engineers to establish suitable landing zones quickly in enemy territory and contributed substantially to the rapid movement of troops into and out of Laos.

All the while, the war raged in other regions of Southeast Asia. From January through April 1971, the USAF launched numerous retaliatory strikes against surface-to-air missile and antiaircraft sites in North Vietnam, and USAF pilots also frequently flew close air support missions in Cambodia and northern Laos. Meantime, on February 18 the North Vietnamese delegation once again boycotted the Paris peace talks, although on April 8 it reappeared to resume negotiations.

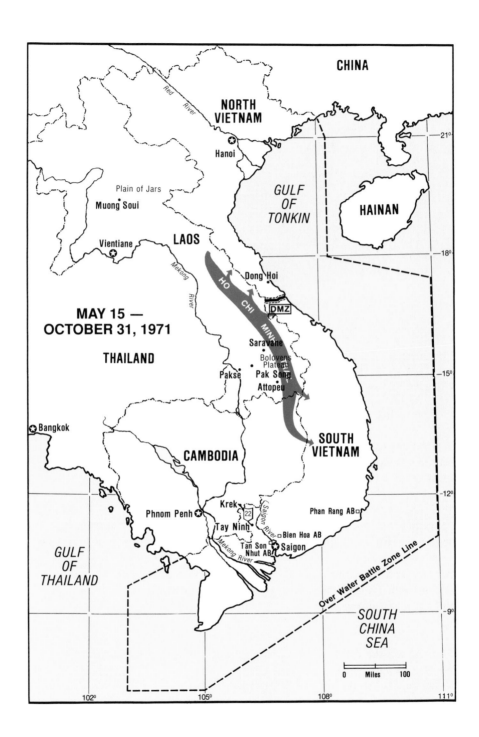

MAY 15 —
OCTOBER 31, 1971

CHINA

NORTH
VIETNAM

Red River

Hanoi

Plain of Jars

Muong Soui

Vientiane

LAOS

Mekong River

THAILAND

Bangkok

Pakse

Saravane

Bolovens
Plateau

Pak Song

Attopeu

GULF
OF
TONKIN

HAINAN

Dong Hoi

DMZ

HO CHI MINH

SOUTH
VIETNAM

CAMBODIA

Phnom Penh

Krek

22

Saigon River

Tay Ninh

Tan Son
Nhut AB

Saigon

Bien Hoa AB

Phan Rang AB

Mekong River

GULF
OF
THAILAND

Over Water Battle Zone Line

SOUTH
CHINA
SEA

0   Miles   100

21°

18°

15°

12°

9°

102°   105°   108°   111°

272

COMMANDO HUNT VI:
May 15–October 31, 1971

During the wet season from May to October 1971, when bad weather restricted air attacks along the Ho Chi Minh Trail in Laos, North Vietnamese troops lengthened and improved roads and added to their air defenses. For the first time, they installed surface-to-air missile sites in Laos. Meanwhile, the USAF flew as many interdiction missions in the Laotian panhandle as weather permitted.

Allied pilots also supported Royal Laotian forces struggling to hold the Bolovens Plateau, an area in the panhandle encompassing the towns of Saravane, 315 miles southeast of Vientiane; Pakse, 60 miles southwest of Saravane; and Attopeu, about 65 miles southeast of Saravane. On May 17, 1971, the North Vietnamese took the last Laotian positions on the Bolovens Plateau; Royal Laotian forces subsequently began an offensive to recapture the area. On July 28 they recaptured Saravane and began an advance on Pak Song, a hamlet some 30 miles east of Pakse and 35 miles south of Saravane. The Laotians recaptured Pak Song on September 14. The royal forces were successful despite the fact that poor weather and lack of coordination between the Laotian government and the Seventh Air Force combined to limit the U.S. role to occasional close air support and the airlift of some troops and supplies.

In northern Laos the Seventh Air Force also aided Royal and irregular Laotian troops which recaptured most of the Plain of Jars during the summer of 1971. Unfortunately, the Pathet Lao and North Vietnamese remained entrenched on the northern and eastern rims. On September 26 the Laotians recaptured their former base at Muong Soui. Then, in mid-September, as the roads dried, the Pathet Lao and North Vietnamese began moving men and supplies from North Vietnam into northern Laos preparatory to a new offensive. To counter this threat, USAF tactical aircraft flew interdiction and close air support missions during the day, and at night AC–130 and AC–119 gunships flew armed reconnaissance and close air support missions for the Laotian government and irregular forces.

Throughout the fall of 1971 the USAF also conducted periodic raids on North Vietnam. For example, on September 21 almost 200 fighter-bombers, escorted by 50 other aircraft, dropped bombs on petroleum and logistical storage areas and military barracks near Dong Hoi. The bombers, using all-weather tactics and equipment, achieved excellent results despite the poor weather. The all-weather tactics, based on the use of advanced electronic equipment for navigation and target selection, would serve the USAF well in subsequent missions against North Vietnam.

In Cambodia the USAF flew frequent interdiction missions and occasional close air support missions. On June 2, 1971, U.S. bombers and helicopters struck Communist troop concentrations to forestall an imminent invasion of South Vietnam. The ARVN reentered Cambodia on September 20, as it had done a number of times since June 1970. This time the troops cleared the road between Tay Ninh, South Vietnam, 50 miles northwest of Saigon, and Krek, Cambodia, about 30 miles northwest of Tay Ninh and 70 miles east of Phnom Penh, capital of Cambodia. The USAF supported this operation with tactical air strikes and B–52 missions.

During COMMANDO HUNT VI, U.S. forces continued to withdraw from South Vietnam. On July 12, 1971, the 35th Tactical Fighter Wing inactivated at Phan Rang Air Base, on the coast 160 miles northeast of Saigon. The Seventh Air Force received a new Commander, Gen. John D. Lavelle, on August 1. The 460th Tactical Reconnaissance Wing inactivated at Tan Son Nhut Air Base in Saigon on the last day of the month. Shortly afterwards the USAF transferred operation of Bien Hoa Air Base to the Vietnamese Air Force, and on September 20 the 14th Special Operations Wing inactivated at Phan Rang. The VNAF, meantime, activated several squadrons to operate aircraft received from the USAF, such as the AC–119 gunship, and to perform new functions, such as airlifting fuel from 1 locale to another. By October 31, 1971, less than 200,000 U.S. troops remained in South Vietnam.

Commando Hunt VII:
November 1, 1971–March 29, 1972

With the onset of the dry season, the USAF began another air interdiction campaign on November 1, 1971. Commando Hunt VII was primarily directed against enemy traffic over the Ho Chi Minh Trail in Laos, although USAF pilots also flew missions in South Vietnam and Cambodia. The campaign consisted of 3 phases. First, U.S. pilots bombed the Mu Gia and Ban Karai Passes, entry points from North Vietnam into Laos. In phase 2, tactical aircraft attacked chokepoints on key transportation routes, bombing or strafing stalled trucks and full storage sites. Phase 3 began in early 1972, when the Air Force shifted air strikes, including B–52 bombing, to entry points between Laos and South Vietnam. During the 5-month interdiction campaign, B–52s and AC–130s hit enemy traffic at night, while during the day tactical fighters bombed and strafed trucks and other targets of opportunity. From November 1971 through March 1972, U.S. aircraft damaged or destroyed an estimated 10,000 trucks in the Laotian panhandle and about 1,500 more in northeastern Laos.

Besides the interdiction missions along the Ho Chi Minh Trail, USAF pilots flew close air support sorties for Laotian forces now under increasing pressure from the enemy on the Bolovens Plateau and the Plain of Jars. On November 25 Royal Laotian troops held most of the Bolovens Plateau, but within 2 weeks, on December 6, the North Vietnamese once again drove the Laotian forces from Saravane, on the northern edge of the plateau. On January 3, 1972, Pak Song, a town 35 miles south of Saravane, fell to advancing Communist troops, and by January 11 the Bolovens Plateau was in the hands of the Communists. In northern Laos, on December 18, 1971, the Pathet Lao and North Vietnamese forces mounted a major offensive on the Plain of Jars and on January 31, 1972, cut the highway between the capital, Vientiane, and the old Royal city of Luang Prabang.

By this time, interdiction and close air support missions in Laos had become much more dangerous because of greatly improved air defenses. For example, on March 29, 1972, the U.S. Air Force lost an AC–130 ten miles southwest of Tchepone to a surface-to-air missile. On May 5, when the Communists first introduced the shoulder-fired infrared heat-seeking missile, the SA–7 Strela, 1 of the missiles damaged an AC–130 near An Loc, South Vietnam, about 55 miles northwest of Saigon.

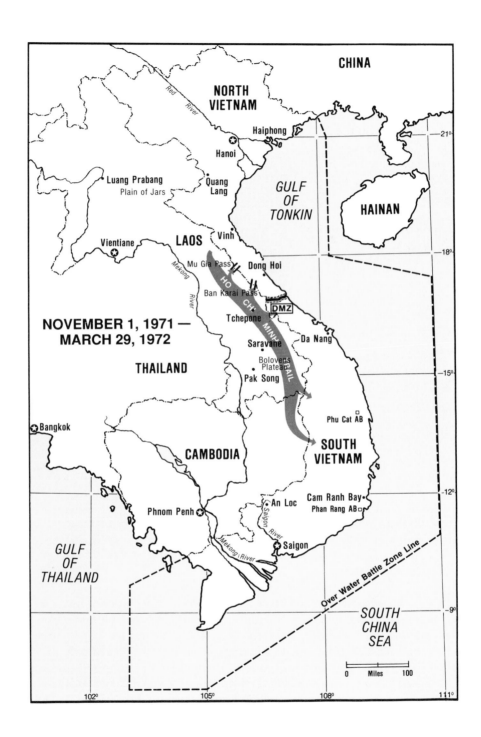

CHINA

NORTH
VIETNAM

Red River

Haiphong

⊕ Hanoi

• Luang Prabang
Plain of Jars

GULF
OF
TONKIN

HAINAN

• Quang
Lang

LAOS   • Vinh

Mekong River

Mu Gia Pass   • Dong Hoi

Ban Karai Pass

HO CHI MINH TRAIL

DMZ

• Vientiane ☆

NOVEMBER 1, 1971 —
MARCH 29, 1972

• Tchepone

THAILAND

• Saravane   • Da Nang

Bolovens
Plateau

• Pak Song

⊕ Bangkok

Phu Cat □ AB

SOUTH
VIETNAM

CAMBODIA

An Loc   Cam Ranh Bay •
              Phan Rang AB □

• Phnom Penh

Saigon River

Mekong River

☆ Saigon

GULF
OF
THAILAND

Over Water Battle Zone Line

SOUTH
CHINA
SEA

0   Miles   100

276

During COMMANDO HUNT VII, the USAF mounted several air raids against targets in North Vietnam in retaliation for enemy fire on reconnaissance aircraft. On November 7 and 8, 1971, U.S. aircraft bombed 3 airfields—at Dong Hoi, on the coast 35 miles north of the DMZ; at Vinh, 90 miles further up the coast and about 160 miles south of Hanoi; and at Quan Lang, on the 20th parallel near the Laotian border and less than 100 miles southwest of Hanoi. From December 26 to 30 the United States conducted the heaviest air attacks on North Vietnam since October 1968, flying 1,025 sorties against military installations south of the 20th parallel.

In spite of the escalating air and ground war, the U.S. continued to withdraw its forces from Southeast Asia. On November 17, 1971, the USAF inactivated the 12th Tactical Fighter Wing and on December 1 the 834th Air Division, at Phu Cat Air Base. Later that month, the USAF transferred base operations at Phu Cat to the VNAF. By the end of December only 158,000 U.S. troops of all services remained in South Vietnam. The withdrawal of American forces continued, although no progress had as yet been secured in the Paris peace talks. Indeed, in February and March 1972 Communist delegates again boycotted the sessions for 4 weeks. In March the 315th Tactical Airlift Wing inactivated at Phan Rang Air Base, and the 504th Tactical Air Support Group inactivated at Cam Ranh Bay. While the USAF inactivated or redeployed units, reduced its manpower, and gave up various functions, South Vietnamese, Laotian, and Cambodian pilots increasingly flew interdiction and close air support sorties, as well as airlift and other support missions.

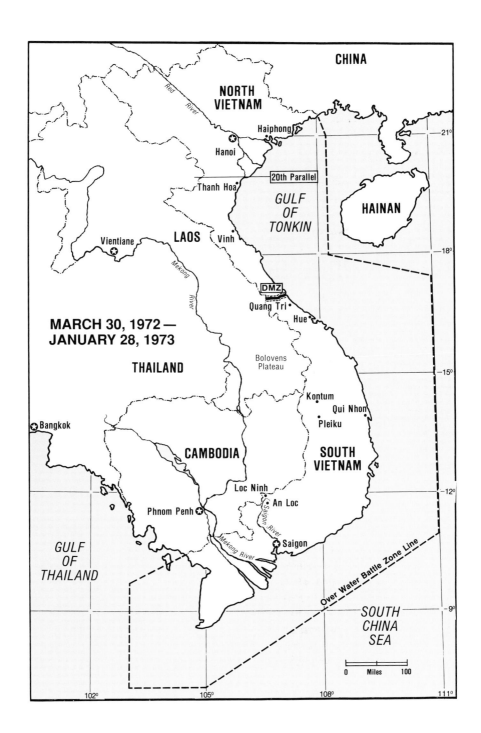

CHINA

NORTH
VIETNAM

Haiphong

Hanoi

20th Parallel

Thanh Hoa

GULF
OF
TONKIN

HAINAN

LAOS

Vientiane

Vinh

MARCH 30, 1972 —
JANUARY 28, 1973

DMZ

Quang Tri

Hue

Bolovens
Plateau

THAILAND

Kontum

Qui Nhon

Pleiku

Bangkok

CAMBODIA

SOUTH
VIETNAM

Loc Ninh

An Loc

Phnom Penh

Saigon

GULF
OF
THAILAND

Over Water Battle Zone Line

SOUTH
CHINA
SEA

0   Miles   100

Red River

Mekong River

Mekong River

Saigon River

21°

18°

15°

12°

9°

102°   105°   108°   111°

278

Vietnam Ceasefire:
March 30, 1972–January 28, 1973

On March 30, 1972, the North Vietnamese and Viet Cong opened a 3-pronged offensive, with the intention of defeating the Republic of Vietnam and reuniting Vietnam under a Communist regime. In a conventional attack supported with artillery and tanks, the North Vietnamese crossed the DMZ into Quang Tri Province, occupying Quang Tri, the provincial capital, on May 1 and attacking Hue. In a second thrust, the Communists invaded the Central Highlands from Laos, isolating Kontum and cutting the highway between Pleiku and Qui Nhon. On April 5 North Vietnamese and Viet Cong forces crossed the border from Cambodia in the third phase of the offensive, capturing Loc Ninh on April 6 and besieging An Loc. By May 8, however, the enemy offensive had stalled; on June 10 the Communists withdrew from Kontum and on the 26th from An Loc. Two days later the North Vietnamese retreated from Quang Tri, and on June 30 the South Vietnamese reopened the road to Pleiku.

U.S. air power contributed significantly to the battle. Although the USAF had reduced its forces in Southeast Asia to half of those present in mid-1968, it moved quickly to augment them. U.S. Navy, Marine, and Army aviation elements joined the USAF to provide airlift, interdiction, tactical reconnaissance, and close air support for the South Vietnamese.

A week after the Communist offensive began, on April 6, the United States resumed systematic, sustained bombing of military and industrial targets in North Vietnam as far north as the 20th parallel. The next day Gen. John W. Vogt, Jr., USAF, became the Seventh Air Force Commander. On May 4 South Vietnamese and U.S. leaders suspended peace negotiations in Paris, and 4 days later, the United States imposed a naval blockade of North Vietnam, mining harbors at Haiphong, Vinh, and elsewhere along the coast. The United States also initiated LINEBACKER on May 8—1 of the largest air campaigns of the war. Targets included the rebuilt Paul Doumer Bridge in Hanoi, the Thanh Hoa Bridge, rail lines, a petroleum pipeline from China to Hanoi, power plants, marshaling yards, and other strategic and tactical objectives throughout North Vietnam. During Linebacker, on June 28, Gen. Frederick C. Weyand, USA, became the Commander of MACV.

Peace negotiations, suspended for ten weeks, resumed in Paris on July 13. Anticipating a successful conclusion to the renewed peace talks, the United States halted the bombing of North Vietnam above the 20th parallel as of October 23. But when negotiations stalled, the United States conducted an intensive aerial offensive, LINEBACKER II, from December 18 to 30, against North Vietnam. B–52s and USAF and Navy tactical aircraft bombed Hanoi and Haiphong and their environs around the clock, concentrating on such targets as railyards, power plants, communication facilities, air defense radars, SAM and antiaircraft gun sites, petroleum tank farms, shipping facilities, ammunition dumps, and MiG bases. On December 30, after peace talks resumed, the United States again ceased bombing north of the 20th parallel.

On January 23, 1973, North Vietnam and the United States agreed to a cease-fire, effective within 5 days. Part of the agreement called for the North Vietnamese to release prisoners of war while the United States withdrew completely from South Vietnam. From February 12 to March 29, following the Vietnam Ceasefire, North Vietnam released 565 American POWs. In OPERATION HOMECOMING, the 9th Aeromedical Evacuation Group flew the POWs from Hanoi to Clark Air Base in the Philippines.

After the Vietnam Ceasefire Campaign, the Royal Laotian government signed a cease-fire agreement with the Pathet Lao on February 21, 1973. USAF B–52s, nevertheless, flew missions against Communist forces in Cambodia until August 15, 1973, when the U.S. Congress mandated an end to U.S. bombing in Southeast Asia.

The fighting had ended for American forces, but the Communists, resupplied and reequipped, soon escalated the ground war throughout Southeast Asia. Within 2 years, on April 17, 1975, the Khmer Rouge occupied all of Cambodia. On April 30 North Vietnam conquered South Vietnam and unified the country. And on December 3, 1975, the Pathet Lao seized power in Laos, marking an end to an era of U.S. influence in Southeast Asia.

Appendices

Appendix 1
Armed Forces Expeditionary Service

Armed Forces Expeditionary Medal

On the obverse side of the Armed Forces Expeditionary Medal, in profile facing left, is an eagle with wings raised, clutching a sword loosed in a scabbard. The eagle is superimposed on a star of 8 points. In a semicircle about the top rim are the words ARMED FORCES and around the bottom, the words EXPEDITIONARY SERVICE. On the reverse side appears the shield of the U.S. Coat of Arms; at the shield's base is an embossed ball, representing a rifle bullet, separating 2 laurel branches. Around the upper rim are the words UNITED STATES OF AMERICA. The medal is worn with a suspension ribbon, although a ribbon bar may be worn instead. Beginning at the edges, the ribbon features narrow vertical stripes of green, yellow, brown, and black. Within the black stripes are broad bands of blue, and in the ribbon's center, the colors of the U.S.—blue, white, and red.

Executive Order 10977, December 4, 1961, authorized the Armed Forces Expeditionary Medal. Any member of the United States Armed Forces participating in certain overseas operations after July 1, 1958, qualifies for the Armed Forces Expeditionary Medal and Ribbon. To receive the medal, the individual must have been a member of a unit engaged in the operation and have served directly in support of the operation, in the area of the operation, or in actual combat or equally hazardous duty. Except for combat duty, the service member must have served during the entire operation if less than 30 days in length, or have served 30 consecutive or 60 nonconsecutive days if the operation extended beyond 1-month duration. An individual who does not otherwise meet the basic criteria may still receive the Armed Forces Expeditionary Medal for duty of such value in an operation as to merit special recognition.

A military member receives only 1 of these medals and ribbons. If he or she participates in more than 1 overseas operation, a Bronze Service Star is awarded for each additional operation. Individuals who received the Armed Forces Expeditionary Medal for participation in Vietnam operations between July 1, 1958 and July 3, 1965, may convert it to the Vietnam Service Medal.

Armed Forces Expeditionary Streamer

The Armed Forces Expeditionary Streamer is identical to the ribbon in design and color. The name and date of each operation are embroidered on separate streamers.

Lebanon:
July 1–November 1, 1958

The operation in Lebanon, codenamed BLUE BAT, involved a U.S. military deployment to that strife-torn nation at the request of its government to assist in restoring and maintaining order. The U.S. Air Force primarily provided airlift for the U.S. Army forces, but also contributed to the "show of force." On July 15, 1958, U.S. Marines made an amphibious landing near the capital city of Beirut. Over the next 5 days, C–130s, C–119s, C–123s, and C–124s assigned to the 322d Air Division, United States Air Forces in Europe, flew Army troops from West Germany more than 2,100 miles to Incirlik Air Base at Adana, Turkey. Incirlik became the operations base for the Air Force during BLUE BAT. Between July 19 and 29, the 322d Air Division moved the Army forces into Beirut. Meanwhile, on July 15–20, the Air Force deployed from the United States to Turkey a Composite Air Strike Force composed of Tactical Air Command F–100 fighters, B–57s, KB–50 tankers, a composite reconnaissance squadron, a communications and control element, and a command element. The strike force provided air defense, reconnaissance, weather forecasting, aerial refueling, and other support for BLUE BAT. Several Air Force organizations contributed to the operation: Tactical Air Command C–130s transported the Composite Air Strike Force; United States Air Forces in Europe F–86Ds provided nighttime air defense of Incirlik; and the Military Air Transport Service sent C–124s. Three C–124 squadrons were on rotational duty attached to the 322d Air Division from the beginning, and 36 more C–124 aircraft arrived later to augment the airlift resources. The Air Force redeployed the strike force to the United States between mid-September and October 24. Meantime, the 322d Air Division on October 19–25 flew the Army troops from Beirut to West Germany. A joint operation in which the USAF played a key role, the Lebanon deployment successfully restored order at that time.

Taiwan Straits:
August 23, 1958–January 1, 1959

On August 23, 1958, the Chinese Communist government began a massive bombardment of the offshore island, Quemoy, which Nationalist Chinese troops occupied. The United States sent the Seventh Fleet to the Taiwan Straits to protect efforts to resupply the Nationalist Chinese garrisons. Air Force personnel on Taiwan numbered about 1,000 when, on August 29, the Pacific Air Forces moved an F–86D squadron from Okinawa to Taiwan. At the same time, the USAF began to deploy Tactical Air Command's Composite Air Strike Force of F–100 and F–101 fighters, RF–101 reconnaissance aircraft, and C–130 transports from California to Taiwan. Receiving aerial refueling from KB–50 tankers on the long overwater stretches, the first F–100s made the trip in 5 days. The rest of the strike force had arrived by September 26 aboard C–118s, C–121s, and C–124s of the Military Air Transport Service. Meantime, Tactical Air Command B–57s and Air Defense Command F–104 interceptors supplemented the Composite Air Strike Force. The F–104s made a particularly impressive contribution to the show of force put on by the Air Force, Navy, a Marine Air Group, and an Army Nike-Hercules battalion. The USAF limited its operations primarily to air defense missions over Taiwan. By the end of September, there were 4,814 Air Force personnel on Taiwan. Meantime, the USAF section of the Military Assistance Advisory Group provided technical aid and assistance to the Nationalist Chinese Air Force, which performed creditably in aerial resupply and air-to-air conflict. On October 7 the Chinese Communists announced a cease-fire, effectively ending the crisis, although they continued the shelling erratically after October 20. The Composite Air Strike Force redeployed to the United States on December 9–18, 1958, but the F–104s and F–86Ds remained on Taiwan. In the Taiwan Straits Operation, the USAF successfully demonstrated its ability to deploy a sizeable tactical force to the Far East, and the Chinese Communists failed to force the Nationalist Chinese from the offshore islands.

Quemoy and Matsu Islands:
August 23, 1958–June 1, 1963

On Taiwan, the Air Task Force Thirteen, Provisional, (also known as the Formosa Defense Command) assigned to the Thirteenth Air Force, had primary responsibility from August 23, 1958, for the air defense of the island, so that most aircraft of the Nationalist Chinese Air Force could patrol the Taiwan Straits. The U.S. Air Force Section of the Military Assistance Advisory Group quickly equipped the Nationalist Chinese F–86s with Sidewinder air-to-air missiles. The USAF also transferred F–100Fs and RB–57Ds to the Nationalist Chinese Air Force and provided maintenance and aircrew training. For the aerial resupply of Quemoy and Matsu Islands, the Nationalists received C–119Gs. In 1959 the Commander of Air Task Force Thirteen became the Air Component Commander of the United States Taiwan Defense Command and Chief, Air Force Section of the Military Assistance Advisory Group. The task force commander subsequently established a Joint Operations Center as part of the defense command. The Military Air Transport Service provided strategic airlift for the Air Task Force Thirteen and for the Air Defense Command F–104 unit. Eventually, the F–104s returned to the United States, but Pacific Air Forces continued to deploy temporarily various units, particularly reconnaissance squadrons, to Taiwan.

In May and June 1960, the Chinese Communists, in reaction to President Dwight D. Eisenhower's June visit to Taiwan, increased their forces, especially air power, in the Fukien area across the Taiwan Straits and greatly stepped up the rate of shelling on Quemoy Island. On June 5–12, in a show of force, the USAF deployed a squadron of F–100 aircraft from Japan to Taiwan. The Pacific Air Forces airlifted personnel to Taiwan for maintenance and housekeeping support of the fighter squadron. Almost 2 years later, in March 1962, the Chinese Communists once again concentrated forces in Fukien Province. Fearing an invasion of Quemoy and Matsu Islands, the United States sent a naval task force into the Taiwan Straits. Supported by the Air Task Force Thirteen, the Nationalist Chinese Air Force shot down several Communist aircraft. By June 1, 1963, the Chinese Communist threat against Quemoy and Matsu had lessened considerably, with only light shellings to remind the Nationalist Chinese that they were still at war with the Communists.

Vietnam:
July 1, 1958–July 3, 1965

On July 1, 1958, the United States Air Force's involvement in Vietnam consisted of a small section in the Military Assistance Advisory Group. This Air Force element advised and assisted the fledgling Vietnamese Air Force, composed at the time of only a few C–47s and obsolete French aircraft. The Communist guerrillas (Viet Cong) launched their armed struggle against the South Vietnamese government in September 1959. But the United States did not send additional aircraft to South Vietnam until late 1960. By early 1961 the Vietnamese Air Force had combat ready an AT–6 fighter squadron, 2 C–47 transport squadrons, 2 L–19 liaison squadrons, and a helicopter squadron. In April and May 1961 the United States substantially increased the Military Assistance Advisory Group, adding around 100 advisors, and during the summer Air National Guard C–97s flew a substantial tonnage of military cargo to South Vietnam. By the fall Viet Cong strength permitted pitched conventional battles against South Vietnamese troops. Meantime, the Air Force moved a mobile combat reporting post, in September and October 1961, to Tan Son Nhut Air Base on the outskirts of Saigon, the capital city. Representing the first sizeable group of USAF personnel in South Vietnam, the reporting post provided air traffic control and warning. A photo reconnaissance detachment of 4 RF–101s followed on October 18, but remained in the country for only a few weeks. The Military Air Transport Service provided airlift support for these deployments via its scheduled channel operations. Its aircraft flying into Vietnam included C–118s, C–121s, and C–124s. From November 1961 until the official closing date of July 3, 1965, the Armed Forces Expeditionary Service, Vietnam Operation, overlaps the designated Vietnam Campaigns.*

---

*See Vietnam Advisory Campaign, pp. 231–32, and Vietnam Defensive Campaign, pp. 233–235.

Congo:
July 14, 1960–September 1, 1962

From July 1960 to September 1962, the U.S. Air Force supported United Nations (UN) operations in the newly independent Democratic Republic of the Congo—an effort that eventually became known as OPERATION NEW TAPE and proved to be the largest airlift operation since the 1948–1949 Berlin Airlift. At the request of the Congolese government, the United Nations Security Council voted to send a peace-keeping force to the Congo. The UN Secretary General, on July 14, 1960, requested the United States and several other nations to airlift and support a multi-national, largely Third World, force. The United States Air Forces in Europe (USAFE) provided air traffic control resources, dispatching C–130s and a combat airlift support unit from Evreaux, France, to Leopoldville, the Congo. From mid-July until September, USAFE C–130s from Evreaux and Military Air Transport Service (MATS) C–124s from Chateauroux, France, transported UN troops from 16 nations, some as far away as India and Canada, to the Congo. In all, the Air Force airlifted 90 percent of the 20,000 United Nations troops flown into the Congo. The airlifters also evacuated 2,640 refugees. By September 1, 1960, the UN force and its equipment were in place. The 322d Air Division controlled the airlift until the Military Air Transport Service assumed that responsibility in October 1961. In December, the U.S. Navy began supporting OPERATION NEW TAPE with C–118s. Later, MATS used C–133s and C–135s on special missions. The Congo Airlift demonstrated the USAF's capability to support a large and continuing operation overseas in spite of linguistic, communications, and navigational difficulties and operational constraints. USAF airmen, with professional and diplomatic conduct, overcame long hours, non-existent or primitive billeting, and even, on one occasion, beatings from Congolese soldiers.

Laos:
April 19, 1961–October 7, 1962

President John F. Kennedy on April 19, 1961, established a Military Assistance Advisory Group to work closely with Laotian government troops in battling the country's Communist guerrillas, the Pathet Lao. In May an international conference opened in Geneva, Switzerland, to negotiate a neutral Laos. Then, in November 1961, Fifth Air Force RF–101s, stationed in Thailand, began flying reconnaissance missions over Laos. The Laotian Government and the Pathet Lao agreed to a cease-fire in April 1962, but the next month, the Pathet Lao overran most of northern Laos. In response, the United States sent a Seventh Fleet task force to Southeast Asia and increased from 1,000 to 5,000 the number of troops in Thailand. Subsequently, in July 1962, the Geneva Conference agreed to make Laos neutral. The USAF stopped flying the RF–101s over Laos, and by October 7, 1962, the United States announced that it had withdrawn all its military advisers.

Berlin:
August 14, 1961–June 1, 1963

To halt defectors fleeing from East Germany via West Berlin, the East German government on August 13, 1961, began constructing a wall in Berlin along the border. In response, President John F. Kennedy mobilized about 154,000 reservists in September–November 1961. Of these, 25,900 were Air Force reservists, mostly members of Air National Guard units. While the Guard units prepared to go overseas, in September the Air Force sent an interim Composite Air Strike Force of F–100s, F–104s, RF–101s, RB–66s, and C–130s to bases in the United Kingdom, France, West Germany, Spain, Italy, and Greece. Most of these Tactical Air Command units redeployed between mid-November and mid-December 1961, but 1 F–104C squadron remained in West Germany. Meantime, the Air National Guard units began the largest overseas transfer of tactical aircraft since World War II. On October 27–29 the Guard flew to Europe 228 jet aircraft—F–84Fs, RF–84Fs, F–86Hs, and T–33s—as well as 6 C–47s. The Military Air Transport Service provided airlift support, including the transport of the 2,200-man 152d Tactical Control Group to handle air traffic control and warning in West Germany. The airlifters also transported 60 partially disassembled F–104s and their squadron personnel to Europe between November 10 and December 12, 1961. United States Air Forces in Europe tasked the Guard units to meet normal conventional alerts, to escort traffic in the air corridors to West Berlin, and to train for combat operations. The escort missions proved the most challenging, because Soviet flyers often harassed U.S. aircraft in the corridors. The first Air National Guard unit to redeploy was the tactical control group, which operated from January 19 to May 19, 1962, before being replaced with a newly activated control unit with more sophisticated equipment. Other Guard units followed, with MATS flying over 260 airlift support missions between July 1 and August 31, 1962. The USAF activated a tactical fighter wing to fly the 80 F–84Fs that the Guard left in Europe. The Berlin Operation officially continued until June 1, 1963, because the United States recognized the Cuban Missile Crisis as an extension of the Soviet power play in Berlin.

Cuba:
October 24, 1962–June 1, 1963

The Cuba Operation officially commenced at 1000 hours on October 24, 1962, with the establishment by the U.S. Navy of a quarantine line in the Atlantic Ocean, 500 miles from Cuba. Ten days earlier, an Air Force U–2 aircraft had photographed ballistic missile sites being built in Cuba. Over the next few days, as President John F. Kennedy planned a strategy, the U.S. Armed Forces prepared to deal with the Cuban Missile Crisis. In the Air Force, the Strategic Air Command placed its aircraft and missiles on full alert, increased the number of B–52s on constant airborne alert, and dispersed its B–47s. Aircraft of the Military Air Transport Service and Tactical Air Command transported Marines to Guantanamo Naval Base in Cuba and U.S. Army troops to posts in the southeastern United States. Tactical Air Command moved aircraft, including RF–101s, RB–66s, KB–50s, F–100s, F–104s, and F–105s, with crews and support personnel, to Florida. The Air Defense Command also contributed aircraft and personnel to the buildup in Florida. During the quarantine, the Military Air Transport Service continued airlift support of the Army, Navy, and Marine forces, while the Strategic Air Command cooperated with the Navy in the aerial surveillance of seaborne shipping. Soviet ships bearing military equipment turned back on October 24, but Air Force reconnaissance flights revealed that missile site construction continued at a quicker pace. The Soviets and Cubans were also assembling IL–28 nuclear-capable bombers that had been shipped in crates. On the 25th, President Kennedy reiterated to the Soviet government the U.S. demand that all intermediate and medium-range missiles be withdrawn from Cuba. On October 27 the Cubans shot down and killed a U–2 pilot. A USAF ready reserve force of 24 troop carrier squadrons reported for active duty on the 28th, but the Soviets halted construction on the missile sites and a few days later began reloading missiles on ships. Aerial reconnaissance and the U.S. Navy's inspection of Soviet ships confirmed the withdrawal. In mid-November the Soviets also removed the bombers. On November 20, 1962, the U.S. Navy lifted the quarantine, and the next day the Air Force released its reservists from active duty. Air defense units remained deployed in the southeastern United States until the summer of 1963. USAF contributions were vital to the outcome of the Cuban Operation. The discovery of the missiles in Cuba and confirmation of their dismantlement came from aerial photography. Also, the Soviets were very aware of the strategic alert and the call-up of troop carrier units.

Congo:
November 23–27, 1964

In November 1964 rebels of the Democratic Republic of the Congo threatened to kill hostages they had held for over 3 months if the central government did not immediately withdraw its troops from the Stanleyville area. With the support of the Congolese government, Belgium and the United States mounted a rescue effort. United States Air Forces in Europe, given operational control of the airlift, prepositioned at Kamina Air Base, the Congo, a Tactical Air Command squadron of C–130E aircraft. The squadron was on rotation in Europe from the 464th Troop Carrier Wing at Pope Air Force Base, North Carolina. Flying from Kamina, on November 24, 1964, five C–130s airdropped an element of Belgian paratroopers on the Stanleyville airport. After the soldiers cleared the runway of obstacles, another 7 C–130s landed the remainder of the Belgian force. The aircraft came under fire, and several were damaged. The soldiers rescued most of the hostages in Stanleyville, but the rebels killed 29, including 2 Americans, during the battle. U.S. aircraft flew the refugees to Leopoldville. As evacuation of the hostages continued, on November 26, seven C–130s airdropped Belgian paratroopers in an assault on Paulis, the Congo. The aircraft received fire, but suffered little damage. The next day the American C–130 aircrews flew the Belgian paratroopers from Stanleyville and Paulis to Kamina and prepared for redeployment to Europe. In all, the Belgian soldiers and the USAF airmen rescued about 2,100 hostages from 18 nations.

Dominican Republic:
April 28, 1965–September 21, 1966

In response to a violent, possibly Communist-inspired, revolution in the Dominican Republic, the United States sent a Navy task force, which arrived offshore on April 26, 1965. On April 28 over 500 U.S. Marines from the task force on April 28 came ashore a few miles from downtown Santo Domingo, the capital city, to ensure the safety of American citizens gathered for evacuation. The next day 1,500 more Marines came ashore, and President Lyndon B. Johnson ordered Army paratroopers to land at San Isidro airfield near Santo Domingo. C–130s belonging to the Tactical Air Command and Military Air Transport Service airlifted 1,800 paratroopers and their equipment from Pope AFB, North Carolina, to the Dominican Republic. An EC–135 out of Ramey AFB, Puerto Rico, guided the C–130s, arriving very early on April 30, into San Isidro. But 65 of the 144 C–130s diverted to Ramey because of overcrowding at San Isidro. The paratroopers moved later in the day into Santo Domingo and the next day fought to link up with the Marines. By May 3 the U.S. forces had isolated rebel elements in the Ciudad Nueva section of Santo Domingo. Meantime, on May 1, the Air Force moved a squadron of F–100s, later augmented by F–104s, to Ramey AFB. Until the squadron returned to the United States on June 1, at least 2 fighters flew over the Dominican Republic at all times. The USAF also deployed a reconnaissance squadron of RF–101s and RB–66s to Ramey on May 2 to provide aerial reconnaissance and photography. U.S. troops reached a peak of nearly 24,000 by May 17, most having arrived in a massive airlift by C–130s, C–124s, and C–119s. On May 29, 1965, U.S. troops, along with soldiers from 6 Latin American nations, became the Inter-American Peace Force established by the Organization of American States. Over the next 15 months, the United States gradually withdrew its forces as the Dominicans established a stable government. The last U.S. units left the country on September 21, 1966, having helped to restore order and avert an allegedly Communist takeover.

Korea:
October 1, 1966–June 30, 1974

From October 1966 the North Korean government had infiltrated numerous agents into South Korea and provoked firefights along the demilitarized zone. Then, on January 23, 1968, the North Koreans seized the USS *Pueblo*, an intelligence ship operating a few miles offshore Wonsan, North Korea. The United States immediately expanded its forces, particularly air power, in the area while trying to negotiate a release of the 82 surviving crewmembers (1 was killed during the ship's capture). Within 2 weeks, USAF personnel in South Korea doubled, and the Pacific Air Forces sent F–102s, F–105s, and RF–4Cs from bases in Okinawa, Japan, and the Philippine Islands. The Fifth Air Force established, on January 30, 1968, an advanced headquarters at Osan Air Base, South Korea. The Tactical Air Command sent F–4s, F–100s, C–130s, and EB–66s, and the Air Defense Command sent F–106 fighter-interceptors from the United States to South Korea. Strategic Air Command tankers refueled these overseas flights. Meantime, the Military Airlift Command organized a strategic airlift using C–141s, C–133s, C–124s and C–130s. It also deployed operations, traffic, and maintenance specialists to handle its aircraft at Osan, Kimpo, Kunsan, and Suwon Air Bases in South Korea. During the summer, Air National Guard units, flying F–100s, replaced regular Air Force tactical fighter units in South Korea. Beginning in July a Guard tactical reconnaissance wing rotated its squadrons in succession to Japan; each squadron sent a detachment to South Korea. The United States finally negotiated the release of the *Pueblo*'s crewmembers on December 23, 1968. But hostilities intensified when, on April 14, 1969, the North Koreans shot down a U.S. Navy EC–121. The Air Force helped search for survivors, but none was found. The Air National Guard units redeployed in April–June 1969. The U.S. left about 68,000 personnel in South Korea, and the Air Force upgraded its facilities there. In 1970–1971, as the North Korean threat subsided, the United States withdrew about 26,000 personnel while increasing military aid to the South Korean forces. By mid-1974 the USAF had only 1 wing of F–4s and some 7,500 people in South Korea.

Cambodia:
March 29–August 15, 1973

Following the official withdrawal of U.S. forces from South Vietnam on March 29, 1973, the Air Force continued its support of the Cambodian government in the battle against Communist forces, known as the Khmer Rouge.* By 1973 the Khmer Rouge controlled most of the countryside east of the Mekong River, but the Cambodian government held the capital, Phnom Penh, and the provincial capitals. The Communists laid siege to Phnom Penh from March to May, having cut all land routes and the Mekong River supply route. The Air Force repeatedly attacked enemy targets on the outskirts of the capital with B–52s, F–111s, A–7s, and AC–130s. F–4s flew escort for other aircraft and provided close air support to Cambodian forces. RF–4s provided tactical reconnaissance to support air attacks against Communist positions. C–130s airlifted from U-Tapao, Thailand, to Phnom Penh supplies, such as rice, fuel, military equipment, and especially munitions. River convoys, under USAF aerial escort, finally broke the blockade. During the siege, air traffic over the capital became so congested that a C–130 Airborne Command and Control Center (ABCCC) orbited nearby around the clock to control air traffic. A USAF ground-based combat control team handled aircraft descents into the airfield at Phnom Penh. While C–130s occasionally landed at other Cambodian airfields, most resupply in the countryside was by airdrop from specially rigged aircraft. The C–130s frequently had to evade surface-to-air missiles (SA–7s) and consequently dropped the supplies, mostly munitions, from altitudes over 10,000 feet. The U.S. Congress mandated an end to bombing in Cambodia, effective August 15, 1973, but the C–130s continued to deliver needed supplies to Cambodia after that date.

---

*USAF support of Cambodian forces dated back to 1969. See the Tet 69/Counter Offensive Campaign, pp. 255–256.

Thailand (in support of Cambodia): March 29–August 15, 1973

USAF resources operating in Cambodia after March 29, 1973, were based in Thailand. When the Military Assistance Command, Vietnam, closed on that date in Saigon, it was replaced by a new United States Support Activities Group at Nakhon Phanom Royal Thai Air Force Base (RTAFB). The Air Force transferred Seventh Air Force headquarters to Nakhon Phanom and merged it with the Support Activities Group. The merged headquarters maintained a limited forward military force in Thailand while providing military assistance to Laos, Cambodia, and South Vietnam. The Pacific Air Forces established an advanced Thirteenth Air Force headquarters at Udorn RTAFB in place of the Seventh/Thirteenth Air Force. The USAF also had a large training program at Korat, particularly Cambodian personnel learning to fly and maintain C–123s that the U.S. government transferred to the Cambodian forces. F–4s operated out of Udorn and Ubon RTAFBs, flying strike and escort missions to Cambodia. A USAF airlift control center at U-Tapao RTAFB scheduled the C–130 airlift to Cambodia. From U-Tapao, the Strategic Air Command continued to operate B–52s that bombed Cambodian targets and KC–135s that refueled combat aircraft bound for Cambodia. At Nakhon Phanom, the 56th Special Operations Wing flew CH–53 helicopters, EC–47s, and OV–10s. Search and rescue units operated from Ubon and Korat RTAFBs in support of USAF aircraft bound for Cambodia. F–111s operating from Takhli RTAFB provided pathfinder support to other tactical aircraft by guiding them to targets during darkness and inclement weather. In short, the Air Force used its personnel and aircraft to stem the tide of Communist forces in Cambodia, but to little avail.

Cambodia
(Evacuation—OPERATION EAGLE PULL): April 11–13, 1975

The Khmer Rouge gradually tightened their grip on Cambodia in spite of continuing, but limited, military aid from the United States. In early April 1975, Communist forces threatened the capital city, Phnom Penh. The United States prepared to evacuate its ambassador, other American citizens, and Cambodians closely associated with the U.S. presence. By April 11 a small Navy task force stood off the coast of Cambodia. The next morning a USAF HH–53 helicopter landed an Air Force combat control team at a soccer field only a quarter mile from the U.S. Embassy. Immediately afterwards, U.S. Marine Corps helicopters, CH–53s, landed a Marine ground security force to guard the landing zone. The Marine helicopters in about 2 hours evacuated 276 people, of whom 82 were U.S. citizens, from Phnom Penh to the Navy ships. RF–4s provided photographic reconnaissance before and after the evacuation. Air Force A–7s and AC–130s escorted the helicopters to the landing zone while 2 C–130s provided airborne control of the air traffic and relayed messages from the U.S. Embassy to the Joint Rescue Coordination Center in Thailand. HC–130s refueled the HH–53s orbiting near Phnom Penh on rescue alert. Shortly before noon, 2 USAF HH–53s landed to remove the combat control team and the ground defense force. The helicopters had been under small arms fire frequently during the morning, and the last HH–53 was damaged as it lifted off. No one was injured, and the crew managed to fly the helicopter back to Ubon Royal Thai Air Force Base. OPERATION EAGLE PULL ended on April 13, but proved to be a rehearsal for a much larger evacuation, OPERATION FREQUENT WIND.

Vietnam
(Evacuation—OPERATION FREQUENT WIND): April 29–30, 1975

In March 1975 the North Vietnamese launched an attack that resulted in the collapse and retreat of the South Vietnamese forces. During the last half of April, as the Communists advanced on Saigon, the U.S. government began to fly refugees out of Vietnam. Early in the morning of April 29, 1975, as USAF C–130s loaded refugees at Tan Son Nhut Air Base, the Communists launched a rocket attack. One loaded and 1 empty aircraft took off, but a rocket destroyed the third C–130, although its crew escaped unscathed. The U.S. authorities recognized that continued evacuation would have to be by helicopter, and that afternoon the Marines and the Air Force began shuttling Americans and South Vietnamese from several landing zones in Saigon to Navy ships off-shore. Air America, a private firm under contract to the Central Intelligence Agency, also participated in the helicopter evacuation. The helicopters came under fire from small arms, antiaircraft guns, and SA–7 missiles. F–4s, A–7s, AC–130s, and F–111s suppressed hostile fire and escorted the helicopters and, in some instances, ships and boats carrying evacuees down the Saigon and Mekong Rivers to the sea. Other Air Force support aircraft included electronic countermeasures, rescue, and radio relay airplanes, as well as KC–135 and HC–130 tankers. A USAF C–130 Airborne Command and Control Center (ABCCC) controlled air operations over land. The U.S. Navy and Marine Corps added their air power support to the evacuation, as well. Initially Air Force security police helped provide crowd control at the major landing zones. Before midnight on April 29, the helicopters had evacuated slightly more than 7,000 people from Saigon to the ships. The U.S. government halted the evacuation, but the next day hundreds of South Vietnamese refugees made their way, mostly by boat but some by aircraft, to the U.S. task force offshore. In April 1975 about 130,000 South Vietnamese fled their country; most eventually resettled in the United States. Even as OPERATION FREQUENT WIND ended, another crisis developed in Southeast Asia.

Mayaguez:
May 15, 1975

On May 12, 1975, Cambodian forces seized the *Mayaguez*, an American-registered cargo ship. On May 15 the U.S. government ordered the recapture of the *Mayaguez* and its 40-man crew. Just before dawn, USAF helicopters approached Koh Tang Island, near the anchored *Mayaguez*, which an F–111 aircrew had spotted earlier. The crew was assumed to be held on the island. The CH–53s and HH–53s attempting to land Marines on the beach came under heavy fire from about 200 well-armed Cambodian soldiers. In the initial wave of 8 helicopters, 6 unloaded, 1 pulled back, and another crashed before unloading. Two more crashed on or near the island, and only 2 escaped undamaged. By mid-morning the Cambodians had returned the *Mayaguez* crew from the mainland to a U.S. Navy ship, and a U.S. destroyer had seized the abandoned cargo ship. There was no longer any reason to assault Koh Tang, but the hard-pressed Marines had to be reinforced before they could be withdrawn. The USAF helicopters eventually placed about 230 servicemen on the island. Air Force and Navy tactical aircraft, along with the ships, blasted enemy positions on the island. Air Force F–111s, A–7s, and AC–130s sank or drove off enemy gunboats trying to reach the island. Navy aircraft hit military targets on the Cambodian mainland. USAF AC–130s provided effective close air support, and KC–135s and HC–130s refueled aircraft as needed. USAF OV–10s arrived in mid-afternoon to serve as airborne forward air controllers, and later a C–130 dropped a 15,000-pound "daisy-cutter" bomb near the island's center. As the tactical aircraft suppressed hostile fire and darkness fell, the Air Force HH–53s plucked the Marines from their precarious positions on the beach. By 2000 hours, the Americans were off the island. Total U.S. casualties during the day were 15 killed, 3 missing, and 49 wounded. Of the 15 helicopters participating, 4 were destroyed and 9 damaged. The Mayaguez Operation ended U.S. combat involvement in Southeast Asia.

Lebanon:
June 1, 1983–October 1, 1987

The U.S. Marine Corps in May 1983 rotated its Marine Amphibious Unit, the U.S. element of a multinational peacekeeping force that had arrived the previous year in Lebanon. A sizeable U.S. Navy task force offshore supported the Marines, who were stationed at the Beirut International Airport, adjacent to the Moslem-controlled sector of West Beirut. The Air Force provided regular air transport of mail and personnel for the Marines, the U.S. Embassy, and U.S. military advisors. On October 23, 1983, a terrorist bomb destroyed the Marines' headquarters building, killing 241 and wounding over 100 servicemen. The Air Force diverted Military Airlift Command C–9s, C–130s, and C–141s already in Europe to evacuate wounded personnel to U.S. Army and Air Force hospitals in Germany. Meantime, 4 C–141s flew a complete battalion headquarters from the Marine Air Station at Cherry Point, North Carolina. They delivered the Marine personnel, vehicles, and equipment to Beirut on October 24, less than 36 hours after the bombing. Between October 23 and 30, Military Airlift Command aircraft flew to Beirut badly needed medical and other supplies, including body bags and military caskets. The C–130s and C–141s carried out personnel, classified materials, and the personal effects of the wounded and dead. The aircraft transported the bodies to a morgue in Germany for identification and embalming. In the weeks following the terrorist attack, the Marines suffered repeated shelling of their positions, and in February 1984 they began to withdraw, the last leaving on March 31. Six months later, on September 20, terrorists bombed the U.S. Embassy Annex, killing 24 people. A Military Airlift Command aircraft transported 8 wounded people from Beirut to Ramstein Air Base, Germany, for treatment. Shortly after this bombing, the U.S. Ambassador moved the embassy from West Beirut to Christian-held East Beirut. Subsequently, first the U.S. Navy, then the U.S. Army, provided helicopter support for the embassy, since it was isolated from the airport. U.S. Navy forces remained offshore Lebanon for several more months.

Grenada:
October 23–November 21, 1983

On October 23 President Ronald Reagan, backed by the Organization of Eastern Caribbean States and the British Governor General of Grenada, ordered a 2-pronged assault to protect American citizens on the island. These were tourists, resident retirees, and, mostly, medical students whom an increasingly hostile government might hold hostage. OPERATION URGENT FURY started 2 days later when Marines from a Navy task force went ashore near Pearls Airport on the northeast coast. Meantime, Military Airlift Command C–130s flew 2 Army Ranger battalions from Georgia and airdropped 1 on Port Salines Airport at the southern tip of Grenada. The Rangers cleared runway obstacles that an MC–130E had spotted earlier with sophisticated sensors. AC–130H gunships, refueled by Strategic Air Command tankers, suppressed hostile fire while the transports landed the rest of the Rangers and an Air Force combat control team to direct aircraft landings and takeoffs. EC–130 Airborne Command and Control Center (ABCCC) and E–3A Airborne Warning and Control System (AWACS) aircraft from Tactical Air Command directed air traffic over Grenada. Tactical Air Command F–15s and A–10s flew numerous sorties in direct support of the rescue mission. Over the next 4 days, while the Marines and Army troops subdued the opposition, C–130s and C–141s, many manned by air reservists, transported 4 battalions of Army airborne forces from the United States to Grenada. Military Airlift Command aircrews evacuated over 700 American citizens to Charleston AFB, South Carolina, while C–5As carried medical evacuation helicopters to Barbados. From there, the Army flew the helicopters to Grenada. Beginning on October 26, USAF security police helped secure the Point Salines airfield perimeter and guarded the Cuban prisoners. An Air Force medical evacuation unit cared for 164 wounded soldiers transported from Grenada by C–9As, C–130s, and C–141s. A USAF aerial port unit unloaded and loaded aircraft at Pearls Airport and Point Salines, and Air National Guard EC–130s flew psychological warfare missions until the cessation of hostilities on November 2. From November 4 to 9, the Military Airlift Command flew over 755 Cubans to Barbados, where they boarded airliners bound for Havana. By November 21 the Air Force had redeployed the Army troops to the United States. OPERATION URGENT FURY succeeded in evacuating American citizens, in eliminating the Cuban military presence, and in permitting Grenada to establish a stable government.

Libya (ELDORADO CANYON):
April 12–17, 1986

The United States planned an attack, code-named ELDORADO CANYON, against Libya to discourage state-sponsored terrorism against American citizens and facilities. On April 12–13, 1986, Navy ships in the Mediterranean Sea moved off Libya's coast, and Air Force units in the United Kingdom prepared for a nighttime flight to Libya. On April 14 Strategic Air Command tankers, KC–10s and KC–135s, launched from Royal Air Force (RAF) Fairford and RAF Mildenhall. F–111s and EF–111s assigned to United States Air Forces in Europe departed RAF Lakenheath and RAF Upper Heyford less than 1/2 hour later. The tankers refueled the aircraft several times as they flew 2,800 miles over international waters to Libya. At midnight on April 15, the fighter aircraft, flying at an altitude of approximately 400 feet to avoid Libyan radar detection, attacked targets near Tripoli. One flight bombed the Azziziyah barracks, headquarters for Libyan-based terrorists, but lost 1 F–111. Another flight destroyed the Sidi Bilal terrorist camp, while the last element bombed facilities and aircraft at Tripoli International Airport. One of the KC–10s provided command and control for the USAF aircraft and communications with the Navy. Carrier-based aircraft bombed targets at Benghazi, Libya, while the F–111s were bombing the Tripoli facilities. Naval aircraft also provided coverage against hostile aircraft attacks, which never occurred, and helped suppress Libyan ground-to-air defenses. Immediately following the attacks, Navy search and rescue forces unsuccessfully looked for the downed F–111 and its 2 crewmembers. The Navy and Air Force strikes in ELDORADO CANYON discouraged Libyan-sponsored terrorist activities for a time and showed that the United States would apply force to deter state-sponsored terrorism.

Persian Gulf:
July 24, 1987–Date to be Determined

When the Iran-Iraq War broke out in 1980, the United States had already stated its Persian Gulf policy: To maintain the flow of petroleum, deny the Soviet Union control of the area, and support friendly Gulf states. In 1987 the government of Kuwait asked the United States to place its flag on Kuwaiti tankers and protect them from Iranian attacks. The U.S. accepted the challenge, augmenting its naval forces in the Persian Gulf and establishing convoy escorts for reflagged tankers. The first convoy through the Persian Gulf got underway on July 22, but 2 days later an Iranian underwater mine disabled a reflagged tanker. The Navy had no minesweeping capabilities in the Gulf; consequently, before the end of the month, Military Airlift Command C–5s airlifted 8 RH–53D helicopters and other minesweeping equipment from the United States to Diego Garcia Island in the Indian Ocean. A Navy ship carried the helicopters to the Persian Gulf to start operations by mid-August. Military Airlift Command C–141s and C–5s flew personnel and supplies to airfields near the Persian Gulf, and Strategic Air Command KC–10 and KC–135 tankers refueled aircraft of all the services in support of the Persian Gulf operations. E–3A Airborne Warning and Control System (AWACS) aircraft assigned to the Tactical Air Command and operating from Ridyadh and Dhahran, Saudi Arabia, conducted air defense operations, controlled U.S. and other nations' air traffic in the Gulf area, and served as aerial refueling coordinators. The AWACS aircraft also provided near real-time intelligence day and night on ship and aircraft movements until Iran and Iraq established a cease-fire on August 20, 1988. In November, the U.S. Navy began withdrawing forces, and in December it dropped the convoy system, eventually downgrading operations to simple monitoring of U.S. flagged tankers. The United States had successfully enforced its Persian Gulf policy.

Panama (OPERATION JUST CAUSE): December 20, 1989–January 31, 1990

On December 20, 1989, U.S. military forces invaded Panama to protect American citizens, support a democratic regime, ensure the operation of the Panama Canal, and capture General Manuel Noriega. The United States wanted Noriega, Panama's dictator, to stand trial in U.S. courts for dealing in illegal drugs. Military Airlift Command C–5s, C–141s, and C–130s transported combat troops from the United States to Panama. Of the initial 111 aircraft, 84, flying at 500 feet, dropped close to 5,000 troops at various sites in Panama in the largest nighttime airborne operation since World War II. The rest of the aircraft landed at Howard AFB and near Panama City at Omar Torrijos International Airport, after Army Rangers had secured it. Tactical Air Command F–117A stealth aircraft of the 37th Tactical Fighter Wing on their first combat mission dropped bombs near the Rio Hato barracks to daze and confuse the Panama Defense Forces. The airdrop of Army troops at that location met minimal opposition. AC–130s of the 1st Special Operations Wing, Military Airlift Command, from Hurlburt Field, Florida, provided close air and special sensor support. Other 1st Special Operations Wing aircraft, MC–130Es, MH–53Js, and MH–60s, flew mostly at night in coordinated operations with Army and Navy special forces. HC–130s refueled helicopters, and Strategic Air Command tankers provided aerial refueling for fixed-wing aircraft. C–5s landed medical teams and supplies at Howard AFB. Eight C–141s and 1 C–130 airlifted 257 wounded to Kelly AFB, Texas, and evacuated the bodies of 23 military personnel killed in action to Dover AFB, Delaware. Air Force Reserve or Air National Guard crews manned several Military Airlift Command aircraft. Air Force personnel at Howard AFB also provided communications, loaded and unloaded aircraft, refueled aircraft, and guarded Panamanian Defense Force prisoners. Organized resistance ended on Christmas Day. Noriega surrendered to the United States on January 3, 1990, and an MC–130 transported him to Florida to stand trial. About 200 1st Special Operations Wing personnel remained in Panama during January to help with humanitarian operations, while Military Airlift Command crews transported the Army troops back home.

Appendix 2

Combat Devices

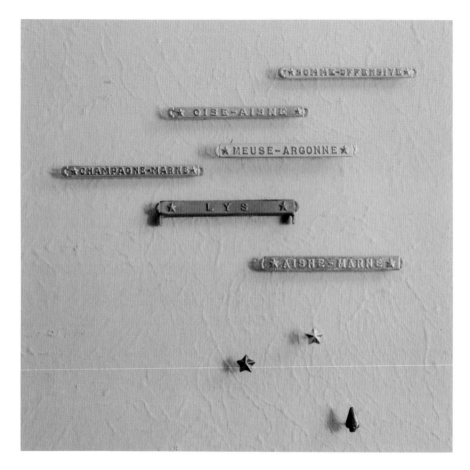

World War I Campaign Clasps
(for aviation credit)

Silver Service Star
(denotes 5 campaign credits for World War II and later)

Bronze Service Star
(denotes single campaign credit for World War II and later)

Arrowhead
(denotes credit for amphibious or airborne assault)

Glossary

AAF	Army Air Forces (United States)
AAFAC	Army Air Forces Antisubmarine Command
ABCCC	Airborne Command and Control Center
AD	Air Division
ADC	Air Defense Command
ADVON	advanced echelon
AEF	American Expeditionary Forces
AFEM	Armed Forces Expeditionary Medal
AFMPC	Air Force Military Personnel Center
ANG	Air National Guard
AP	Asiatic–Pacific
ARVN	Army of the Republic of Vietnam
ATF 13	Air Task Force Thirteen, Provisional
AVG	American Volunteer Group
AWACS	Airborne Warning and Control System
CACW	Chinese-American Composite Wing
CASF	Composite Air Strike Force
CATF	China Air Task Force
CCF	Chinese Communist Forces
CHECO	Contemporary Historical Examination of Current Operations
DMZ	Demilitarized Zone
EAME	European–African–Middle Eastern
FEAF	Far East Air Forces
GHQ	General Headquarters
IMA	individual mobilization augmentee
LST	landing ship tank
MAAF	Mediterranean Allied Air Forces
MAAG	Military Assistance Advisory Group
MAC	Military Airlift Command

MACV	Military Assistance Command, Vietnam
MATS	Military Air Transport Service
MiG	Communist jet fighter aircraft
NAAF	Northwest African Air Forces
NCAF	Nationalist Chinese Air Force
NVA	North Vietnam Army
PACAF	Pacific Air Forces
POW	prisoner of war
RAAF	Royal Austalian Air Force
RAF	Royal Air Force (Great Britain)
RFC	Royal Flying Corps (Great Britain)
RLAF	Royal Laotian Air Force
ROK	Republic of Korea
RTAFB	Royal Thai Air Force Base
RVNAF	Republic of Vietnam Armed Forces
SA–7	hand-held ground-to-air missile
SAC	Strategic Air Command
SAM	surface-to-air missile
TAC	Tactical Air Command
UN	United Nations
UNC	United Nations Command
U.S.	United States
USA	United States Army
USAF	United States Air Force
USAFE	United States Air Forces in Europe
USAFHRC	United States Air Force Historical Research Center
USAMEAF	U.S. Army Middle East Air Force
VNAF	Vietnamese Air Force

Note on Sources

I used primary sources to write the descriptions of the medals, ribbons and streamers and determine the correct names, dates, and locations of the campaigns. War Department General Orders established the Mexican Service Medal and the Victory Medal of World War I. Executive orders established the other 5 medals. Descriptions of the medals, ribbons, and streamers came from Air Force Regulation 900–48 and the *Army Almanac*. The campaigns are listed in War Department and U.S. Army orders, Air Force Regulation 900–48, and Air Force Pamphlet 900–2. The Secretary of the Air Force approved the names and dates of the Vietnam Campaigns; the correspondence establishing these campaigns is part of the document collection at USAFHRC.

I relied mostly on secondary sources to write the campaign descriptions. Dr. Maurer Maurer, former Senior Historian at the USAFHRC, included as an appendix in *Air Force Combat Units of World War II* synopses of campaigns from World War I through the Korean War. These formed the foundation for many campaign descriptions. The information for the synopsis of the Mexican Expeditionary Campaign came basically from Benjamin D. Foulois's report on the 1st Aero Squadron, and from Juliette A. Hennessy, USAF Historical Study #98, *The United States Army Air Arm, April 1861 to April 1917*, Chapter IX, "The 1st Squadron with Pershing's Punitive Expedition, 1916." Information for World War I came from James J. Hudson's *Hostile Skies*, on the American Air Service and Maj. Gen. Mason M. Patrick's *Final Report on the Air Service in Europe*. The World War II campaign synopses contain information drawn mostly from Wesley F. Craven and James L. Cate's 7-volume work, *The Army Air Forces in World War II*. Dr. Frank Futrell's classic history of the air war in Korea provided the information in the Korean War campaign descriptions. The major sources for the Vietnam synopses are the Office of Air Force History's publications on the conflict in Southeast Asia and CHECO reports on file at USAFHRC.

CHECO is an acronym for contemporary Historical Examination of Current Operations. Air Force historians stationed in Southeast Asia during the war compiled these reports to provide objective contemporary histories of USAF operations in Southeast Asia, and many have been recently declassified.

Governmental Sources

Books

American Battle Monuments Commission. *American Armies and Battlefields in Europe.* Washington: Government Printing Office, 1938.

Ballard, Jack S. *The United States Air Force in Southeast Asia; Development and Employment of Fixed-Wing Gunships, 1962-1972.* Washington: Office of Air Force History, 1982.

Berger, Carl, ed. *The United States Air Force in Southeast Asia, 1961–1973: An Illustrated Account*, Revised Edition. Washington: Office of Air Force History, 1983.

Bowers, Ray L. *Tactical Airlift: The United States Air Force in Southeast Asia.* Washington: Office of Air Force History, 1983.

Buckingham, William A., Jr. *Operation Ranch Hand: The Air Force and Herbicides in Southeast Asia, 1961–1971.* Washington: Office of Air Force History, 1982.

Carter, Kit C. and Robert Mueller. *The Army Air Forces in World War II: Combat Chronology, 1941–1945.* Washington: Albert F. Simpson Historical Research Center and Office of Air Force History, 1973.

Choinski, Walter F. *Country Study: Republic of Vietnam.* Washington: Department of Defense, Military Assistance Institute, 1965.

Craven, Wesley F. and James L. Cate, eds. The Army Air Forces in World War II. 7 volumes. Chicago: University of Chicago Press, 1948–1958. [Reprinted by the Office of Air Force History, 1983]

Fox, Roger P. *Air Base Defense in the Republic of Vietnam, 1961–1973.* Washington: Office of Air Force History, 1979.

Futrell, R. Frank, *et al. Aces & Aerial Victories: The United States Air Force in Southeast Asia, 1965–1973.* Washington: Albert F. Simpson Historical Research Center and Office of Air Force History, 1977.

_____. *The United States Air Force in Korea, 1950–1953.* Revised Edition. Washington: Office of Air Force History, 1983.

_____. *The United States Air Force in Southeast Asia: The Advisory Years to 1965.* Washington: Office of Air Force History, 1981.

Gorrell, Edgar S. *History of the Air Service, American Expeditionary Forces in France, 1917–1918.* Washington: U.S. Air Service, 1919.

Howland, C. R. *A Military History of the World War.* Fort Leavenworth, Kansas: The General Service Schools Press, 1923.

Lane, John L. Jr. *Command and Control and Communications Structures in Southeast Asia.* Maxwell Air Force Base, Alabama: Air University, Airpower Research Institute, 1981.

Lavalle, A. J. C., ed. *USAF Southeast Asia Monograph Series.* Volumes I–VII. Washington: Government Printing Office, 1976–1979.

Maurer, Maurer, ed. *Air Force Combat Units of World War II.* Washington: Government Printing Office, 1961. [Reprinted by the Office of Air Force History, 1983]

_____, ed. *The U.S. Air Service in World War I.* 4 volumes. Washington: Albert F. Simpson Historical Research Center and Office of Air Force History, 1978–1979.

Momyer, William W. *Air Power in Three Wars (World War II, Korea, Vietnam).* Washington: Department of the Air Force, 1978.

Nalty, Bernard C. *Air Power and the Fight for Khe Sanh.* Washington: Office of Air Force History, 1973. [Reprinted 1986]

Patrick, Maj. Gen. Mason M. *Final Report of the Chief of Air Service, A.E.F. to the Commander in Chief, American Expeditionary Forces*, Air Service Information Circular #180, February 15, 1921. Washington: Government Printing Office, 1921. [Published in Maurer, Maurer, ed. *The U.S. Air Service in World War I.* Volume I. Washington: Albert F. Simpson Historical Research Center and Office of Air Force History, 1978–1979.

Ravenstein, Charles A. *Air Force Combat Wings: Lineage and Honors Histories, 1947–1977.* Washington: Office of Air Force History, 1984.

Tilford, Earl H., Jr. *Search and Rescue in Southeast Asia, 1961–1975.* Washington: Office of Air Force History, 1980.

Tolson, John J. *Air Mobility 1961–1971.* Washington: Department of the Army, 1973.

Historical Studies

Directorate of Operations, DCS/Plans and Operations. "Air Power in Southeast Asia." Washington: HQ USAF, 1969.

Eckwright, Royce E. *Air National Guard Deployment to USAFE Area, 1961–1962.* Ramstein Air Base, West Germany: USAFE Historical Division, December 1962.

Ferguson, Arthur B. *The Antisubmarine Command.* U.S. Air Force Historical Study #107. Maxwell Air Force Base, Ala.: USAF Historical Division, Air University, April 1945.

Hennessy, Juliette A. "The 1st Squadron with Pershing's Punitive Expedition, 1916," Chapter IX, pp. 167–176, in *The United States Army Air Arm, April 1861 to April 1917.* U.S. Air Force Historical Study #98. Maxwell Air Force Base, Ala. : USAF Historical Division, Air University, 1958.

NOTE ON SOURCES

Little, Robert D. and Wilhelmine Burch. *Air Operations in the Lebanon Crisis of 1958.* Washington: USAF Historical Division Liaison Office, 1962.

Ravenstein, Charles A. *A Guide to Air Force Lineage and Honors.* 2d Edition, Revised. Maxwell Air Force Base, Ala.: USAF Historical Research Center, 1984.

Tustin, Joseph P. *USAFE Humanitarian Missions, 1945–1962.* Ramstein Air Base, Federal Republic of Germany: USAFE Historical Division, January 1963.

Van Staaveren, Jacob. *Air Operations in the Taiwan Crisis of 1958.* Washington: USAF Historical Division Liaison Office, 1962.

Reports

Anno, Col. Stephen E., and Lt. Col. William E. Einspahr. *Command and Control and Communications Lessons Learned: Iranian Rescue, Falklands Conflict, Grenada Invasion, Libya Raid.* Maxwell Air Force Base, Ala.: Air War College, May 1988.

Build-up in Korea: A Fifth Air Force Report. Fuchu Air Station, Japan: Headquarters Fifth Air Force, Office of Information, n.d.

Carter, G. A., et. al. "Chronology of Events in Southeast Asia: 1945–1975," in *User's Guide to Southeast Asia Combat Data,* A Report Prepared for Defense Advanced Research Projects Agency. Santa Monica, Calif.: Rand Corp., June 1976.

CHECO Southeast Asia Reports, Hickam Air Force Base, Hawaii: HQ, Pacific Air Forces, 1964–1976.

Frondren, Lt. Col. James W., Jr. *Joint Task Force Operations in the Persian Gulf.* Maxwell Air Force Base, Ala.: Air War College, May 1989.

Harris, Walter P. *The Cuban Missile Crisis and its Aftermath.* Carlisle Barracks, Pa.: Army War College, October 1974.

Sharp, U. S. G., Admiral, USN, and Gen. W. C. Westmoreland, USA. *Report on the War in Vietnam (As of June 30, 1968).* Washington: Government Printing Office, 1969.

Spiller, Roger J. *"Not War But Like War": The American Intervention in Lebanon.* Fort Leavenworth, Kans.: U.S. Army Command and General Staff College, Combat Studies Institute, January 1981.

Willeford, Major Hugh B. *Airlift in Grenada.* Maxwell Air Force Base, Ala.: Air Command and Staff College, 1988.

Yates, Lawrence A. *Power Pack: U.S. Intervention in the Dominican Republic, 1965–1966.* Fort Leavenworth, Kans.: U.S. Army Command and General Staff College, Combat Studies Institute, 1988.

Histories

History, Air Force Task Force Thirteen, Provisional. Taipei Air Station, Taiwan, July 1–December 31, 1958 and January 1–June 30, 1960.

History, 3d Aerospace Rescue and Recovery Group. Nakhon Phanom Royal Thai Air Force Base, Thailand, January 1, 1975–June 30, 1975.

History, 437th Military Airlift Wing. Charleston Air Force Base, South Carolina, October 1–December 31, 1983.

History, 464th Troop Carrier Wing. Pope Air Force Base, North Carolina, July–December 1964. Volume I.

Regulations, Orders, Pamphlets

Air Force Pamphlet 900–2. *Unit Decorations, Awards, and Campaign Participation Credits.* June 15, 1971, November 27, 1981, May 8, 1984, May 18, 1987.

Air Force Regulation 900–3(C2), *Department of the Air Force Seal, Organizational Emblems, Use and Display of Flags, Guidons, Streamers, and Automobiles and Aircraft Plates.* August 31, 1988.

Air Force Regulation 900–48, *Decorations, Service, and Achievement Awards, Unit Awards, Special Badges, and Devices.* March 25, 1982.

Department of the Army General Orders No. 80, Sec 1, *Battle Credits and Assault Landings for Korea.* November 22, 1954.

Executive Order No. 9265, *American, European-African-Middle Eastern and Asiatic-Pacific Campaign Medals.* November 6, 1942.

Executive Order No. 10179, *Establishing the Korean Service Medal.* November 11, 1950.

Executive Order No. 11231, *Establishing the Vietnam Service Medal.* July 8, 1965.

War Department General Orders No. 155, Sec. IV, *Mexican Service Badge.* December 12, 1917.

War Department General Orders No. 48, *War Service Medal.* April 9, 1919.

War Department General Orders No. 24, Sec. I, *Campaigns, World War II.* March 4, 1947.

NOTE ON SOURCES

Articles

"Bluesuiters Back 'Just Cause'." *Airman* (January 1990).

Caldwell, Dan, ed. "Department of Defense Operations During the Cuban Crisis: Report by Adam Yarmolinsky, Special Assistant to the Secretary of Defense, 13 February 1963." *Naval War College Review* (July–August 1979).

Gross, Charles J. "A Different Breed of Cats." *Air University Review* (January–February 1983).

"Operation New Tape: A History of MATS Operations in the Congo." *The MATS Flyer* (January 1965).

Sights, Albert P., Jr. "Lessons of Lebanon: A Study in Air Strategy." *Air University Review* (July–August 1965).

Taylor, Capt. John B. "Air Mission Mayaguez." *Airman* (February 1976).

Watkins, Brig. Gen. Tarleton H. "The Congo Airlift." *Air University Quarterly Review* (Summer 1961).

Other Sources

"Chronology of Significant Events in Southeast Asia—FY 1961 Through FY 1973," pp. XXIII–XXXI in *United States Air Force Statistical Digest, Fiscal Year 1974.* Washington: HQ USAF, April 15, 1975.

Document Collection. Miscellaneous correspondence among CINCPAC, USAFMPC, Secretary of the Air Force, and Joint Chiefs of Staff concerning designation of campaigns in Vietnam. April 1966–May 1974. Maxwell Air Force Base, Alabama: HQ USAFHRC, 1988.

Letter, Maurer Maurer to HQ USAF Military Personnel Center, Awards Division. "Regarding Air Combat Campaigns." June 3, 1965.

Non-Governmental Sources

Books

Barnds, William J. *The Two Koreas in East Asian Affairs.* New York: New York University Press, 1976.

Belden, Bauman L. *United States War Medals.* New York: The American Numismatic Society, 1916. [Reprinted by Norm Flayderman, Greenwich, Connecticut, 1962].

Clendenen, Clarence C. *Blood on the Border: The United States Army and the Mexican Irregulars.* New York: The MacMillan Co., 1969.

Clough, Ralph N. *Deterrence and Defense in Korea: The Role of U.S. Forces.* Washington: The Brookings Institution, 1976.

Epstein, Howard M. *Revolt in the Congo, 1960–1964.* New York: Facts on File, Inc., 1965.

Esposito, Vincent J., Brig. Gen., USA, ed. *The West Point Atlas of American Wars: Volume II, 1900–1953.* New York: Frederick A. Praeger, Publishers, 1959.

Grosvenor, Gilbert, ed. *Insignia and Decorations of the Armed Forces*, Revised Edition. Washington: National Geographic Society, 1944.

Hammel, Eric. *The Root: The Marines in Beirut, August 1982– February 1984.* San Diego, California: Harcourt Brace Jovanovich, Publishers, 1985.

Harding, Stephen. *Air War Grenada.* Missoula, Mont.: Pictorial Histories Publishing Co., 1984.

Hudson, James J. *Hostile Skies: A Combat History of the American Air Service in World War I.* Syracuse, N. Y.: Syracuse University Press, 1968.

Laslo, Alexander J. *The Interallied Victory Medals of World War I.* Albuquerque, N. M.: Dorado Publishing Co., 1986.

Schick, John M. *The Berlin Crisis: 1958–1962.* Philadelphia: University of Pennsylvania Press, 1971.

Tompkins, Frank. *Chasing Villa: The Story Behind the Story of Pershing's Expedition Into Mexico.* Harrisburg, Pa.: Military Service Publishing Co., 1934.

Articles

"DOD Commission Reports on Beirut Terrorist Attack. " *Marine Corps Gazette* (February 1984).

Hughes, David. "Night Airdrop in Panama Surprises Noriega's Forces." *Aviation Week & Space Technology* (January 1, 1990).

Kuter, Gen. Laurence S. "The Meaning of the Taiwan Strait Crisis." *Air Force Magazine* (March 1959).

McGlasson, W. D. "Mobilization for Deterrence: The Berlin Crisis of 1961." *National Guard* (December 1986).

O'Rourke, Ronald. "Gulf Ops." *U.S. Naval Institute Proceedings* (May 1989).

Steele, Dennis. "Operation Just Cause." *Army* (February 1990).

"US Airpower Hits Back." *Defense Update International* (July 1986).

Wyllie, Robert E., Col, USA. "The Romance of Military Insignia." *The National Geographic Magazine* (December 1919).

Index

INDEX

INDEX

INDEX

INDEX